Macbeth

THE ARDEN SHAKESPEARE STATE OF
PLAY SERIES

General Editors: Lena Cowen Orlin and Ann Thompson

Macbeth: The State of Play, edited by Ann Thompson
Othello: The State of Play, edited by Lena Cowen Orlin

Further titles in preparation

Macbeth

The State of Play

Edited by Ann Thompson

B L O O M S B U R Y

LONDON • NEW DELHI • NEW YORK • SYDNEY

Bloomsbury Arden Shakespeare

An imprint of Bloomsbury Publishing Plc

50 Bedford Square
London
WC1B 3DP
UK

1385 Broadway
New York
NY 10018
USA

www.bloomsbury.com

Bloomsbury is a registered trade mark of Bloomsbury Publishing Plc

British Library Cataloguing-in-Publication Data
A catalogue record for this book is available from the British Library.

ISBN: HB: 978-1-4725-0320-6
PB: 978-1-4081-5982-8
ePDF: 978-1-4725-0321-3
ePub: 978-1-4725-0319-0

Library of Congress Cataloging-in-Publication Data
A catalog record for this book is available from the Library of Congress.

Typeset by Fakenham Prepress Solutions, Fakenham, Norfolk NR21 8NN
Printed and bound in Great Britain

CONTENTS

SERIES PREFACE

The Arden Shakespeare
State of Play
Series Editors: Ann Thompson and Lena Cowen Orlin

This series represents a collaboration between King's College London and Georgetown University. King's is the home of the London Shakespeare Centre and Georgetown is the home of the Shakespeare Association of America (SAA). Each volume in the series is an expedition to discover the 'state of play' with respect to specific works by Shakespeare. Our method is to convene a seminar at the annual convention of the SAA and see what it is that preoccupies scholars now. SAA seminars are enrolled through an open registration process that brings together academics from all stages of their careers. Participants prepare short papers that are circulated in advance and then discussed when the seminar convenes on conference weekend. From the papers submitted, the seminar leader selects a group for inclusion in a collection that aims to include fresh work by emerging voices and established scholars both. The general editors are grateful for the further collaboration of Bloomsbury Publishing, and especially our commissioning editor Margaret Bartley.

In the Series:
Macbeth, edited by Ann Thompson
Othello, edited by Lena Cowen Orlin

NOTES ON CONTRIBUTORS

Dermot Cavanagh teaches English at the University of Edinburgh. He is currently editing *King John* for the Norton Shakespeare and contributing to a revised edition of Geoffrey Bullough's *Narrative and Dramatic Sources of Shakespeare* (ed. John Drakakis) by editing a volume on *Earlier English History Plays*. He is also working on a critical study of Shakespeare and the commonwealth.

Sandra Clark is Professor Emerita of Renaissance Literature, Birkbeck, University of London, and Senior Research Fellow, Institute of English Studies, University of London. She is Series Editor of the Arden Shakespeare Dictionaries. Her publications include *The Elizabethan Pamphleteers: Popular Moralistic Pamphlets, 1580–1640* (1984), *The Plays of Beaumont and Fletcher: Sexual Themes and Dramatic Representation* (1994), *Women and Crime in the Street Literature of Early Modern England* (2003) and *Renaissance Drama* (2007). She is currently completing an edition of *Macbeth* for the Arden Shakespeare.

Anthony B. Dawson is Professor Emeritus at the University of British Columbia. He has written extensively on performance history and theory, on early modern theatre and culture, especially religious culture, and on matters relating to editing and textual theory. His books include *Hamlet* (for the *Shakespeare in Performance* series, 1995), *The Culture of Playgoing in Shakespeare's England* (written with Paul Yachnin, 2001) and editions of *Troilus and Cressida* (New

Cambridge Shakespeare series, 2003), *Timon of Athens* (with Gretchen Minton, Arden 2008) and *Richard II* (with Paul Yachnin, Oxford, 2011). He is currently editing versions of *Hamlet* for the Norton Shakespeare and has begun work on *Macbeth* for Internet Shakespeare Editions.

Darlene Farabee is Assistant Professor of English at the University of South Dakota, where she teaches Shakespeare and early modern drama. Her current book project is titled *Shakespeare's Staged Spaces and Audience Perception*.

Brett Gamboa is Assistant Professor of English at Dartmouth College, where he teaches courses on Shakespeare and other dramatic literature. He also directs plays, on and off campus, and has staged ten of Shakespeare's. He is currently working on performance commentaries for each play in the Norton Shakespeare and is completing a book about doubling roles in Shakespeare's plays.

Jonathan Hope is Professor of Literary Linguistics at Strathclyde University, Glasgow. He has published widely on Shakespeare's language and the history of the English language. His most recent book, *Shakespeare and Language: Reason, Eloquence and Artifice in the English Renaissance* (2010), seeks to reconstruct the linguistic world of Shakespeare's England and measure its distance from our own. With Michael Witmore (Folger Shakespeare Library), he is part of a major digital humanities project, funded by the Mellon Foundation, to develop tools and procedures for the linguistic analysis of texts across the period 1450–1800. Early work from this project is blogged at: winedarksea.org

Kevin A. Quarmby is Assistant Professor of English at Oxford College of Emory University, Atlanta. He is co-director of the World Shakespeare Project, a model for interactive pedagogy in a new media world. His book, *The Disguised Ruler in Shakespeare and His Contemporaries* (2012), considers

Measure for Measure as one of several interrelated disguise plays. His previous career was as a professional UK actor, appearing in Shakespeare productions throughout the country, including *Macbeth* at the Old Vic (1980). He has published journal articles on *As You Like It*, *Hamlet*, *Macbeth* and *The Tempest*; forthcoming work explores contemporary productions of *Measure for Measure* and *King Lear*.

Debapriya Sarkar is completing her doctoral dissertation on 'Possible Knowledge: Forms of Literary and Scientific Thought in Early Modern England' on a Mellon/ACLS Dissertation Completion Fellowship in the English Department at Rutgers University, New Brunswick. Her research interests include poetry and poetics, epic and romance, history of science and possible worlds in fiction and philosophy. She is also currently working on a series of essays on romance and early modern epistemology.

Philippa Sheppard lectures for the Department of English at the University of Toronto. She also lectures regularly for the Shakespeare Festival in Stratford, Ontario. She has published chapters in *Approaches to Teaching Renaissance Drama*, *Latin American Shakespeares*, *Renaissance Medievalisms*, *Faith and Fantasy in the Renaissance* and *Who Hears in Shakespeare*. She has also published essays about Shakespeare and adaptation and is currently completing her book on film adaptations of Shakespeare.

Geraldo U. de Sousa is Professor of English at the University of Kansas, and Deputy Executive Director and Fellow of the Mediterranean Studies Association. His research explores the intersection of various disciplines, including Renaissance literature and history, theatre and stage history, anthropology, history of architecture and art history. His publications include *Shakespeare's Cross-Cultural Encounters* (1999, new edition 2002), *At Home in Shakespeare's Tragedies* (2010) and *Shakespeare: A Study and Research Guide* (with David

Bergeron, 3rd edition 1995). He served as editor of the journal *Mediterranean Studies* for ten years and has published on Luso-Brazilian, Mediterranean and global studies. He is currently working on a book on Jacobean City Comedy and everyday life in early modern London.

Ann Thompson is Professor of English at King's College London and Director of the London Shakespeare Centre. She is a General Editor of the Arden Shakespeare and has (with Neil Taylor) edited all three texts of *Hamlet* for Arden. Other publications include an edition of *The Taming of the Shrew* (1984, updated 2003), *Shakespeare's Chaucer* (1978), *Shakespeare, Meaning and Metaphor* (with John O. Thompson, 1987), *Teaching Women: Feminism and English Studies* (edited with Helen Wilcox, 1989), *Women Reading Shakespeare, 1660–1900* (edited with Sasha Roberts, 1996) and *In Arden: Editing Shakespeare* (edited with Gordon McMullan, 2003). Current projects include an edition of *Cymbeline* for the Norton Shakespeare, and a book on Shakespeare and metonymy.

Michael Witmore is Director of the Folger Shakespeare Library, Washington DC. His publications include *Landscapes of the Passing Strange: Reflections from Shakespeare* (2010), *Shakespearean Metaphysics* (2008), *Pretty Creatures: Children and Fiction in the English Renaissance* (2007) and *Culture of Accidents: Unexpected Knowledges in Early Modern England* (2001). With Jonathan Hope (Strathclyde University, Glasgow), he is part of a major digital humanities project, funded by the Mellon Foundation, to develop tools and procedures for the linguistic analysis of texts across the period 1450–1800. Early work from this project is blogged at: winedarksea.org

Ramona Wray is Reader in Renaissance Literature at Queen's University, Belfast. She has edited Elizabeth Cary's *The Tragedy of Mariam* for Arden Early Modern Drama (2012).

She is the author of *Women Writers in the Seventeenth Century* (2004) and co-author of *Great Shakespeareans: Welles, Kurosawa, Kozintsev, Zeffirelli* (2013). She is also the co-editor of *The Edinburgh Companion to Shakespeare and the Arts* (2011), *Screening Shakespeare in the Twenty-First Century* (2006), *Reconceiving the Renaissance: a Critical Reader* (2005), *Shakespeare, Film, Fin de Siècle* (2000) and *Shakespeare and Ireland: History, Politics, Culture* (1997).

Introduction

Ann Thompson

Despite its status as one of the 'big four' mature Shakespearean tragedies (along with *Hamlet*, *Othello* and *King Lear*), *Macbeth* has been somewhat neglected during the critical revolution that has galvanized Shakespeare studies since the 1980s. The seminal collections of essays on topics such as *Alternative Shakespeares*, *Political Shakespeare* and *Shakespeare and the Question of Theory*, all of which were published in 1985, typically contain new readings of *Hamlet*, *Othello* and *King Lear*, a couple of histories, notably the *Henry IV* plays and *Henry V*, and a few comedies, such as *Measure for Measure* and *The Tempest*, but not one of them has an essay on *Macbeth*.[1] The agenda set by new historicist, feminist and post-colonialist critics has continued to omit or implicitly downgrade this play, despite its relevance to the 'gender and power' issues that have often been dominant.

It is not obvious why this should be so. Perhaps one reason is that most people today, at least in the UK and North America, read *Macbeth* in high school, alongside *A Midsummer Night's Dream* and *Julius Caesar*, so they may regard it, consciously or not, as a play for juniors, one they 'grow out of' as they get older. It has never quite entered the competition for being regarded as 'Shakespeare's greatest tragedy', a title contested in the later twentieth century between *Hamlet* and *King Lear*, as R. A. Foakes demonstrated in *'Hamlet' versus 'Lear'*.[2] *Macbeth* does not have the overtly racial dimension that has made *Othello* a more popular (because more controversial) play among teachers at least, and its 'fiend-like queen' presents performers and critics with a less satisfactory part than that of Cleopatra.

Although it has always been popular on the stage, productions have somehow not managed to achieve the 'iconic' status of many productions of *Hamlet* and *King Lear*. This may relate to some problems with the Folio text itself (perhaps arising from early revision or adaptation, as we shall see), or indeed to the extent to which it has been conceived as a star vehicle for two performers who need to be unusually well matched. This has turned out to be difficult to achieve. In the earlier stage history of the play it seems notable that David Garrick stopped performing it after his co-star Hannah Pritchard retired, and that John Philip Kemble's performance as Macbeth was less exceptional than that of his sister, Sarah Siddons, as Lady Macbeth. Ellen Terry and Henry Irving should have been more evenly matched, but her performance, although visually striking as recorded in the portrait by John Singer Sargent,[3] was described as a 'whitewashing' of the character.[4] Laurence Olivier was unequally matched by Vivien Leigh, and he never made the film of the play that he planned in the 1950s. A rare case of fully satisfying performances in both roles was when Ian McKellen and Judi Dench were directed by Trevor Nunn at the tiny Other Place theatre in Stratford-upon-Avon in 1976, a production subsequently recorded on film. But similarly, there has been no cinematic version of the play that has been considered unequivocally a 'great' one: the closest contender is probably Akira Kurosawa's Japanese adaptation, *Throne of Blood* (1957), while the English-language version most (though not universally) admired is probably Roman Polanski's film from 1972.

Nevertheless, terms such as 'neglected' and 'downgraded' have to be relative in this context. There has of course been considerable interest in the witches (for example, in Christina Larner's *Witchcraft and Religion*, 1984; Diane Purkiss' *The*

Witch in History, 1996; and Deborah Willis' *Malevolent Nurture: Witch-Hunting and Maternal Power in Early Modern England*, Cornell, 1995) and in the specifically Jacobean nature of the play (e.g. Alvin Kernan, *Shakespeare, the King's Playwright: Theater in the Stuart Court, 1603–1613*, New Haven, 1995; Arthur F. Kinney, *Lies Like Truth: Shakespeare, 'Macbeth' and the Cultural Moment*, Detroit, 2001; David Norbrook, '*Macbeth* and the Politics of Historiography' in Sharpe and Zwicker, 1987). Its inclusion in the 2007 *Collected Works of Thomas Middleton* (edited by Gary Taylor and John Lavagnino, Oxford, 2007) has sparked new controversy over its textual puzzles as well as its authorship. Much has been written about recent productions (see, for example, Bernice W. Kliman's *Shakespeare in Performance: 'Macbeth'*, Manchester, 2004; *Weyward 'Macbeth': Intersections of Race and Performance* edited by Scott L. Newstok and Ayanna Thompson, Palgrave Macmillan, 2010, which discusses over one hundred cross-racial productions) and on film, with recent versions ranging from the relatively 'straight' adaptation of the 2007 stage version directed by Rupert Goold with Patrick Stewart and Kate Fleetwood (2010) to Billy Morrissette's *Scotland, PA* (2001) set in a fast-food outlet. Mark Thornton Burnett's recent book, *Shakespeare and World Cinema* (Cambridge, 2012), discusses a number of contemporary films from outside the Anglo-American tradition.

Most of the essays in this collection arose from a double research seminar on *Macbeth* that I led at the Shakespeare Association of America meeting in Bellevue, Seattle, in April 2011, and I am grateful to the programme committee for accepting my seminar proposal. Such seminars are open to all members of the Association (which is an international association, not limited to citizens of the United States) and provide rare and valuable opportunities for scholars at all stages of their careers, from postgraduate students to senior professors, to share their new ideas on all aspects of research in Shakespeare studies. Short papers are exchanged among the participants well in advance of the meeting, and responses are also circulated, so that by the time the group meet face to face they have already begun their discussion. For the purpose of this volume, I selected nine papers from the total of thirty submitted and invited the authors to expand them to their current length. I also commissioned two additional essays to fill what seemed to me obvious gaps in an attempt to provide a balanced coverage of 'the state of play' concerning contemporary debates about *Macbeth*.

In the first section, 'The Text and its Status', Anthony B. Dawson and Brett Gamboa address these issues from very different perspectives, Dawson focusing on the textual problems of the play and their provenance in the context of debates about authorship and revision, while Gamboa looks at what might be seen as the consequence of these problems, namely the tendency of the play to disappoint in performance, especially in its second half. Dawson outlines eight puzzling features of the First Folio text of *Macbeth* and asks whether revision (and specifically revision by Middleton) is the only explanation for them. Further, he uses this instance to reflect more generally on the evidence that editors and other scholars use to mount arguments about authorship, collaboration and revision, cautiously reminding us that Macbeth himself evokes the fiend that 'lies like truth' (5.4.43). Gamboa discovers a pattern whereby reviewers of the play repeatedly find that productions of *Macbeth* fail to live up to expectations and dares to ask whether the play may be failing the theatre practitioners rather than vice versa. He analyses the various ways in which the second half of the play can seem an anti-climax: 'Macbeth is killed by the wrong man', for example, since both Malcolm and Fleance have a better case for acting as primary revenger, but neither is allowed to assume the role.

Under the heading, 'History and Topicality', Dermot Cavanagh re-examines the notion of the body in *Macbeth*, arguing that the play contains a profound debate on the values that should govern the body politic, and that this can be understood by following the account it offers of bodily experience. He suggests that Shakespeare engages with this topic, not just through Jacobean writings about sovereignty, but also contemporary notions of the 'common weal' or commonwealth, invoking James I's reading of Jean Bodin's *The Six Bookes of a Commonweale*. His essay aims to avoid the sometimes polarized political readings of the play and to acknowledge that, while it was written in a volatile political climate, it is not of course a political treatise. Similarly combining close reading with a historical approach, Debapriya Sarkar places the treatment of prophecies and prescriptions in the play in the context of a contemporary epistemic shift regarding the nature and interpretation of prophetic discourse. She considers writings about prophecy by late sixteenth-century authors such as Henry Howard and John Harvey in a careful analysis of the distinction between predictions which will certainly become true (Banquo's descendants will become kings, including James I) and those that will only become true if the hearer snatches 'the nearest way' (Macbeth's own route to the throne).

As the average man or woman on the street in London, New York or Delhi can quote a line like 'To be or not to be', or 'Romeo, Romeo, wherefore art thou Romeo?', so he or she has a general vague knowledge of 'Lady Macbeth' as the type of a powerful (and malign) woman. Kevin A. Quarmby traces the popularity of the label as a pejorative description of powerful women in politics, especially 'First Ladies', from Abigail Adams to Michelle Obama, and from Cherie Booth Blair to Asma al-Assad. His analysis demonstrates the astonishing longevity of the analogy and its popularity with headline-grabbing commentators in the UK and North America, who are not afraid to apply it to public figures in the Middle East and China as well as in their own countries. As he also shows, topical allusions often haunt productions of the play, whether the company intends them or not.

Two of the essays in the 'Critical Approaches and Close Reading' section focus on aspects of disorientation in *Macbeth*. Darlene Farabee considers Macbeth's deteriorating spatial orientation and the disintegration of his ability to separate time and space, arguing that his confusion leads to a similar disorientation of the audience's perceptions. (This argument might recall William Empson's discussion of 'the fog of war' in the play, advanced in his case as deliberate effect created by Shakespeare, not the result of revision, as Dover Wilson had argued in his 1947 edition.[5]) Geraldo U. de Sousa explores perceptual disorientations associated with the concept of the home in the play, picking up on the associations between witchcraft and cookery to link ordinary home cooking, criminality and sorcery. In Farabee's reading, the contrast between Macbeth and Banquo is that between a man who is continually confused about his location and one whose direction is clear. De Sousa draws on contemporary accounts of food and cookery in Scotland, contrasting the domestic associations and the rules of hospitality on the one hand with their inversion into the witches' 'hell-broth' on the other, and finding that the two become intimately intertwined.

Taking a very different approach to 'close reading', Jonathan Hope and Michael Witmore use quantitative techniques from linguistics to explore aspects of the language of the play which have often been observed by literary critics but never precisely analysed. They move from traditional literary approaches, such as metrical analysis and patterns of verbal repetition and echo, to computer-aided statistics of word frequency, while remaining aware of the potentially misleading nature of crudely mathematical measures. Arguing that the frequency of the word 'thane' in *Macbeth* is statistically true but not particularly surprising or interesting, they provide a thoughtful discussion of the numerous 'extra' occurrences of the word 'the' in the text – a word often dismissed as too common to be of interest – which turns out to support Stephen Booth's insight into the importance of 'indefinition' in the play.[6]

Whether or not the text we have of *Macbeth* in the First Folio is already a revised or adapted version of Shakespeare's original play, it has frequently been rearranged and rewritten over the last four hundred years, as the three essays in the section on 'Adaptation and Afterlife' demonstrate. Sandra

Clark discusses how the play has been both abbreviated and expanded on stage. Some patterns of cuts have been repeated frequently, while the ongoing influence of Davenant's Restoration version has added to the roles of the witches, and Garrick's dying speech for Macbeth persisted well into the nineteenth century. Philippa Sheppard and Ramona Wray write about recent film adaptations: Geoffrey Wright's 2006 Australian version of the narrative set amongst drug-smuggling gangsters in twenty-first century Melbourne, and the 2005 version in the BBC 'Shakespeare Re-Told' season which set it in an upmarket London restaurant. Sheppard finds Wright's adaptation essentially reductive, despite brief flashes of wit in acknowledging the original play. It becomes an excuse for revelling in violence, which she contrasts unfavourably with both *Scotland, PA* and the BBC adaptation. Wray is much more positive about the latter, defending its director from comparable charges of 'butchering' the play and applauding his ingenuity in numerous aspects of the adaptation, including his maximization of the power of the leading female role.

Audiences in London in 2013 have been offered an extremely visceral *Macbeth* set in a dystopian Scotland brutalized by war at the Trafalgar Studios, starring James McAvoy and directed by Jamie Lloyd, as well as a 'traditional practices' version at Shakespeare's Globe, starring Joseph Millson and directed, unusually, by a woman, Eve Best, who had moreover played Lady Macbeth to Jasper Britton's Macbeth in Tim Carroll's 2001 production at the Globe. Meanwhile, tickets for Kenneth Branagh's version, co-directed with Rob Ashford and set in a deconsecrated church in central Manchester, sold out immediately they went on sale. A new film version directed by Justin Kurzel and starring Michael Fassbender and Natalie Portman has been announced. The National Theatre of Scotland is to take Alan Cumming's one-man show to Broadway, and Alex Johnstone, a Member of the Scottish Parliament, has suggested, in the wake of the discovery of the remains of Richard III in Leicester, that it is time to review the reign of Macbeth, who might similarly have been maligned by

Shakespeare. For an unlucky, neglected, and arguably flawed play, this tragedy is not doing too badly after all.

Notes

1   John Drakakis ed., *Alternative Shakespeares* (London, 1985); Jonathan Dollimore and Alan Sinfield (eds), *Political Shakespeare* (Manchester, 1985); Patricia Parker and Geoffrey Hartman (eds), *Shakespeare and the Question of Theory* (New York and London, 1985).

2   R. A. Foakes, *'Hamlet' versus 'Lear'* (Cambridge, 1993).

3   This 1889 portrait is in the Tate Britain Gallery, London.

4   See A. R. Braunmuller, ed., *Macbeth* (Cambridge, 1997), pp. 56–88, 78.

5   William Empson, *Essays on Shakespeare* (Cambridge, 1986), pp. 137–57. This version of the essay is 'substantially revised' from 'Dover Wilson on *Macbeth*' which appeared in *The Kenyon Review* 14 (1952).

6   See Stephen Booth, *'King Lear', 'Macbeth', Indefinition, and Tragedy* (1983).

PART ONE

The Text and its Status

1

Notes and Queries Concerning the Text of *Macbeth*

Anthony B. Dawson

I want to begin by outlining a few salient features of the text of *Macbeth*. Many of these are well known but tend to be forgotten in the rush to interpretation.

I. The Folio (F) text is among the shortest in the collection (only *Comedy of Errors* and *The Tempest* are shorter). In comparison especially with the other tragedies, its brevity would seem to be anomalous.

II. It contains two scenes (3.5 and parts of 4.1) that feature a character called Hecate who appears unexpectedly, is mentioned nowhere else in the play, and graces no other drama of the whole period except Middleton's *The Witch*.

III. The latter play (*The Witch*) gives the full text of two songs which are cited in F but (uniquely for songs in the Folio) are not printed (or, to be precise, a part line of each is printed).

IV. *Macbeth* was first composed some time around 1606. The date of *The Witch* is unknown but the Oxford Middleton,

following other recent scholars, argues for a date of mid-1616.[1]
Musical settings for the two songs named in F and printed in
The Witch exist, and are attributed to composers who worked
with the King's Men at Blackfriars in the second decade of the
seventeenth century.

V. In April 1611, Simon Forman saw *Macbeth* at the Globe
and recorded his impressions in the idiosyncratic style which
he adopted for his theatrical criticism. There are a number of
small discrepancies between what he writes and the play as we
have it, plus there are several important parts of the play that
he fails to mention (including the Hecate scenes).

Va. Forman describes the figures called *Witches* or *weyard/
weyward sisters*[2] in the play as 'women feiries or Nimphes'.

VI. The opening stage direction of 1.2 uses the word
'meeting' for the arrival on stage of a) Duncan and his train,
and b) the 'bleeding captain'. This formulation recurs at the
opening of 3.5 (*Enter the three Witches meeting Hecat*) and
occurs frequently in Middleton (much more often than in the
work of any other contemporary playwright) and only once in
Shakespeare's undisputed plays (*King Lear* [quarto only] 2.1.0).

VII. The sequence from 3.6 to 4.1 has been questioned
as introducing contradiction, with particular reference to
Macduff's flight to England and its effect on Macbeth. In
3.6, an unnamed Lord tells Lennox that Macduff 'Is gone
to pray the holy king [Edward] upon his aid / To wake
Northumberland and warlike Siward … And this report / Hath
so exasperate their king that he / Prepares for some attempt
at war' (3.6.29–39).[3] Exactly what the report consists of is
ambiguous, and the phrase 'their king' which appears to refer
to Edward has frequently been emended to 'the king' and hence
made to refer to Macbeth. The reason for this is that Lennox's
response ('Sent he to Macduff?'; l. 40) almost certainly refers to
Macbeth, and is so understood by the Lord, who then goes on
to describe Macduff's frosty reception of Macbeth's messenger.
Despite this indication that Macbeth knows about Macduff's
flight, Macbeth soon afterwards (at 4.1.139ff.) expresses shock
at Lennox's news that 'Macduff is fled to England' and resolves

on immediate violent action. Critics who are concerned about this discrepancy tend to ascribe it to revision.

VIII. F's stage directions for the final duel between Macbeth and Macduff are contradictory: the combatants exit *'fighting'* and, after *'Alarums'*, they re-enter, *'Fighting, and Macbeth slaine'*; Malcolm and his men then enter, paying no attention to the apparently slain Macbeth or his vanquisher (in fact they are anxious that Macduff is 'missing'). Shortly thereafter comes the climactic stage direction: *Enter Macduffe, with Macbeths head*. Editors have found their way around this problem by adding directions such as *'Exit Macduff with Macbeth's body'*[4] after the duel and sometimes by beginning a new scene.[5] Several have suggested that the two sets of directions indicate different stagings: one in which Macbeth is killed offstage and his head carried on and displayed; the other, more dramatic perhaps, where he is killed (and beheaded?) onstage.

Here are some recurrent questions relating to the peculiarities just described:

1 Is the text we have a product of adaptation or revision?

2 If so, was the play radically abridged in the process of undergoing adaptation?

3 Assuming the answer to (1) is yes, is Thomas Middleton the likely candidate for the role of adapter?

4 Is the Folio text a 'theatrical' one – i.e. a 'promptbook' or a transcript thereof?

Some of the elements listed above lend weight to the proposition that the play was indeed revised. The references to the two songs from *The Witch* along with the unexpected appearance of a new head-witch in act 3, when no mention has been made of her earlier, suggest that Hecate may be an addition; this view is supported by the fact that she does nothing to advance the plot, and the verse she is given differs

materially from the trochaic tetrameter of the witches' earlier
speeches (it's a mix of doggerel pentameters and iambic
tetrameter). One thing that the Hecate scenes do provide,
however, is an enhanced witchy spectacle and some singing.
That these elements of the play were at some point popular is
attested to by Davenant's revival in the 1660s, a text of which
was published in 1674, where the operatic opportunities
offered by the witches are given full voice.[6] So, I think we are
safe in concluding what scholars since the nineteenth century
have argued, namely that the Hecate material was added to
Shakespeare's original text at some point (probably around
1616, when *The Witch* and the extant musical settings were
composed). Can we also conclude that Thomas Middleton
was the culprit? If the revisions were indeed composed in
1616, then Middleton is certainly the best candidate. Most
recent editors have argued that he was involved – even
Braunmuller, who is more careful and cautious than propo-
nents such as Gary Taylor and Nicholas Brooke.[7] But Brian
Vickers, armed with statistical evidence, has suggested that
Shakespeare himself was the reviser, and that these scenes
should be dated earlier – for a revival in 1610–11[8]. Whoever
added the Hecate scenes, there is nothing to indicate that
either the 'contradiction' discussed in VII or the inconsistency
of staging outlined in VIII, both of which could be ascribed to
changes made for a revival, is linked to the additions.

One odd feature of the apparently additional material is
that Hecate's role in 3.5 is slightly different from that in 4.1.
In 3.5, she is clearly in command; she scolds the weird sisters
for acting without her authority, and prepares them and
the audience for the coming interview with Macbeth and its
'illusion[s]', which will 'draw him on to his confusion' (28–9).
In 4.1, she displays much less authority; indeed, the sisters have
stirred up the cauldron on their own before Hecate's arrival
and, despite her earlier chastisement, she restricts herself to
commending them for their work and there is another '*Song.
Blacke Spirits, &c.*'. She then has nothing to say or do for the
rest of the scene; there is no suggestion that she, rather than

the sisters, is responsible for the apparitions, which, almost
everyone thinks, were part of the original text.[9] Should she
and her three attendant witches (i.e. those who entered with
her, not the three original sisters) exit at this point (4.1.43)?
Such is what many editors, dating back to the mid-nineteenth
century, have thought. This would make her stay onstage
very brief – five lines plus the song, which, as G. K. Hunter
pointed out some time ago,[10] needn't be sung in full. It might
be comprised of just a few lines to cover the (noisy?) exit of
Hecate via some kind of flying machine. Perhaps, indeed, that
is the reason it isn't given in full in F. If, on the other hand,
we recall that F seems to be derived from a theatrical text
(perhaps a transcript of a play-book), the allusion to the song
could be a kind of bookkeeper's shorthand for the full song.
Thus the existence of just a few words, both here and in 3.5,
can be used as an argument for either view: that the song was
performed *in toto* or that it was merely a short transitional
strategy. In any case, there seems little dramatic justification
for the intervention.

Responding to the perceived need for fuller theatrical
treatment of both 3.5 and Hecate's brief appearance in 4.1,
and perhaps, in the latter case, seeking to provide some
dramatic advantage to a seemingly pointless sequence, Oxford
and Brooke insert interludes derived from Middleton's *The
Witch* at both points. In doing so they also draw on
Davenant's operatic rendition from after the Restoration as
well as on other versions of the song; for the 4.1 sequence,
they keep Hecate onstage until the moment, signalled in F's
stage direction, when all '*The witches dance and vanish*'
(131 stage direction). (In this scenario, she presumably
directs the show in which her attendants sing and dance.)
It seems extraordinary to me that in editing a text from
F, editors interpolate two substantial sequences from a
completely different play (and by a different playwright),
with the authority only of '*Come away, come away, &c.*'
and '*Blacke Spirits &c.*'

Since the two scenes pose somewhat different problems, I

will deal with them separately. In 3.5, the sequence goes like this:

> *Musicke, and a Song.*
> Hearke, I am call'd: my little Spirit see
> Sits in a Foggy cloud, and stayes' for me.
>   *Song within. Come away, come away, &c.*
> 1 Come, let's make hast, shee'l soone be
> Backe again.

(TLN 1464–9)

Here the song is clearly called for as a beckoning from offstage. We can assume that the *Song* mentioned in the two stage directions is the same one, and is heard coming from *within*, there being no indication at all that the spirits(s) appear onstage. (Hecate's admonition to the witches to 'see' the little Spirit no doubt implies a gesture offstage and up, and needn't be taken to refer to a literal descent of a cloud-riding spirit.) If, as in Oxford and Brooke and now also the Oxford Middleton, a long sequence is inserted before she exits, we have to ask why, after being called away, does she remain behind for so long? In *The Witch* there is some dramatic justification for this long-drawn-out exit, but here, immediately after the banquet scene and just before Macbeth's confrontation with the apparitions and his resolution to make the 'very firstlings of [his] heart ... the firstlings of [his] hand', to extend the sequence is simply to dilute the theatrical effect. I'm operating on the assumption here that in thinking about the text, it's important to ask questions about the play in the theatre. Would Middleton, if we presume that he is responsible for 3.5 and the relevant part of 4.1, deliberately undermine the reckless speed with which Macbeth is moving the action towards its devastating conclusion? It could, I suppose, be argued that inserting Hecate in the first place, even in such small doses, dilutes the effect, and so what's wrong with simply extending the interruption? Is it possible to speculate that Middleton used the Witch material for different reasons: to wind up the dark effect rather than undermine it? One could perhaps imagine a staging that does that, but not if we include drifting clouds and descending cat-spirits. What about the possibility that Shakespeare wrote these scenes, as Vickers argues? Again we have to ask why. If we assume that the original version of the play represents something like Shakespeare's intention, it's hard to square that with the interpolation of scenes that seem to undermine the tragic trajectory.

Augmenting 4.1, as these editors do, does give Hecate the prominent part in the scene that seems appropriate given her role in 3.5. If, as Taylor both advocates and practises in the Oxford Middleton, she is also assigned the speeches given to First Witch ('I.' in F) during the display of apparitions, her prominence is given an additional boost. The way to these emendations had already been paved by the Oxford editors and Brooke, who both assign the speech after the show of kings ('Ay, sir, all this is so ...; 124ff.) to Hecate (as of course Taylor does as well), though the F speech prefix is simply 'I.'. Thus a character unambiguously called Hecate (*Hecat*) in stage directions and speech prefixes (*Hec.*) in F suddenly, in these editors' eyes, is to be identified with 'I.' in this section of the play, though in the rest of the F text 'I.' designates the character usually known as the First Witch.

Making these moves depends on the presumption that Middleton is answerable not only for the additions but for a number of revisions as well. If he is, and if he sought to make the play more spectacular and less intense, and if one wants as an editor to enhance his role, then it makes sense to get as much Middleton in as one reasonably can and still claim to be acting responsibly. But at the same time, adding a sequence clearly not by Shakespeare, and with only a tenuous connection to the play as it appears to have been originally conceived, does raise questions about what editors do or are supposed to do.[11]

Brian Vickers, to turn now more fully to his perspective, published a broadside in the *TLS* (28 May, 2010) in which he attacks Taylor's conclusions and both cleverly and convincingly undermines most of Taylor's argument. Vickers' article

aims at all the passages Taylor thinks are Middleton's. But if
we confine ourselves to the Hecate scenes, which are the only
passages that most recent editors think are not by Shakespeare
(though there have in the past been disputes, now brought
back into currency by Taylor, over other segments, such as the
bleeding captain's speech in 1.2 and parts of the apparition
scene), the status of these scenes is far from clear. Vickers and
his colleagues use a system of three- and four-word colloca-
tions to test the disputed passages and end up affirming that
everything, including Hecate's speeches, is from Shakespeare's
hand. However, looking at the evidence provided on the
webpage (but not in the *TLS*) yields less definitive results. In
his *TLS* article Vickers claims that the team's results 'point
unmistakably to Shakespeare's hand'. But the evidence is far
from conclusive. In the web article,[12] the authors list twelve
instances in 3.5 of three- or four-word matches with other
Shakespeare texts, which do not appear in Middleton, and one
that is found in both authors. This at first seems impressive.
But many of the phrases are commonplace ('the mistress of',
'was never called', 'the glory of our', etc.). One or two are
a little less so and could be Shakespearean (e.g. '**draw him
on to** his confusion', which matches *Hamlet*, 'So by your
companies / To **draw him on to** pleasures'[13]). But what is
to stop Middleton, if any such phrases did originate with
Shakespeare, from simply, no doubt unconsciously, echoing
them? When we check the five-line speech in 4.1 together
with the stage directions that precede and follow it, the ratio
is reversed. There we have one string unique to Shakespeare
('the other three', hardly a startling one) and *five* unique
to Middleton. Consistency would seem to demand that if
the high number of matches in the forty lines in 3.5 'prove'
Shakespeare's authorship, then the matches in 4.1 (five in five
lines) 'prove' Middleton's.

More fundamental than such questions, however, is the
matter of motivation. If Shakespeare revised the text for a
production sometime around 1610–11, as Vickers suggests,
we can only wonder why he would have taken this strange

direction. What might he have found unsatisfying about the original play? Why, in an attempt supposedly to improve upon it, would he have inserted this semi-operatic sequence with a new and negligible character whose speeches are written in bad verse – and verse, we might add, that, while it superficially resembles the speech of characters such as Jupiter in *Cymbeline* and Iris and Ceres in *Tempest,* has little in common with what we know about Shakespeare's late style?[14] I find it interesting that in his book, *Shakespeare Co-Author*, Vickers acknowledges the value of intuition in readers and critics who are deeply immersed in Shakespeare's works, and quotes Gary Taylor approvingly when Taylor asserts the value of 'the intuitions of a practised and perceptive reader'.[15] The fact is that many such readers have indeed recoiled from the Hecate speeches on just such intuitive grounds. So what does one do when statistics are contradicted by practised readers? In his eagerness to use statistical evidence as yielding 'truth', Vickers ignores the contradiction and the kind of professional insight he had championed in his masterly 2002 book.

Even more knotty is the matter of abridgement. *Macbeth*, as noted above, is a surprisingly short play – the shortest of the tragedies and shorter than most of the comedies. But the differences in length between it and the rest of the tragedies are often exaggerated. *Timon of Athens* and *Titus Andronicus* are also quite short in comparison with the other tragedies and not that much longer than *Macbeth*.[16] Since *Timon* was written in collaboration with none other than Thomas Middleton, its brevity might be seen as parallel to that of *Macbeth*, i.e. as the product of Middleton's role in its composition.[17] But the two cases are very different. *Timon of Athens* is clearly collaborative, while just as clearly *Macbeth* is not. It is possible to trace in the *Timon* text the patterns of collaboration between Shakespeare and Middleton – at least in general terms.[18] Nothing of this is visible in *Macbeth*, the form and development of which is entirely Shakespeare's. The – to me uncertain – claim that *Titus* is also collaborative has similarly been used to argue that its relative brevity should be discounted as a parallel to *Macbeth* and hence to bolster the claim for *Macbeth* as an anomaly. (Why in principle collaborative plays should be shorter than single-authored ones is left unexplained.) Let us, despite such complications, admit that *Macbeth* is somewhat anomalous. And, if we subtract the added Hecate scenes, it becomes even shorter, suggesting that perhaps something was left out when those additions were inserted (or perhaps at some other time). If the additions belong to Middleton, it seems likely that he also would have made some adjustments to the text to fit them in. But that he did anything beyond that is much less likely. Taylor suspects (indeed is certain) that he did, though the internal verbal 'proofs' he brings to bear are not all that convincing (more on that later).[19]

What was cut? Here the path becomes thorny – how can we tell? Something from the beginning of 1.2, perhaps? So Brooke, Taylor and even, cautiously, Braunmuller suggest, pointing to R. V. Holdsworth's demonstration that the formulation in the stage direction, '*meeting* ... [in this case] *a bleeding Captaine*' (see VI. above) is a favourite of Middleton's and occurs only once in Shakespeare's unassisted works.[20] Since it occurs twice in *Timon,* once in a Middleton scene and once in a scene of mixed or uncertain authorship, it is at least possible that Shakespeare, writing *Macbeth* soon after his work on *Timon,* used it here under the influence of Middleton (indeed, that authors influence each other is too often forgotten in these kinds of discussion); not to mention the fact that the same phrasing occurs in the quarto version of *King Lear* (1608) and, in two other places, Shakespeare's formulation is similar.[21] Taylor suggests that perhaps in the original there was a scene involving Duncan and his supporters prior to the entrance of the bleeding captain which, having been cut, necessitated a new stage direction, which Middleton supplied with his characteristic '*meeting*' formulation. Again, this is possible, but the mere presence of *meeting* seems insufficient to ground the evidence. Taylor also suggests that there may have been a battle scene (old-fashioned and fusty by 1616?) which Middleton took out, retaining only the aftermath with the Captain and his message. This seems much less likely for at least two reasons: 1) no other Shakespeare tragedy features battle scenes at both the beginning and the end – to do so would be to flirt with anti-climax;[22] and 2) why would we need the Captain's elaborate description of the battle (which even Taylor recognizes to be mostly Shakespearean) if we had just seen it enacted?

Other candidates for disappeared scenes are one involving Edward the Confessor, and one or two involving Angus, a mysterious and, with Ross and Lennox, rather undeveloped character. But none of these seems at all necessary, or even likely, and even if we were to imaginatively reinsert them, the play would still be unusually short. Those critics who have ascribed the play's brevity to its intensity of focus, its taut concentration on Macbeth, his wife, their crimes and the consequences of those crimes, may well be right. There are no visible gaps – although of course it is the business of effective theatrical cutting to cover any potential gaps. Taylor, among others (Brooke, for example), thinks that the play was shortened by the removal of clauses starting with 'by', which seems fanciful if not downright absurd.[23] Of course, some trimming of speeches could have been undertaken, but not only is it hard to tell, it's hard to imagine where; most of the speeches seem appropriately weighted, and there are even places (especially in the Malcolm/Macduff dialogue) where one might well have wished for some judicious cuts which appear not to have been made. Would an experienced playwright such as Middleton, who clearly admired Shakespeare's work even though he may have become impatient with it at times, have cut Macbeth's or Lady Macbeth's intense speeches down and let the insipid Malcolm go on at such length?

Brooke claims that the text's shortness is 'entirely the result of its derivation from performance' (p. 56) and 'forcefully refutes' (the phrase is Taylor's; p. 386) the point that its compression of language is accompanied by a parallel compression of structure. But Brooke merely says that this argument 'does not impress me' (p. 55) and ignores entirely the matter of the play's tightly compressed structure (he merely shows that the play's *language* is not uniformly and universally concentrated). His 'refutation' is more groundless than 'forceful'. If, then, there is no evidence for the elimination of particular scenes, and there is at least some tenuous evidence for the claim that the play's overall structure is indeed somewhat compressed, we are left with the view that what abridgement there might have been was confined to some shortening of certain speeches – not enough to make the imagined original all that much longer than the F text, with its Hecate additions, now is.

This does not mean that the F text is not a product of theatrical revision. Indeed, if the F text is derived from a theatrical playbook, then some of the anomalies discussed above could be the result of deletions or insertions missed or other gaps. It is possible to imagine that the copy that reached the printer (probably a transcript and not the play-book itself) was in a sense palimpsestic, the result of different stagings with different directions, additions or cuts. The apparently contradictory directions for the final duel (VIII) certainly point to different possible stagings, and the problems concerning what Lennox tells Macbeth in 4.1 about Macduff's flight (VII) could have arisen from adjustments made to the text for a revival. The apparent inconsistency between what Macbeth seems to know in 3.6 and what he says in 4.1 (or seems not to know) could have arisen from cuts made when the Hecate section was added to 4.1, though as I puzzle over this I am at a loss to figure out how.[24] Both 3.6 and the relevant part of 4.1 are clearly Shakespearean, though it is remotely possible that Shakespeare added 3.6 somewhat later (perhaps for the revival which saw a change in the final duel) to replace a longer scene in which Macduff resolves on flight. Our forgetful author might then have inadvertently introduced the inconsistency. However, as we all know, little inconsistencies that can bother editors tend to fly past in performance and go unnoticed by hard-working authors (indeed Shakespeare is often nailed for such failures by eagle-eyed critics). So it's just as likely that the inconsistency, such as it is, was there in the original version.

What about Simon Forman? For Taylor, two features of Forman's account indicate revision after 1611: one the description of the weird sisters as 'women feiries or Nimphes' and the other that Forman speaks of Macbeth and Banquo as 'Ridinge thorowe a wod'. On the latter, Taylor takes Forman to mean that they really did come onstage on horseback, which seems awfully literal-minded to me; it's true that there are three references in the period to a horse being brought on stage,[25] and Taylor seizes on this. But if we are to take Forman at his word, *two* horses would be required, which is unheard of in any stage direction through the whole period. It seems much simpler to interpret Forman as having inferred that Banquo and Macbeth arrive on horseback (which would be what he would expect, given their rank), and this may indeed have been indicated by offstage sounds (a frequent feature of contemporary stage directions). As for the 'Nimphes', Taylor thinks that Banquo's line, 'you should be women / And yet your beards forbid me to interpret / That you are so' (1.3.43–5) is an obvious sign of revision, since what Forman witnessed in 1611 is belied by the reference to beards – nymphs and fairies don't have beards. But Taylor ignores the phrase 'you should be women' and he apparently thinks that 'beards' means full bushy male beards, not straggly bits of facial hair on a person who is apparently female.[26] Forman's phrasing comes from Holinshed, though there is no other indication that he knew the *Chronicles*. His reference is a bit odd, but he is not always a reliable witness; his musings were written some time after he saw the performances he reports on, and they speak to his interests and in no way purport to be a full and accurate description.

Before concluding, I'd like to think a little more directly about evidence. This is a topic that I have written about elsewhere,[27] and all I want to reflect on here is a particular instance of a more general problem. In his attempt to prove the persistent presence of Middleton's revisions and adaptations throughout *Macbeth*, Taylor relies on internal evidence in ways that seem to me problematic. He isolates bits of text and then adduces parallels to the known work of one or the other writer to establish authorship. In a sharply argued article written over fifty years ago,[28] Ephim Fogel questioned the then widespread use of internal evidence to establish authorship, showing that the presence of 'salmons in both' the rivers near which two great kings grew up did not necessarily establish a parallel between them. His reference is to the comic exaggerations of the partisan Fluellen in extolling the merits of his well-loved commander (*Henry V* 4.7). In his conclusion, Fogel concedes that there is something exhilarating about such isolated parallels, which are seductive because they 'marshal us the way that we were going'; but, he argues, they must be 'rejected as unreal mockeries even, paradoxically, when they are genuine' (p. 308). The submerged allusions to *Macbeth* caught my eye. Macbeth's famous imaginative powers, his tendency (noted by Bradley) to live within the fantastical, to project his imagination onto the world, are here enlisted to warn against a critical fallacy, a willingness to trust in chimeras. It's a clever move on Fogel's part, and he ends his essay with yet another Shakespearean allusion, this time quoted, though not identified (in 1959, scholars of whatever speciality were expected to know their Shakespeare): 'To vouch this is no proof / Without more wider and more overt test ...'

Under the brunt of such attacks, impressionistic marshalling of parallels in pursuit of internal 'evidence' lost its cachet, and was gradually replaced by linguistic and statistical evidence of a more telling kind. But it makes a comeback in Taylor's exhaustive attempt to prove the presence of Middleton's hand in many passages of *Macbeth*. Taylor's proselytizing zeal, his ingenuity, his copiousness, his extraordinary command of the *oeuvre* of both writers, his frequently stated and hence disarming awareness of the pitfalls of the kind of 'evidence' he adduces, all contribute to a sense of depletion on the part of the reader that tends to make me, at least, susceptible: 'OK, OK, yes I see you must be right because there are so many examples ...' But once one begins looking more closely, the amassing of presumed parallels comes to rest on an uneasy foundation. I want to isolate just a couple of examples (added to those already mentioned) as a kind of sceptical counter-point. Take the following claim, adduced to help prove that 4.2.39–57, part of the dialogue between Lady Macduff and her witty son, is a Middletonian interpolation: 'Middleton frequently, and Shakespeare rarely, uses the oath *i'faith* or the contraction *''em*' (p. 395). However, a quick glance at an online search engine reveals that the oath occurs at least sixty times in Shakespeare, while *''em*' (certainly a common Middletonism) occurs around 170 times – more often than can credibly be described as 'rarely'. To take a second example: Taylor suggests that a passage in 4.1 (the exchanges with Lennox concerning the witches' exit and Macduff's flight discussed above) 'contain[s] nothing notably Shakespearean', while Macbeth's comment 'I did hear / The galloping of horse' (138–9) is adduced as evidence of Middleton's authorship of the passage, since 'Shakespeare never elsewhere uses the word "galloping"; Middleton does' (p. 390).[29] This is true; Middleton does use *galloping* once, in *Black Book* 348 (though there it is a verb form while in the *Macbeth* passage it is a substantive).[30] But Taylor neglects to mention that Shakespeare uses 'gallop(s)' more often than Middleton (11 times to 4)[31] and ignores the use of the word 'galloping' as a noun – the very first instance of that usage cited in *OED* and hence perhaps 'notably Shakespearean'. Of course this doesn't *prove* that Shakespeare is the author of the passage either, though the burden of proof would seem to rest with the would-be 'disintegrator'.[32]

All this comes down to what counts as evidence and what kind of proof we seek to establish or will allow. Evidence is malleable – it depends on desire and intention and hence has a rhetorical character. This is true even of generally more reliable statistical evidence, such as that used by Vickers and his colleagues, which can be deployed tendentiously and often is. At the very least it requires substantial chunks of text to work with, though it is clearly more dependable than the method used by Taylor. 'Facts', such as they are, only become 'evidence' when they are marshalled as part of an argument. This of course doesn't invalidate all evidence, even the circumstantial kind, or even verbal parallels for that matter. It merely speaks to the need for caution and precision in our disposition and assessment of data. In the case of *Macbeth*, to come down to the focus of the present volume and how we might think about the evidence for addition, revision and abridgement, we should perhaps consider just what role these features of the text might or should play in our interpretations.

In doing so, we would do well to remember the play's recurrent motif of equivocation, its delight in the possibilities of 'lying like truth',[33] its mingling of foul and fair as a mode of thinking. The play, like the characters etched by the garrulous Porter, undermines expectation and swears 'in both scales against either scale'. As the witches' equivocal prophecies undo Macbeth's reiterated desire for consequence to be squarely trammelled up, so the F text offers what looks at first like a relatively simple set of problems, which become the more uncertain the longer one pores over them. And yet it seems nevertheless to be true that the play, as originally composed, has been tampered with, abridged perhaps, adapted maybe, added to almost certainly, and in the process given what looks like a Middletonian twist.

Notes

1   Gary Taylor et al. (eds), *Thomas Middleton: The Collected Works* and *Thomas Middleton and Early Modern Textual Culture* (Oxford: Oxford University Press, 2007), vol. 1, p. 1128 (text cited as 'Oxford Middleton').

2 Usually (and rightly) spelled 'weird' in modern editions; see the extended note to 1.3.30 in A. R. Braunmuller, ed., *Macbeth,* NCS (Cambridge: Cambridge University Press, 1997), pp. 239–40.

3 Here and throughout the Chapter, when I quote from a modernized text, I follow Braunmuller.

4 Stanley Wells et al. (eds), *The Oxford Shakespeare* (Oxford: Oxford University Press, 1987) (cited as 'Oxford').

5 See, for example, G. L. Kittredge, ed., *Complete Works of Shakespeare* (Boston, MA: Ginn, 1936); J. D. Wilson, ed., *Macbeth*, New Shakespeare (Cambridge: Cambridge University Press, 1947); Kenneth Muir, ed., *Macbeth,* Arden 2nd series (London and New York: Routledge, 1986), and Braunmuller.

6 William Davenant, *Macbeth* (1674), Christopher Spencer, ed. (New Haven, 1961). Of course this doesn't mean that a version like Davenant's ever appeared on the Jacobean stage.

7 Gary Taylor, '*Macbeth*' in vol. 2 of Oxford Middleton (pp. 383–98, 693–703), and Brooke, ed., *Macbeth*, Oxford Shakespeare (Oxford: Oxford University Press, 1990).

8 Brian Vickers, 'Disintegrated: Did Thomas Middleton really adapt Macbeth?' *TLS*, 28 May 2010, pp. 14–15. See pp. 17–19 for a discussion of Vickers' argument.

9 Taylor thinks the prophecies are original and the apparitions interpolated (p. 391).

10 See the note to 3.5.36 in his edition for New Penguin (London, 1967).

11 I've explored this question at length in 'What do editors do and why does it matter?' in Laurie Maguire, ed., *How to Do Things with Shakespeare* (Oxford: Oxford University Press, 2008), pp. 160–80.

12 See Marcus Dahl, Marina Tarlinskaya and Brian Vickers, 'An Enquiry into Middleton's supposed "adaptation" of Macbeth', 2010. PDF file downloaded from http://www.ies.sas.ac.uk/networks/london-forum-authorship-studies

13 In this as in several other of the examples, the meanings of the matched phrase are somewhat different (entice him to pleasures, lead him to destruction).

14 Vickers sees similarities between some of the supernatural
   material in the late plays and Hecate's speeches, but the
   pronounced differences far outweigh the similarities. See
   Gordon McMullan, *Shakespeare and the Idea of Late Writing:
   Authorship in the Proximity of Death* (Cambridge: Cambridge
   University Press, 2007) for a thorough account of late
   Shakespeare.

15 *Shakespeare Co-Author* (Oxford: Oxford University Press,
   2002), p. 46, quoting Taylor, 'Shakespeare and Others:
   The authorship of *Henry VI Part One*' *MRDE* 7 (1995),
   pp. 145–205, 177.

16 The TLN count for the three plays is as follows: 2528
   (*Macbeth*), 2607 (*Timon*), 2708 (*Titus*). Other counts yield
   somewhat different results, with *Macbeth*, in E. K. Chambers'
   reckoning, being about 250 lines shorter than *Timon* (*William
   Shakespeare: A Study of Facts and Problems* [Oxford: Oxford
   University Press, 1930]). Comparing the Arden 3 *Timon* with
   the Cambridge *Macbeth* produces similar results (*Macbeth*
   2087, *Timon* 2307).

17 Taylor declares that *Timon* 'combines Middleton's compression
   with Shakespeare's expansiveness' (p. 385), but if we compare
   1.1 (Shakespeare) and 1.2 (Middleton) the opposite seems to
   be the case; the two scenes are of similar length (Middleton's a
   bit shorter) but the writing in 1.1 is more condensed and events
   more compressed.

18 See Anthony B. Dawson and Gretchen Minton (eds), *Timon of
   Athens*, Arden edition (London, 2008), pp. 1–10 *passim*.

19 Taylor argues that *Macbeth* must have been cut by somewhere
   between 700 and 1200 lines. Since, by his count, the play,
   without the added Hecate material, would have been 2049
   lines long, this would mean that as much as 40 per cent of the
   original play could have been cut. This seems to me a massively
   unfounded claim.

20 R. V. Holdsworth is much cited in Middleton attribution
   studies, even though he has never published his findings.

21 See *1HIV* 3.3.87 (*Enter the Prince marching, and Falstaffe
   meets him* ...) and *AC* 4.3.6 (*They meete other Soldiers*).
   However, in both of these, one of the parties is already on stage,

whereas in the typical Middleton formulation, as in *Mac.* 1.2, both parties seem to be entering more or less simultaneously.

22 *Coriolanus*, with its extensive act 1 battle, plays brilliantly on the expectation of further battle at the end, which never materializes. Battles are more pervasive in the early histories, of course, but are carefully positioned in the tragedies.

23 Taylor did a study of function words and finds *Macbeth* anomalous for plays written between 1603 and 1608 when it comes to the frequency of this preposition, but no other (p. 386).

24 Taylor, arguing for a wholesale redoing of 4.1, thinks that Middleton wrote the passage in question, but doesn't ascribe the inconsistency directly to Middleton's intervention. He believes that the Lord's speech in 3.6 was marked for omission in the copy and inadvertently printed, but offers no real evidence for this position (pp. 697–8) beyond the existence of the inconsistency itself.

25 See Alan Dessen and Leslie Thomson, *A Dictionary of Stage Directions in English Drama, 1580–1642* (Cambridge: Cambridge University Press, 1999).

26 See p. 389 for his long and, to me, tendentious and unpersuasive argument, which I don't have space to deal with here. I may simply say that while insisting that the post-1611 witches were conceived of as male and played by male actors with beards, he neglects to say why, given the extensive revisions throughout the text that he ascribes to Middleton, the reviser made no attempt to take out the many references to the witches as 'sisters'.

27 'Staging Evidence', in P. Holland and S. Orgel (eds), *From Script to Stage in Early Modern England* (Basingstoke and New York: Palgrave Macmillan, 2004), pp. 89–110.

28 Ephim Fogel, 'Salmons in Both, or Some Caveats for Canonical Scholars', *Bulletin of the New York Public Library* 63.5–6 (May–June 1959), pp. 223–36, 292–308. Fogel's general target is 'Fluellen's fallacy', i.e. 'the "proof" of a thesis by carefully selected fragments of a total pattern, [which] can vitiate historical as well as literary and statistical analysis' (p. 236).

29 Note that, though Taylor doesn't say so directly, his argument

here supports the view that the inconsistency cited in VII is a product of Middleton's revision.

30 Dahl et al. add that 'of horse' is common in Shakespeare.

31 I am using a rather crude and perhaps incomplete pair of files (or dramatic and non-dramatic works respectively) to do these searches, supplied to me before the Middleton project was finished. I have no access to a full Middleton concordance. Hence the numbers cited may be less accurate than I would hope, but they reveal the general trend.

32 The kinds of evidence favoured by Jonathan Hope (*The Authorship of Shakespeare's Plays* Cambridge: Cambridge University Press, 1994), among others (i.e. linguistic/socio-linguistic) depends on the availability of more data than is possible in this case – so Taylor is driven to adopt Fluellen's methodology.

33 In act 5, Macbeth finally begins 'To doubt the equivocation of the fiend / That lies like truth' (5.5.42–3). See Steven Mullaney ('Lying Like Truth: Riddle, Representation, and Treason in Renaissance England,' *ELH*, 1980), among many other critics who have explored the ramifications of this theme.

2

Dwelling 'in doubtful joy': *Macbeth* and the Aesthetics of Disappointment

Brett Gamboa

Few plays are more widely admired or more frequently staged than *Macbeth*.[1] But while its reputation, supernatural subjects and set speeches help explain its popularity with producers, its history with audiences does not. No other play by Shakespeare has so extensive a history of disappointing audiences. And no other finds reviewers so determined to praise the play in the midst of panning its productions, so where expectations are concerned *Macbeth* excels at falling short.[2] Carolyn Sale notes the play's tendency to fail onstage in her review of Michael Boyd's 2011 production for the RSC:

> I have seen poor productions of *Macbeth*. We all have. It's a beguiling play, apparently so simple, that no production company thinks it beyond its ambitions. But no matter how poor the production, I have always walked away from the theatre thinking that the play itself is indestructible.[3]

Like many reviewers, Sale goes beyond the problems of the moment to comment on the play's unusual rate of failure. She assumes that failed attempts at the play are so common that everyone has seen one.[4] But as interesting as the number of poor productions she supposes is her effort to distance the play from them. For Sale, it is not that *Macbeth* has a habit of failing – it is 'indestructible' – but that its producers fail it.

Steven Winn likewise shields the play from his criticism of Michael Donald Edwards' 2001 *Macbeth* for Shakespeare Santa Cruz: 'the production never finds the true measure of the play'; and Michael Billington extends the theme in his review of Grzegorz Bral's 2010 production at the Barbican: 'at no time did I feel that I had been led towards the heart of darkness in Shakespeare's magnificent dramatic poem'.[5] Like Sale, each reserves signal praise for *Macbeth* despite its momentarily failing iterations. While good and bad reviews exist in plenty for all of Shakespeare's plays, productions of *Macbeth* lead to rarely personal expressions of disappointment, often commingled with glowing tributes to the text. Reviewers repeatedly insinuate that the play deserves better, as if aware of a wide and unfortunate gap between th' effect and it. Bob Hoover called Des McAnuff's 2009 production for the Stratford Festival of Canada a 'letdown', noting how 'All the elements were there for an outstanding production, but they never added up'.[6] And Chris Kompanek typified the frustration many reviewers of *Macbeth* experience in his account of Aquila Theatre's 2012 off-Broadway production: 'how Aquila has managed to strip this great play of all its joys is a mystery and a grave disappointment'.[7] Reading reviews can give one the sense that *Macbeth* merits both its reputation for greatness and consideration as Shakespeare's greatest theatrical flop.

This essay is an attempt to account for why productions of *Macbeth* routinely fall short of expectations. But rather than asking how practitioners fail the play, it asks how the play may be failing them. I entertain the possibility that failure and disappointment are products of *Macbeth*'s design, and that the recurrent dissatisfaction that audiences experience owes much to the discomfort and confusion brought about by the play's efforts to mislead them during its second half, and by its pervasive lack of conflict. In *Macbeth*, Shakespeare appears to work purposefully to avoid conflict, and to deny audiences the logic-driven sequences and interactions they anticipate, thereby contributing to perceptions that a given performance has lost its way. A well-known example of the play's unusual logic occurs when Malcolm, the Hamlet-like son to a dear father murdered, and Macbeth, the object of his revenge, miss each other entirely in the last act.

But though I explore related examples for how they contribute to the audience's sense of frustration and disappointment, my end is not to show that the play is a great *failure* so much as a *great* failure. In other words, I argue that performances can thrive on the play's inevitable disappointments, that *Macbeth* is great at – even great by – failing its audience. In the right hands, *Macbeth*'s problems in logic can increase its power by likening the playgoer's situation to that of the protagonist, involving us in an experience of tragedy that parallels the one we witness onstage. In the foregoing examples, theatre critics appear to intuit the possibility that failure and success are indivisible in *Macbeth*. The sense of loss they experience – the realization of a gap between any performance and their ideal of it – is itself a dramatic outcome and the result of a productive engagement, even if the drama disappoints in some superficial elements. Some elements of failure are thus aesthetically productive and worth preserving in *Macbeth*, a play that intensifies the engagement of audiences by exploiting their attachment to what is progressively denied them.

Of course, the notion that *Macbeth* is built to fail may not surprise those aware of the many superstitions and accidents associated with its production history.[8] Any cast of *Macbeth* is more than usually mindful of the risks of failure, and the efforts of actors to avoid attracting the play's 'curse' adds tension to the process of staging it. It may be that practitioners, like reviewers, sense that failure is central to the play, and of its essence. The cast of *Macbeth* thus provides an analogue for its audience, whose increased engagement owes to the play's own flirtations with failure. Whether real (Diana Wynyard's Lady Macbeth falling from a platform while 'sleep-walking'), or imagined (Shakespeare taking on Lady Macbeth after a boy player's sudden death), the incidents and legends that add colour to the play's production history indicate what can go wrong with the play – how it can fail.[9] And however suspicious the stories, it is curious that an extensive mythology of failure should crop up around a play that disappoints in production as often as *Macbeth* does.

When it comes to the play's failures onstage, the sites of displeasure are mostly consistent.[10] Critics fault nearly any actor in the title role, and they are underwhelmed, confused, or otherwise let down by what happens after Duncan's murder, especially by what follows the departure of Banquo's ghost in 3.4. Regarding the lead, Kenneth Tynan declared that before Laurence Olivier 'no actor [had] ever succeeded in the role of Macbeth', a view supported by unsuccessful turns from some of the most admired actors of their generations.[11] Ralph Richardson, Anthony Hopkins, Peter O'Toole and Mark Rylance are just a few that have been blamed for not bringing the part – and the play – off.[12] More recently, Patrick Stewart was praised in Rupert Goold's production for Chichester Festival Theatre, but Liev Schreiber (Public Theater), Colme Feore (Stratford Festival of Canada) and Elliot Cowan (Shakespeare's Globe) starred in disappointments.[13] We generally concede the difficulty of staging *King Lear* or *Hamlet*, likely contributing to the result that a host of actors have been appreciated, or at least tolerated, in the leading roles. But we are not as lenient with producers of *Macbeth*, whose stage history may best be described as a series of spectacular failures.[14]

Reflecting on twentieth-century performances at Stratford-upon-Avon, Gareth Lloyd Evans describes a range of miscarried attempts at the lead:

[Ralph] Richardson simply failed dismally, [Paul] Scofield's was consistently out of sorts with its surrounding production, [Eric] Porter's had the dullness of intellectual clarity almost totally devoid of emotional vibrancy and Nicol Williamson, again predictably, confused eccentric behavior with perceptive acting.[15]

Of the nine actors surveyed, only Olivier and Ian McKellen were considered successful by a majority of critics. And only McKellen starred in a production that was admired as much as he was, since Glen Byam Shaw's version was 'generally regarded as an unsatisfactory complement to Olivier's acting'.[16] In his analysis Evans stresses the starkly different approaches the actors took: 'Where Macbeth is concerned it would be impossible to devise a set of actors whose interpretation differed so much in nature and quality than those at Stratford'.[17] Yet despite the differences in their talents and individual characterizations the results were similar: seven of the nine were considered deficient in a role commonly held to be one of Shakespeare's greatest. That so many good actors fell short in distinct ways argues that the role may be the problem and that actors may be victims to it.[18]

The play's second half attracts as much blame as the lead actor. Reviewers regularly notice sudden fallings off in pace and clarity after strong starts, and directors come under fire for derailing promising productions and contributing to a sense of anticlimax.[19] Mark Cofta faults Blanka Zizka's 2010 production at the Wilma Theater for just that, concluding: 'the play peters out rather than climaxes'.[20] Charles Isherwood praises the first half of Declan Donnellan's 2011 staging for Cheek by Jowl, which moved 'at the fluttering pace of an anxious heartbeat', but then observes 'how sparing the play's action is' in the latter half, and how the production 'loses some of its fleet pacing in the final innings'.[21] And Terry Doran recalls that 'the theater-wise at Stratford [Canada] had great hopes' for Robert Beard's 1990 *Macbeth,* but 'by the time Brian Bedford comes to the "Is this a dagger" speech, disappointment has set in'. [22] The way audiences often

experience the play is reflected in Lyn Gardner's account
of Zoe Seaton's 2002 *Macbeth* for Creation Theatre. She
applauds a production that 'begins strongly' and with welcome
'speediness', then singles out the arrival of Banquo's ghost as a
high point before describing a director losing her way: 'by the
second half, Seaton is just throwing everything she can think
of at the play'.[23] Though it began with promise, Gardner joins
her voice to the chorus, 'Creation could have done so much
better'.

But just as the widespread lack of success by talented actors
in the title role argues that the role may be more to blame than
they are, so recurring problems at predictable sites in the latter
acts may tell us more about the play's construction than the
skill of its directors. We can no more assume that directors
of *Macbeth*, after a successful act or two, suddenly lose their
sense of proportion and pace, or their ability to facilitate
dramatic climax, than we can imagine that so many talented
actors save their worst performances for one particular play.
Though Cofta is focused on Zizka's production, his comment
that 'the play peters out rather than climaxes' is valuable in
thinking about the play's structure. The play does peter out.
Climaxes are lacking in every production of *Macbeth,* because
climaxes are lacking in *Macbeth*.

The series of slayings in the play is illustrative. The deaths
that most concern audiences are those they do not witness.
The play takes time to show the deaths of Banquo and
little Macduff, each at the hands of tertiary characters, but
Macbeth's murder of Duncan occurs offstage. Macbeth does
kill someone onstage, but it is Young Siward, a character
whose death is almost irrelevant, a distraction from the death
that matters in the moment – that of Macbeth himself.[24] And
when the play comes to Macbeth's death, in most productions he is killed offstage, and in all productions he is killed
by the wrong man, since Malcolm has the prior claim and is
the primary generic revenger. If someone should replace him,
Fleance is next in line, while Macduff doesn't take the stage
until nearly two acts are out, and his family is unknown until

act 4. The play thus bars the audience from the deaths in which it is most concerned and allows it a privileged position for deaths that are comparatively insignificant. The play thus works against its own climaxes, allowing them to occur in the wings while extraneous plot points take centre stage.

In an attempt to contextualize Olivier's rare success in the role, Tynan ties the difficulties of the role to the character's diminished ability to participate, noting the absence of a climactic death scene for Macbeth:

> Instead of growing as the play proceeds, the hero shrinks; complex and many-leveled to begin with, he ends up a cornered thug, lacking even a death scene with which to regain lost stature. Most Macbeths, mindful of this, let off their big guns as soon as possible, and have usually shot their bolt by the time the dagger speech is out.[25]

Tynan anticipates Cofta's critique in blaming the play – and by extension its playwright – for the diminishing energy of the play in production. Since Macbeth is deprived of his role, actors give all they can to the character while it remains viable. But after Duncan's murder they succumb to a role that no longer allows them to be large or complex in it, and their subsequent failure helps to sink the play. Tynan links what reviewers often treat as independent sources of disappointment – Macbeth actors and sputtering second halves – implying that the failure of the Macbeth role *in* the second half helps explain why many productions can succeed early and then fall apart. So *Macbeth* fails to climax because it prevents its protagonist from taking part in one.

Like Tynan, I think Shakespeare forces problems on the Macbeth actor after the revelation of Duncan's murder, problems that explode in number and intensity after the departure of Banquo's ghost. But depriving Macbeth of his death scene is just one way the text compromises its protagonist's ability to play the star part prefigured in the first two acts. Throughout the play, Shakespeare limits chances for his lead player to take action or engage in legitimate conflict – things essential to any character. And when Macbeth achieves the throne of Scotland, at the height of his power, the play works hardest to prevent him from exercising any. Consequently, the audience waits on the Macbeth actor to deliver what he cannot: a sense of possibility, and – what should be fundamental to any dramatic text – confidence that the results of the action depend upon what the protagonist does. The audience is consequently deprived of its role, too, since it remains indebted for its progress to a character that cannot determine the way forward.

Macbeth is a tragedy of inefficacy and impotence. Hamlet is famous for hesitancy and inaction, but Macbeth proves even less capable of directing his course than Hamlet. The emergence of fates that predestine his fall gradually render his attempts at action meaningless. From the first, the play works to sideline its star. In 1.2 Macbeth's exploits in war are reported in detail, but the audience does not see them. When Macbeth appears on the road to Forres, it is Banquo who speaks to the weird sisters while Macbeth is silent. After the prophecies are spoken, the thanes wait on Macbeth while he stands frozen with fear, contemplating the actions that may be necessary to fulfil his destiny: 'why do I yield to that suggestion / Whose horrid image doth unfix my hair, / And make my seated heart knock at my ribs' (1.3.134–7). Macbeth is already less than advertised. Audiences expecting 'Valour's minion', who carved his way to Macdonwald and 'unseam'd him from the nave to th' chops', may sense that the man before them doesn't measure up (1.2.18–22).

If *Macbeth* is a tragedy of impotence, Macbeth is the star actor who cannot act. Like an actor, he takes different roles (Glamis, Cawdor, King), he pretends loyalty to a king that he murders, he pretends friendship to Banquo while leading him to an ambush. And like an actor, agency is implanted upon him, first by the witches and then by Lady Macbeth. But his attempts at action are often characterized by something like stage fright. He experiences it first after the meeting of the witches, and it is highlighted by the verbiage as well as by his behaviour:

Banquo	Look how our partner's rapt.
Macbeth	[Aside.] If Chance will have me king, why, Chance may crown me
	Without my stir.
Banquo	New honours come upon him,
	Like our strange garments, cleave not to their mould,
	But with the aid of use.

$$(1.3.143-7)$$

By observing that his friend is 'rapt', Banquo affirms that Macbeth is powerless to move. His powerlessness is accentuated by his given reason for not moving: he wonders whether he can achieve his goal without taking any action ('why, Chance may crown me / Without my stir'). And Banquo further establishes the connection between Macbeth and a stage actor by shifting to a language of costume: 'New honours come upon him, / Like our strange garments…'. As the play progresses, stage fright returns and with growing intensity, as Macbeth proves that he is not up to his own part. Inexplicably, though, like an actor who has missed his cue, Macbeth does not go with his wife to greet Duncan in 1.6. He then hesitates twice before the murder: first Lady Macbeth must shame him to action and then the 'air-drawn dagger' must invite him to carry out the murder. And his fear paralyzes him entirely after the murder, when Lady Macbeth cannot persuade him to return the daggers to the murder scene, or to exit the stage to wash his hands.

Despite his inaction, the conflicts between Macbeth and his wife, between him and his own ambition, along with the doubt about whether Macbeth will get the crown (and whether Chance or his stir will lead him there), preserve the audience's sense of possibility through two acts. But as the play continues the conflict dissipates, as does the sense of possibility. Macbeth takes the throne and attempts to bar Banquo's heirs the way to succession, but since the forecast of Macbeth's rise has proven true, his fall is likewise assured. He vies with fate for a time – even killing Banquo and little Macduff by proxy – but after the departure of his wife Macbeth struggles as though with foes that have already bested him. Fate ultimately renders all his actions irrelevant. At the height of his power he is powerless, and the play is thereby sapped of its vitality. The result for the audience is not dullness but frustration, since it remains attached to the protagonist and to its opinion that the stakes of the drama should be significant even though the conflicts within it are not. Lady Macbeth never loses steam; Malcolm never has any. If the play falters – and it will – it will be on the shoulders of Macbeth.

It may be that audiences and critics are unfair to the Macbeth actor, faulting him for not taking control in a play that won't let him. If failure in the play is linked to Macbeth's – and the Macbeth actor's – failure as a performer, then actors may do themselves and their productions some harm by trying to play the star part imagined rather than adapting themselves to changes in the role that come with Duncan's murder. The role is weaker and more hesitant than what audiences or star actors expect. Macbeth is yielding, uncomfortable in the 'strange garments' in which the witches dress him, and he is ultimately more comfortable giving way to the witches, his wife and others than he is appropriating agency for himself.

I will return to the unique problems of the role, and the effects of limiting conflict in the latter acts, but it is worth noting that while the problems in those acts involve Macbeth, they do not end with him. Nearly every scene and character in the second half partakes in the play's failure – and helps involve the audience in the fallout. The second appearance of Banquo's ghost marks the halfway point of *Macbeth*. Though every attempt at the play is an odds-on favourite to disappoint, its first hour usually speeds by audiences like a bullet train. But the extreme compression of events is easy to track.[26] Less than ten minutes after the witches forecast Macbeth's rise, Lady Macbeth is plotting Duncan's fall; ten minutes later, Macbeth has 'done the deed'.[27] And ten minutes more finds him safely established on the throne. The audience wants no additional explanations in the early going, despite the blistering pace and the need to reconcile an array of contradictions. The witches 'should be women', yet they have beards that forbid Banquo 'to interpret that they are so' (1.3.45–7). Macbeth is the loyal protector against that 'most disloyal traitor, / The Thane of Cawdor', and he is the Thane of Cawdor – and a most disloyal traitor, too (1.2.53–4).[28] He is 'Bellona's bridegroom', brave and masculine, yet, in the view of his wife, 'too full o'th' milk of human kindness' (1.5.17). Meanwhile, his 'Lady' asks to be 'unsexed', and to trade her 'milk for gall', shortly before citing her experience with a suckling child (1.5.17, 48).

The verse is as enlivened by paradox as the compressed contradictions that stand in for characters. Consider just three phrases from the play's first half: Duncan's praise of Macbeth as 'a peerless kinsman' (1.4.57); Macbeth's description of how the witches 'made themselves air into which they vanished' (1.5.4–5); and his fantastically attractive statement to the murderers concerning Fleance, 'Whose absence is no less material to me / Than is his father's' (3.1.135–6).[29] One who pauses over these lines will find them out as logically impossible, cancelling the meaning they express in the very moments of its expression. Yet, the audience traverses these lines as smoothly as they encounter 'weird sisters' who are man and woman, natural and supernatural, those who tell the future and those who determine it.[30] In the first half of *Macbeth* audiences are unfazed even by equations like 'foul is fair and fair is foul' (1.1.11). The patterning and the insistent repetition of paradoxes allow audiences a privileged position by which they seem to understand, effortlessly, what could not possibly be understood. In the first two acts, action, character and verse empower audiences, causing them to mirror Macbeth's rise to power in Scotland. But something changes, radically, after the exit of Banquo's ghost. The verse continues rich and inventive but the characters lose complexity, the tension and the formerly torrid pace dissipates or grows inconsistent and audiences struggle to understand the details of an action that had formerly progressed with clarity.

If the first half makes audiences feel invincible, the second often confuses or leaves them out altogether. One early instance of the play eluding its audience occurs when Macbeth is left alone with his wife after the banquet:

Macbeth	How say'st thou that Macduff denies his person,
	At our great bidding?
Lady Macbeth	Did you send to him, sir?
Macbeth	I hear it by the way; but I will send.
	There's not a one of them, but in his house
	I keep a servant fee'd. I will to-morrow
	(And betimes I will) to the Weird Sisters:
	More shall they speak; for now I am bent to know,
	By the worst means, the worst. For mine own good,
	All causes shall give way: I am in blood
	Stepp'd in so far, that, should I wade no more,
	Returning were as tedious as go o'er.
	Strange things I have in head, that will to hand,
	Which must be acted, ere they may be scann'd.

(3.4.127–39)

To this point, the play had taken pains to ensure that the audience was keeping up. The Macbeths had walked us through their devices, his to practise on Duncan, hers to practise on him, allowing the audience a favoured place. This speech helps erode that place, since the audience is ignorant of the rumours and Macbeth's arrangement to spy on all of his thanes. Though we anticipate his anxiety concerning Banquo, we cannot understand why everyone suddenly has become a threat. The simplifying of Macbeth's character that Tynan describes has begun, as has his paranoia, but of a less complex kind than what formerly generated the air-drawn dagger and disembodied voices.

Macbeth had then previewed each step for the audience through soliloquies and asides. He proceeded with our consent, if against our moral judgment. But our place in the inner circle is now denied, and we are thrust into an improbable alignment with Lady Macbeth, asked to 'be innocent of the knowledge.../ Till thou applaud the deed'(3.2.45–6). The play and its protagonist have begun to move without us. We may not pause to wonder how Macbeth has come into possession of the witches' home address, but the news that he can visit them when he likes contradicts the understanding that the first encounter was an act of fate. The play had implied that Macbeth could not do what he now so casually plans. Macbeth should have sought more information from the witches already, if he had free access to them all along (1.3.44–5).

Macbeth departs 3.4 planning to act first and ask questions later: 'Strange things I have in head, that will to hand, / Which must be acted, ere they may be scann'd' (3.4.138–9). After 3.4, the play takes the hint, constantly acting things that cannot be scanned – by the audience. Consider the dialogue between Lennox and a Lord in 3.6. Beginning with William D'Avenant's 1664 text, versions of the play have altered, omitted, moved or apologized for 3.6, since nothing can get the scene to play clearly as it exists in the Folio.[31] In just fifty lines, the Folio text gives the audience to understand that: a) Macduff lives in disgrace because he didn't attend the feast – though moments ago Macbeth admits to not inviting him (3.4.127–9); b) Macduff has gone to England to join Malcolm; c) a 'King' (context suggests Macbeth; syntax Siward[32]) has sent to Macduff, who is in England and therefore unavailable

to receive Macbeth's messenger, yet he has it seems received
the messenger; and d) Macduff is not here nor yet there, but on
the way, since Lennox prays that some angel may announce
his message there before Macduff is come. The same audience
that had no trouble with weird sisters that, though 'seeming
corporal melted / As breath into the wind' (1.3.81–2), has
nothing but trouble here, and cannot say with certainty where
Macduff is, whether a message reached him, or who sent it.

But nothing can prepare audiences for the greater confusion
to come, when, at the end of his second interview with the
witches, Macbeth *learns*, as if for the first time, that Macduff
has fled to England:

Macbeth	Who was't came by?
Lennox	'Tis two or three, my lord, that bring you word,
	Macduff is fled to England.
Macbeth	Fled to England?
Lennox	Ay, my good lord.
Macbeth	Time, thou anticipat'st my dread exploits:
	The flighty purpose never is o'ertook,
	Unless the deed go with it.

                                                    (4.1.140–6)

Macbeth is surprised by the news, as though he had not sent
to Macduff or received the answer of defiance described in
the previous scene. He even upbraids himself for his delay in
doing what the audience has understood to be already done.
Again we are pushed off from what had seemed to be firm
ground. From this vantage 3.6 appears to serve the primary
purpose of adding an obstacle for its audience, since all it
established is put in doubt. The lone possibility remaining is
that Macduff was home to receive a message from Macbeth
that did not involve the feast, an explanation the play has
already twice contradicted. And, what is a greater problem,
in the following scene Ross goes in Macduff's place to inform
Lady Macduff of her abandonment, which suggests that
Macduff was not home to inform her himself or to receive

messengers. All paths to understanding the sequence are steep and full of thorns. We can speculate that the playwright was careless with the facts and sequence of his plot, but a pattern is emerging. That Lennox changes from disloyal conspirer in 3.6 to dutiful subject in 4.1 adds another thread of inconsistency.

The inconsistencies are complemented by unsettling instances of compression. After Ross leaves the Macduff home in 4.2, a messenger enters to warn Lady Macduff about a murder plot. But his warning is in vain, since six lines after the message is delivered the murderers appear. Seconds later both mother and son are dead. The result is equal parts trauma and confusion for an audience whose distress is anchored partly in tragedy and partly in a failure of dramatic logic. Since there is no time for the Macduffs to escape, the warning is cruel and superfluous – it feels as unjust outside the bounds of the plot as the murder does within it. One piece of the action treads upon another's heels. In this case, the arrival of the second invalidates the dramatic uses of the first. Whereas formerly the audience maintained their sense of mastery over the plot despite the torrid pace and frequent paradoxes, now it can't keep up with a plot that seems no longer to have control over its own elements.

Something similar happens in the following scene when Ross arrives in England. In response to Macduff's inquiries about his family members, Ross tells him that all are well. Though he parted shortly before the murders, Ross left them well in health, and the audience believes that Ross reports what he thinks to be true. But as soon as the subject turns from Macduff's family to Malcolm's revenge, Ross returns to it:

> Would I could answer
> This comfort with the like. But I have words
> That would be howled out in the desert air,
> Where hearing should not latch them.

(4.3.192–5)

The audience must redefine its understanding, allowing now
that Ross learned about the murders despite leaving hurriedly
for England before they took place. But if he knew, why not
tell Macduff at first? We may guess, of course, that he wanted
to avoid the responsibility of telling Macduff. But the fact that
we are guessing is the problem. There is dramatic irony here
but the audience has no share in it.

The following scene continues to erode the audience's
confidence, since it learns that it has been kept inexplicably
ignorant of Lady Macbeth's *habit* of walking in her sleep.
A doctor reports that he has for 'two nights watched', with
a gentlewoman we have never met, and we are suddenly
indebted to these minor characters to teach us about what has
become customary at the Macbeths' home (5.1.1). The play
is gradually diminishing our access to the central figures of
the plot. There is some injustice in the comparative privilege
assigned to these nameless characters. Audiences do not pause
to complain that they were not informed sooner, just as they
do not fault Ross for knowing about the murders, but they
feel their hold on the plot slipping, and they are forced to
guess at what is transpiring in the gaps. After the murder of
Duncan, Macbeth keeps his wife 'innocent of the knowledge'
of his plots (3.2.45). But her lament, 'The Thane of Fife
had a wife: where is she now?' confirms that information
is travelling through channels unavailable to us (5.1.41–2).
Though momentarily aligned with Lady Macbeth in 3.4, the
audience finds it has as little access to her as to Macbeth.
And her death offstage will continue the trend of denying the
audience access to what most anxiously concerns it.

Lady Macbeth's departure from the play – the couple
never appears together after 3.4 – also helps assure the
audience's lessening appreciation for Macbeth – and for the
Macbeth actor. She had held a kind of mastery over him, like
he did over us. Previously he was partly defensible in our eyes
because of her role in manipulating him. His struggles against
her, and against his own ambition, generated the conflict in
the play and enabled the audience to share his doubts and

hopes regarding the resolutions to come. But her departure leaves nobody to share the blame. Malcolm and Macduff, the logical candidates left to oppose Macbeth, are prevented from joining him onstage. So, isolated from all parties, including the audience, and permitted neither to challenge his adversaries nor to change his fate, the Macbeth of acts 4 and 5 appears as Tynan describes – shrinking, cornered, tyrannical, and gradually bereft of both complexity and fascination.

We may wonder why Shakespeare creates such a character, one set up – and one who helps set audiences up – to fail. One answer is that *Macbeth* risks the audience's relationship to the protagonist, as well as its pleasure, in order that it might experience tragedy as Macbeth does. In other words, audiences face their own powerlessness before a play that had formerly super-empowered them, and their own disappointment in a character that had electrified them, in order to experience a fall that parallels Macbeth's own after being crowned a king. He loses his power to act and we lose the play. In *Macbeth*, then, we do not sympathize with the protagonist's predicament – we live it. Stephen Booth observes that 'to be audience to *Macbeth* is virtually to *be* Macbeth' throughout the performance, noting that Macbeth and the audience are 'the only major parties to the play who see or feel the magnitude of the situations the play presents'.[33] Booth is explaining our inability emotionally to defect from Macbeth, and his comments are valuable in justifying how our relationship to the play and its protagonist parallels Macbeth's relationship to the fates within the play. Each of us is paltered with in a double sense. Each is attached to a mirage that reveals itself as one, yet neither actor nor audience can give over the attachment. That the play can divide us from its protagonist in a way that simultaneously draws us closer to him is a great achievement, even if the process is as frustrating for us as it is for Macbeth.

In describing what ails the audience about *Macbeth*, I have thus far skipped over Malcolm, Scotland's rightful heir.

Malcolm's star turn occurs in 4.3, a scene that creates more problems for the audience than any other. Marvin Rosenberg has described it as the 'most resistant scene in the play', noting its comparatively sluggish pace and the fact that it 'has given trouble to generations of directors and actors ... and audiences'.[34] Indeed, the scene is the play's longest and, by a large margin, its dullest. In 4.3 Shakespeare pursues dullness as if wholly focused on irritating and distancing his audience. We should expect just the opposite, since the anticipated generic result – and the audience's sense of justice – depends on Malcolm unseating Macbeth and regaining the throne. An audience that remains emotionally attached to Macbeth despite feeling increasingly isolated from him would be served by the rise of an attractive hero to whom it can defect. Malcolm is ripe for the part when he takes the stage and begins an elaborate test of Macduff's loyalty. But the test is an obstacle for an audience that – once again – isn't in on the joke. When Malcolm describes how he would be a worse ruler than Macbeth, we have no more idea that Malcolm lies to test Macduff than Macduff does. Again, dramatic irony is available here, but only to Malcolm, and at the expense and frustration of an audience that is left out once more. Were Malcolm to enter alone, explaining in soliloquy his suspicions about Macduff and laying out a plan to test him, the audience could readily take his part. But Malcolm puts on a lengthy performance for himself alone. He is both actor and audience, while Macduff and the audience of the play must take him at his word.

Since our sense of justice demands that Malcolm regain his father's crown, his confessions are lost on us. We have seen the work of a tyrant in Scotland, so Malcolm's imagined evils cannot rival the blood of Duncan, Banquo or young Macduff. Because his claim on the throne is legitimate, Macolm will always be preferable to Macbeth, so his extended self-incriminations are as unproductive as his imposture. We are neither impressed by the one, nor aware of the other. What is more, *we* know Macduff is honest, so the outcome of Malcolm's

game is never in doubt for us – even if we could be certain
that it is a game. Malcolm thus fails to catch on to one of the
few things about which the audience can still be certain. Act
4 scene 3 does nothing to teach audiences what they don't
already know, but it goes on interminably teaching them what
they already do know.

From the first, Malcolm alienates his audience through a
speech as needlessly and ostentatiously complicated as scenes
we have witnessed elsewhere in the second half:

> What I believe, I'll wail;
> What know, believe; and what I can redress,
> As I shall find the time to friend – I will.
> What you have spoke, it may be so perchance.
> This tyrant, whose sole name blisters our
> tongues,
> Was once thought honest: you have loved him
> well,
> He hath not touched you yet. I am young, but
> something
> You may discern of him through me, and
> wisdom
> To offer up a weak, poor, innocent lamb
> T' appease an angry God.

Macduff   I am not treacherous.

Malcolm   But Macbeth is.

> A good and virtuous nature may recoil
> In an imperial charge. But I shall crave your
> pardon:
> That which you are my thoughts cannot
> transpose;
> Angels are bright still, though the brightest fell.
> Though all things foul would wear the brows
> of grace,
> Yet grace must still look so.

                                        (4.3.8–24)

I quote Malcolm at length because the leadenness of his rhetoric operates through excess. In all, Malcolm's test of Macduff runs more than one hundred lines. The stilted phrasing, the platitudes and infelicitous metaphor, the attempts to imply dialogue where none is taking place, the frequent elisions and the curtailed clauses combine to guarantee that the speeches will be delivered slowly, and will prove almost unendurable for us, their victims. Though we encounter the scene with every reason to support Malcolm's position against Macbeth, we soon struggle to remain interested in him at all. Since the rhetoric continues longer than it took to plan and commit the murder of Duncan, and since the subject here is a private performance for insignificant ends, the audience cannot but feel that the play has lost its way. It is in search of a hero, but Macbeth remains preferable to this one. The audience is disappointed here, since it must perform its generic duty and support what it loathes, while remaining attached to Macbeth, whose position on the throne – along with his moral position – is impossible to support.

Macbeth depends for its energy on cultivating simultaneous attractions and repulsions in the audience, presenting a moral problem in the person of Macbeth, but giving that moral problem some of the more attractive speeches in literature. It makes audiences covet what they cannot choose and, by comparison with Malcolm, electrifying an ever more simple, isolated and impotent lead character. And it does the reverse for Malcolm – letting us feel we can do without the only force that can bring moral closure to the play. That is disaster by design. But there is wonder in it, since the play ultimately enables its audience to side with and against both its villain and its victim in the same moments.

On the surface Malcolm underwhelms the audience because he has all the majesty of a linoleum floor. But Malcolm's role is more complicated than it seems. He's incapable of pleasing in the role assigned to him, and yet he's prevented even from playing that role. Malcolm is a revenger like Hamlet, but the play deprives him of his revenge, allowing Macduff to usurp the role of revenger just as Macbeth took his place as king. Malcolm has no exploits in battle and is forced to stand aside not only for Macduff, but also for Young Siward. His identity both as Macbeth's adversary and as royal son is diminished by the sudden primacy of the Siward plot, and, as if that were not enough, the audience is eerily aware throughout the final scenes that Malcolm cannot remain a king for long, since Banquo has been hailed father to a long line of kings. Fleance therefore waits in the wings, yet another potentially royal son and revenger casting shadows over Malcolm, whose piece of the dramatic pie continues to shrink during the very scenes in which he is supposedly coming to power. The audience requires Malcolm's rise but ends up feeling that it is ineffectual and even inappropriate. So the ending of the play feels like one more needlessly crude disappointment. We are left with anticlimax upon anticlimax, deprived of Macbeth's death scene and of Malcolm's proper rise.

What hurts Malcolm most with the audience is the very thing that undermines Macbeth and the play that bears his name – the lack of meaningful conflict. Dramatic structures, we are given to believe, require conflict. But *Macbeth* has little. Everything is always already in motion. Audiences wonder whether Macbeth is destined to murder Duncan or not, whether he has the will to choose once the witches speak. But the problem stands out because it mirrors the problem the play presents to its audience. When Duncan is killed, Malcolm flies to England and is forgotten by the plot. When we see him again, he has Siward and ten thousand men. Those men ride north and immediately vanquish their foes. The battle ends before it is begun, and Malcolm's lone moment of glory rests in the ingenious plot to carry branches from Birnam to obscure the numbers of the army. But even then the audience gives little credit to Malcolm, since he seems to play out a script that the witches have written. If the witches had not first prophesied that Birnam Wood would come, Malcolm would appear resourceful. But their prophecy prevents it. In the end he has no exploits in battle and no exchanges with the tyrant he has come to dethrone. And Malcolm has little better prospects on the throne than Macbeth himself had. After Duncan's murder, Macbeth appears to play out a hand that is already concluded, one that he had every reason to think would win, yet one that he cannot win. Malcolm takes the mantle of inefficacy at the play's close, and the audience is left with a resolution that feels less pleasing and complete than it should.

The audience to *Macbeth* is like Donalbain, asking 'What is amiss?' and encountering the appropriate but still confusing answer: 'you are and do not know it' (2.3.94–5). Just as Macbeth's authority and ability elude him, so the play itself eludes its audience's apprehension. This feeling of loss, one that the audience largely remains ignorant of but that impacts their experience deeply, may figure significantly in explaining why many critics have blamed practitioners more than they have deserved, and why Tynan blamed Shakespeare. Booth suggests that 'the tragedy of plays like *Macbeth* occurs in the audience'.[35] If that is true, then forcing audiences to feel they have the world in their hands for a while and then have lost it is a worthy achievement, particularly when the arc the audience describes mirrors that of the title character in the play unfolding before them. The often-heard conclusions that the director lost control or created a sense of anticlimax are better applied to the play, and they may mask the play's effect of engaging its audience in their own sense of loss regarding the protagonist and the action in which he attempts to participate. That experience is valuable and worth cultivating, since it acquaints the audience with the lead character, and with tragedy, in a more intimate and extensive way than could be accomplished otherwise. The audience may leave the theatre convinced that the production has come short of the play, much as Macbeth might complain of the witches failing to meet his expectations, but its sense of loss, and of the gap between its expectation and what was delivered, argues a richer and more complex experience than Shakespeare could have provided by a more uniform shift in allegiance from Macbeth to Malcolm.

Notes

1   Few theatre companies have operated long enough to help decide the question, but *Macbeth*'s popularity is clear. The Royal Shakespeare Company records seventy-two productions, ranking the play ninth among their repertory and second only to *Hamlet* among tragedies. During the last fifty years (1962–2012) only *Hamlet* and *A Midsummer Night's Dream* have been staged more. At the Stratford Festival of Canada, *Macbeth* is the most frequently produced tragedy (ten productions) and ranks fourth overall. And at the Oregon Shakespeare Festival, *Macbeth* ranks fourth among tragedies (after *Hamlet, Romeo and Juliet, Othello*) and ninth overall.

2   Productions of any play can disappoint. But when audiences come away from *The Merry Wives of Windsor* thinking they have seen something mediocre, they have. Audiences at *Macbeth* are rightly convinced that a masterpiece is before them, so their sense of disappointment tends to be greater.

3   *Shakespeare Bulletin*, 30: 2, Summer 2012, p. 149.

4   In his review of Edward Hall's 2002 *Macbeth* for the Albery Theatre, Paul Taylor provides a similar example, situating Hall's version among a number of dismal precedents: 'I have seen quite a few worse productions [...] but the current account is still a crude and disappointing venture' (*Independent,* 15 November 2002).

5   Winn's review appears in the *San Francisco Chronicle*, 27 July 2001. Billington's review ran in the *Guardian,* 4 November 2010. Of course, there are many positive reviews of the play and its principal actor. I mean to establish only that negative reviews are more common for *Macbeth* than they are for most plays, and that what displeases critics is often predictable.

6   *Pittsburg Post-Gazette*, 27 September 2009.

7   *Macbeth (Review)*, 25 April 2012. http://www.theatermania.

com/ [accessed 15 November 2012]. The production was
directed by Desiree Sanchez.

8   Superstitions regarding the play are well known. Chief among
    them, theatre practitioners avoid uttering the name 'Macbeth'
    in the theatre lest a curse be revived that will lead to a
    catastrophic accident during the run. '*Macbeth*' therefore gives
    way to 'the Scottish play', and the principals are referred to as
    'Mackers' and 'Lady M'.

9   Several sources record Wynyard's fall, including Oscar James
    Campbell's *A Shakespeare Encyclopedia* (London: Methuen,
    1966), p. 488. The legend that Shakespeare had to step in for
    the Lady Macbeth actor is popular but sourceless, so far as I'm
    aware.

10 Here I intend lines of failure that are unique to productions of
    Macbeth. Naturally, any staging of any play may falter or fail
    due to things like uneven pacing, stray motion, confusing or
    distracting concepts, inaudibility, bad acting, etc.

11 Kenneth Tynan, *Curtains* (London: Longmans, 1961), p. 98.

12 Richardson played Macbeth in 1952 at Stratford, in a
    production directed by John Gielgud; Hopkins played the
    role for Michael Blakemore at the National Theatre in 1972;
    O'Toole's turn came in Bryan Forbes' 1980 production at the
    Old Vic; and Rylance directed and starred in a 1995 production
    at the Greenwich Theatre. All four productions were famously
    disastrous.

13 Goold's 2007 production opened at Chichester's Minerva
    Theatre, before travelling to London and New York.
    Schreiber starred in Moisés Kaufman's 2006 *Macbeth* at New
    York's Delacorte Theater, Feore's turn came in Des McAnuff's
    2009 production at the Stratford (ON) Festival Theater, and
    Cowan starred in Lucy Bailey's 2010 version at Shakespeare's
    Globe.

14 O'Toole's performance at the Old Vic became the base metal
    standard by which many failed plays were measured for two
    decades following. Rylance's production was considered 'the
    worst *Macbeth* since Peter O'Toole's', and famously inspired
    Benedict Nightingale to offer to eat the First Folio if the
    decade following offered a version as 'ill-conceived'. Across

the Atlantic, perhaps the biggest flop on Broadway in the past two decades was Terry Hands' production of *Macbeth* starring Kelsey Grammer, which closed after ten days. Regarding O'Toole and Rylance, see Paul Taylor's 'The Knives Came out for Rylance', *Independent*, 20 December 1995. Web. 12 December 2012. http://www.theindependent.co.uk/. For the Kelsey Grammer *Macbeth* see Jesse McKinley's '*Macbeth* Will Close After Just Ten Days on Broadway', in *The New York Times*, 20 June 2000. Web. 12 December 2012. http:www.nytimes.com/

15 '*Macbeth*: 1946–80 at Stratford-upon-Avon', in *Focus on Macbeth*, ed. John Russell Brown (Abingdon: Routledge, 1982), pp. 88–9.

16 Evans, p. 95. McKellen starred in Trevor Nunn's 1977 *Macbeth*; Olivier's performance came in Glen Byam Shaw's 1955 production.

17 Evans, p. 88.

18 Of course, actors who fare poorly in the role may do so for pedestrian reasons. I cannot absolve the actors mentioned from all responsibility for their performances. Still, the trends in reception for the play and its leading player argue that something greater is working against the lead actor than his own deficiencies in speech, movement, characterization, etc.

19 Critics occasionally notice an especially emotive Macduff, an innovative staging of the witches' second coming, or extend their praise or blame of the principals to her somnambulism or his 'poor player'. But the play's second half chiefly inspires criticism along predictable lines.

20 *Philadelphia City Paper*, 13 October 2010. Web. 12 December 2012. http://www.citypaper.net/

21 *New York Times*, 7 April 2011, pp. C1, C5.

22 *Buffalo News*, 29 May 1990. Web. 12 December 2012. http://www.buffalonews.com/. Again, good and bad reviews exist for every play, and one reviewer may praise a production that another has panned. It is the trends among the plentiful negative reviews of productions of *Macbeth* that are of interest here. Collectively, they suggest that when productions are found wanting (which is often) the second halves are faulted. Even in

well-reviewed productions, the play's second half is likely to suffer from neglect or blame.

23 *Guardian,* 7 February 2002.

24 Interestingly, Young Siward is a king's son, and Macbeth spends much of the play trying to kill royal (Malcolm), or potentially royal (Fleance) sons, in order to retain power. But the sons he does kill – little Macduff and Young Siward – do not keep him on the throne. Macbeth kills fathers (Duncan and Banquo) when he should kill sons (Malcolm and Fleance) and sons (little Macduff and Young Siward) when he should kill fathers (Macduff and Old Siward).

25 Tynan, p. 98.

26 A. C. Bradley first noticed the unusual 'rate of movement in the action' and the 'peculiar compression' of the play's language in *Shakespearean Tragedy* (London: Macmillan, 1905), p. 332.

27 There are about 180 lines between the witches' prophecy and Lady Macbeth's first soliloquy. 192 lines separate the decision to kill Duncan in 1.5 from Macbeth's entrance after the murder.

28 All references from the text are taken from *Macbeth,* ed. Kenneth Muir for The Arden Shakespeare (London: Methuen, 1951).

29 For example, note how the ideational force of 'peerless' works expressly against what the root sense of 'kinsman' is doing, though each seems harmonious in furthering the ends of the other. Duncan's phrase is readily apprehended to mean something like 'Macbeth is a great guy'. But it gets there by saying that he's one of us *and* he's in a category wholly his own.

30 The Porter may have been built into the play in order to beat the drum of 'equivocation' for an audience that has been weaned on variations of equivocation during the first two acts.

31 William D'Avenant first adapted the play in 1664. His version is reprinted in Christopher Spencer's *Davenant's Macbeth from the Yale manuscripts: an edition with a discussion of the relation of Davenant's text to Shakespeare's* (New Haven: Yale University Press, 1961).

32 At 3.6.38 editors often emend 'their King' to 'the King', so that the line indicates Macbeth and accords with the context.

But the emendation cannot be reconciled to Macbeth's clear statements that he did not send to Macduff in 3.6 and 4.1.

33 *King Lear, Macbeth, Indefinition and Tragedy* (New Haven: Yale University Press, 1983), p. 110.

34 'Paul Scofield's Macbeth: *Macbeth in Rehearsal* – A Journal', in *Adventures of a Shakespeare Scholar* (Newark: University of Delaware Press, 1997), p. 230.

35 Booth, p. 117.

PART TWO

History and Topicality

3

Politic Bodies in *Macbeth*

Dermot Cavanagh

As Macbeth makes his way towards the sleeping and defenceless Duncan, he evokes the spirit of an infernal night where 'Nature seems dead', 'Witchcraft celebrates' and the spectre of 'wither'd Murther … Moves like a ghost' with 'stealthy pace, / With Tarquin's ravishing strides, towards his design'. Macbeth also wishes to move soundlessly, as if he was bodiless, over 'the sure and firm-set earth', preserving the silence of 'the time, / Which now suits with' the horror of his enterprise.[1] In this, as in many other respects, the play frustrates his will. Nature returns with alarming vitality to protest the regicide of Duncan and time will not be compelled into the shape he seeks to impose upon it. More immediately, Macbeth finds his desire to be wraith-like or imperceptible overpowered by his sudden and frightening immersion in bodily sensations after the killing. This leaves him rawly vulnerable to sights and sounds, unnaturally sensitive to what he touches, hears and sees: 'How is't with me, when every noise appals me? / What hands are here?' (2.2.57–8).

Beginning with this moment is a reminder of the intense corporeality of *Macbeth* and of how often the body returns to thwart those protagonists who wish to exercise control

over it. Macbeth's desire to be disembodied or spectral is
further rebuked by the alarming physicality of Banquo's ghost,
whose appearance harrows him with fear at the height of his
illicit power. At the play's conclusion, the vengeful Macduff
vanquishes Macbeth in defiance of the latter's belief in his own
invulnerability to anyone born of woman. Lady Macbeth,
too, finds that her own body will not remain obedient to
command. Having disavowed imperiously 'the compunctious
visitings of Nature', her self-control vanishes at the recol-
lection of Duncan's desecrated corpse: 'Yet who would have
thought the old man to have had so much blood in him?'
(1.5.44; 5.1.40–1). During her sleepwalking, Lady Macbeth's
speech and movements betray her involuntarily; haunted by
the smell of blood, her senses too are overcome by her actions:
'her eyes are open ... but their sense are shut' (5.1.25–6).

How should these manifestations of the body in *Macbeth*
be interpreted? They clearly play a critical role in expressing
its political viewpoint, but there is little agreement as to the
nature of this. Traditional moral and political accounts of the
play emphasize, as the examples just cited suggest, that there
is a simple organizing principle at work in its representation
of bodily experience: rightful sovereignty is invested in the
person of Duncan and any attack upon this recoils upon
its perpetrators. After all, Macbeth himself offers powerful
testimony for this view. For example, his stricken account of
the king's violated corpse depicts it as an aperture through
which the apocalypse will enter to consume the world: 'Here
lay Duncan, / His silver skin lac'd with his golden blood; /
And his gash'd stabs look'd like a breach in nature / For ruin's
wasteful entrance' (2.3.109–12). The narrative outcomes of
the work surely endorse this sense of unfolding catastrophe
and, consequently, the unjust suffering endured by Scotland
can be seen to result simply from treachery and regicide. In
this respect, the bodies of the living and the dead bear witness
to the horrors of Macbeth's self-defeating tyranny and the
play evidences a protective attitude towards those who oppose
and attempt to redress this.[2]

However, more recent ways of reading *Macbeth* have stressed its capacity to blur rather than to clarify moral distinctions. On this view, the play is troubling because it is so profoundly equivocal. Far from simply representing lawful and beneficent authority, Duncan and his son Malcolm share troubling dependencies upon, or resemblances to, the usurper who seeks their destruction. As a series of penetrating inter-pretations have shown, maintaining distinctions between conflicting forces is hazardous in a work that is replete with echoes, doubling and uncanny resemblances.[3] These gaps in the logic underpinning the play's apparently orthodox message are part of a broader scepticism that pervades *Macbeth* with regard to securing reliable knowledge.[4] On further exami-nation, the presence of the body compounds rather than resolves these uncertainties. To begin with, physical testimony is dismayingly easy to misread in a world where what 'seem'd corporal' as the sinister presence of the weird sisters suddenly melts away 'as breath into the wind' (1.3.81–2). At the play's outset, the 'Norweyan lord' who aids the 'merciless Macdonwald' in his rebellion against Duncan perceives a strategic advantage when he sees the retreating heels of the 'skipping Kernes' being swept off the battlefield. Yet the fresh assault that he then launches leads only to defeat (1.2.31; 9; 30). Duncan is similarly deceived when he follows Macbeth 'at the heels' to his castle and attributes the latter's speed to his 'great love' for his wife (1.6.21–4). As the king acknowledges subsequently: 'There's no art / To find the mind's construction in the face' (1.4.11–12). In this way, the play is deemed to inhibit any straightforward reading of its local details or its broader implications. Identifying who or what embodies political virtue is no exception to this when even the apparent embodiments of rightful power have an unnerving capacity to mirror their opposites. Consequently, Shakespeare writes as an intensely sceptical and disenchanted thinker who takes an essentially pragmatic view of how political actors behave and for whom 'the ethics of authority are deeply compromised'.[5]

The political implications of the body in *Macbeth*, and

most notably its sovereign bodies, have provoked, therefore, uncertainty and dispute. This essay provides an alternative to these polarized traditions of interpretation and sheds new light on the play's political implications. It derives from a simple premise: that *Macbeth* contains a profound debate on the values that should govern the body politic and that this can be understood by following the account it offers of bodily experience. Furthermore, I'll suggest that Shakespeare's way of engaging with this topic is shaped by a crucial, if under-estimated, context for his political theatre: the expansive and deeply influential tradition of commonwealth thought. Indeed, *Macbeth* overlaps markedly with commonwealth thinking not least because it too was habitually conducted in physiological terms. '[T]here is the true common weal,' wrote the Henrician humanist Thomas Starkey, 'whereas all the parts as members of one body be knit togidder in perfit love and unity.'[6] The tragic experience of the play can be understood as a nightmarish inversion of this ideal and this mode of thought is equally prominent in its principal source, Holinshed's *Chronicles*.

However, the play is also composed in a moment when the values intrinsic to this way of thinking were facing new and exceptional challenges: it explores this as well through its representation of bodily experience. *Macbeth* is dominated by an insistence on bodily autonomy and this viewpoint is shared by what appear to be otherwise irreconcilable forces; this is in stark contrast to the corporate understanding of the body politic intrinsic to commonwealth discourse. As we shall see, this emphasis on self-sufficiency is integral to the play's absorption of a tendency in Jacobean political thought associated most notably with Jean Bodin and his follower in this regard, James VI and I. This stressed the singular and distinctive capacities of sovereign power. However, the play also recalls the implications of perceiving political and personal wellbeing in the collective terms proposed by humanists such as Starkey. Such residual reminders of an alternative way of conceiving the body, as well as the catastrophic consequences of its loss, serve to question the recent emphasis on the play's equivocality. It is unsurprising that *Macbeth* has produced such sharply divided responses as critics place different emphases on the oppositions and debates that it stages. However, emphasizing the play's profound engagement with the conflict between 'autonomous and ... corporate selves' provides a new perspective from which to evaluate it.[7] To be sure, *Macbeth* does not provide us with a straightforward embodiment of political virtue. It does give us a vantage point, however, from which to comprehend rival ways of conceiving sovereignty and how these promote or injure the body politic.

1

'Commonwealth' was a much-debated term in the period and, inevitably, the tradition of thought it provoked was equally disputatious. Yet, at the centre of its concern was 'the collective well-being of communities ... and the obligations and reciprocities that *communitas* entailed'.[8] In this respect, the concept of commonwealth became most politically 'emotive and contested' when it was used to define 'a form of polity that enabled the pursuit of the common good and the interest of the people'.[9] Such emphases and ideas may seem remote from the claustrophobic world of Shakespeare's play, which is dominated by murderous conflict among the nobility over possession of the crown. Yet *Macbeth*'s dependence on Holinshed's *Chronicles* means that it draws extensively on an exceptional instance of commonwealth historiography: Hector Boece's *Scotorum Historia* (1527), as translated into Scots by John Bellenden in 1540.[10] This work was one of the key sources used by Francis Thynne, who was primarily responsible for revising and expanding the history of Scotland included within the 1587 edition of Holinshed. Consequently, the perspective adopted by Boece, one of Scotland's leading sixteenth-century humanists, as well as Bellenden, is made evident throughout the chronicle, especially in the treatment of sovereignty.

In Holinshed's narration of Scottish history, those monarchs who hold that their powers are established for the care of the commonwealth are perceived as exemplary. For example, in the account of King Duff – the details of whose murder Shakespeare drew on extensively in portraying the killing of Duncan – the chronicle records that despite suffering debilitating illness caused by bewitchment, 'yet had he still a diligent care unto the due administration of his laws and good orders of his realme'.[11] In contrast, his successor descends into a maelstrom of sexual debauchery and lawlessness that evoke the horrors Malcolm promises Macduff he will visit upon the realm once he becomes king. The text clearly welcomes the assassination of this tyrant and the subsequent succession of the temperate and virtuous Kenneth III, whose goal is 'to advance the common-wealth from decaie to a flourishing state'. The concern of this monarch is 'onelie for the publike preservation of the realme' and he pledges to extirpate all practices that imperil 'the whole state of the Scottish Common-wealth'. Indeed, at the centre of this account is the king's passionate speech on behalf of the commonweal that distils the ideals shaping Boece's historical viewpoint. The 'lords and other high estates lived by the trauell of the commons,' Kenneth declares, 'then if the same commons should in anie wise decaie, the lords and such other high estates could in no wise prosper.' An injury done to any member of the community, regardless of status, is a wrong done to 'the universall state of the whole common-wealth':

> Therfore he that loved the common-wealth, would not seeke onelie to defend the commons from such injuries as theeves and robbers dailie offered them; but also would helpe to see just execution doone upon the same theeves and robbers, according to the laudable lawes and customes of the land. (sig. N5r)[12]

The king makes clear that the latter category of felons includes those of high social status: all are accountable to the law. Boece and his translator Bellenden have an unmistakeable viewpoint, therefore, and it is absorbed by Holinshed: 'royal authority is to be wielded for the common good – for the security, well-being, and integrity of the community as a whole.'[13]

Yet if Kenneth espouses an ideal of preserving the wellbeing of the entire body politic, he is also judged by it. Boece's account does not turn on a simple contrast between virtuous and tyrannical monarchs. Threats to commonwealth principles can emerge even from within those who understand them most fully. In the event, Kenneth is corrupted by his achievement of sovereignty. He murders a potential rival for the succession and asserts his 'private authorite' over the 'old ordinance and law of the realme' by abrogating the principle of elective monarchy in favour of primogeniture.[14] He too is assassinated. After further civil tumult, Duncan becomes king, ushering in the sequence of events familiar from, if reshaped by, Shakespeare's play. This passage of history is also evaluated by Boece, as one might expect, in terms of whether the public good is ensured or impeded. The king's weakness is noted along with his reliance on Macbeth: 'Thus was justice and law restored againe to the old accustomed course, by the diligent means of Makbeth' (sig. P1r). Duncan's assassination flows from the debased power-hunger shared by Macbeth and his wife, but the former proves to be a commonwealth-minded king for some years – committed to 'holesome laws' and the 'publike weale' (sig. P2r). However, these virtues prove too frail to resist his inclination towards cruelty and the reign descends into tyranny and oppression, followed by the welcome invasion and deposition led by Malcolm.

As even this brisk summary indicates, Shakespeare found in Holinshed's history of Scotland a narrative that is shaped by the ideals of commonwealth discourse: accountability to law; collective well-being; mutual reciprocity and obligation.[15] The overriding importance of these virtues and the threats they

confront means that Boece sees both the value of elective and
constitutionally limited kingship as well as the necessity of
tyrannicide. It is also possible that Shakespeare had independent
access to the history of Scotland completed by Boece's successor,
George Buchanan, a renowned monarchomach (and tutor
to James VI); this work was also consulted by Thynne for
the history of Scotland included in Holinshed.[16] Buchanan's
work reinforced and expanded the political implications of
Boece's history in the light of his own profound commitment
to the ideal of commonwealth. In his account, Scottish history
revealed and renewed the importance of crucial principles:
'When an injury is done to the people, it is not done merely
to one single part of the commonwealth [*civitatis*] but reaches
into every limb of the body politic [*civilis corporis*].' Political
authority needed to follow, therefore, a simple overriding
imperative: 'Let the welfare of the people be the supreme law';
and this could only be ensured by affirming the supremacy of
law over all forms of political authority, including monarchy.
Consequently, it was essential to deprive 'the king of the power
not only to enact laws but even to interpret them'.[17]

   Many critics insist that *Macbeth* avoids, even suppresses,
the radical potential of its source material.[18] As is well known,
Shakespeare's play contains in Banquo the historical figure
that James looked back to as the founder of the Stuart line
and the play ensures that he is absolved of any complicity
in Duncan's killing, an unwelcome detail that is recorded by
Holinshed. In addition, the weird sisters reveal, to Macbeth's
horror, the seemingly unbreakable continuity of the Stuart
dynasty in their show of eight kings (4.1.68–132). These
facets of the play may well be attributable to Shakespeare's
membership of the King's Men, a theatrical company that had
been newly elevated by royal patronage, and to *Macbeth*'s
composition in the highly charged atmosphere created by the
Gunpowder Plot. In addition, James had written expansively
on the nature and prerogatives of kingship and his aim had
been precisely to overturn the political beliefs of writers such
as Boece and George Buchanan.[19] Quite understandably,

James' accession and his mode of kingship have featured prominently in attempts to recover the context of the play.[20] In *The Trew Lawe of Free Monarchies* (1598), James addressed 'our so long disordered, and distracted Common-wealth' and showed that the monarch's will lay at the origins of civil government.[21] In founding the kingdom, the monarch had divided and allocated lands with the consequence that the king is 'over-lord' of the whole land and his subjects were his vassals. Hence, James advanced his key claim: that 'kings were the authors and makers of the Lawes, and not the Lawes of the kings' (p. 73). Although the monarch should let 'the health of the common-wealth be his chiefe lawe' and act within it, the king is still 'above the Law' and its provisions can be mitigated, suspended and superseded as he see fit (p. 75). [22] These doctrines have been identified as playing a forceful role in the play, flooding it with horror at regicide and augmenting its commitment to a concept of just order founded on monarchy.

Yet *Macbeth* was composed in a volatile political and intellectual context. Peter C. Herman has pointed out that even James' accession speech proved to be divisive. The Speaker of the House of Commons, Sir Edward Phelips, responded to this, 'rather amazingly', by revising the King's understanding of the body politic and elaborating instead a corporate conception of the commonwealth that envisaged 'law, monarchy, subjects and justice as interrelated and inter-dependent, all equally important, all equally essential, none predominating'.[23] As we've seen, Shakespeare was also drawn to an historical narrative that was informed throughout by similar values and these ran counter to James' ideas. Discovering how Shakespeare responded to Jacobean doctrines of kingship in the play is bound to provoke continuing debate as critics weigh its complexities and reservations against the pressures of its context. Yet there is a way to follow its thinking on sovereignty, I'll now suggest, and this reveals that *Macbeth* does not efface or surrender so readily the heritage of commonwealth principles that was so evident in Holinshed.

In this respect, Alan Sinfield is correct to stress the importance of ideas associated with Buchanan as a source of complication and contradiction in the play.[24] Indeed, we can go further than this. The presence of the values underlying Boece's and Buchanan's thought not only helps to explain many of *Macbeth*'s seemingly equivocal or ambiguous passages, they shape both its tragic experience and its political vision. This can be demonstrated by returning to the play's insistent concern with bodily autonomy; this issue lies at the origin of the political crisis that engulfs Scotland and creates the conditions for the tragedy that unfolds. In this respect also, *Macbeth* remains engaged by commonwealth values.

2

From the outset of the play, Macbeth expresses his own physical responses and reactions with great vividness. After his initial triumph in crushing the rebellion that threatens Duncan, he is disturbed by the 'supernatural soliciting' of the weird sisters. Although they address him as Thane of Cawdor – a new honour whose award is confirmed quickly – and as a future king of Scotland, these predictions invoke bodily apprehension at the disturbing turn his thoughts take:

> why do I yield to that suggestion
> Whose horrid image doth unfix my hair,
> And make my seated heart knock at my ribs,
> Against the use of nature?

(1.3.34–7)

This marks the beginning of a preoccupation with the body that is shared by Macbeth and Lady Macbeth and, more strikingly, a refusal to be inhibited by seemingly instinctive responses. Indeed, this is the crux of Lady Macbeth's fears concerning her husband's nature as being 'too full o' th' milk of human kindness, / To catch the nearest way' (1.5.15–17). In an equally telling formulation, Lady Macbeth equates Macbeth's wavering resolution to act against Duncan with a reluctance to succumb to the 'illness' that attends the pursuit of political ambitions (17–19). Her resolution is to use both rhetorical and corporeal persuasion so as to overcome these resistances:

> Hie thee hither,
> That I may pour my spirits in thine ear,
> And chastise with the valour of my tongue
> All that impedes thee from the golden round,
> Which fate and metaphysical aid doth seem
> To have thee crown'd withal.
>
> (1.5.24–9)

This aspiration is integral to her infamous speech of self-transformation in which, with the demonic assistance of the 'murth'ring ministers' that 'tend on mortal thoughts', she purges herself of remorse, thickens her blood and surrenders her maternal milk for gall (39–53). Subsequently, in the extraordinary dialogue that takes place between them prior to the murder of Duncan, Lady Macbeth continues to use a discourse of vivid bodily sensation; this includes confessing to the infanticide she would commit, even upon 'the babe that milks me', rather than complying with her husband's faltering resolution to dispose of Duncan (1.7.54–9).

Regardless then of any 'natural' promptings, Lady Macbeth determines to compel herself and Macbeth towards the goal of achieving power understood as the capacity to exercise 'solely sovereign sway and masterdom' (1.5.69). This requires the quelling of those processes or parts of the body that would '[s]hake my fell purpose' (45). Later, she confesses during her sleepwalking that to possess such authority will mean they are unaccountable to law or any other restraint: 'What need we fear, who knows it, when none can call our power to accompt?' (5.1.38–40). These emphases are equally prominent in Macbeth's remorseless attempt to resolve his body and will into a 'single state of man' (1.3.140), an instrument as serviceable to his purposes as any other he exploits. This pursuit of sovereign power becomes maniacal in the play; preserving it against threats in both the present and the future leads Macbeth into the play's notorious sequence of atrocities. His logic is clear: to ensure his sovereignty cannot be possessed by or shared with another, as to do so would mean that his own unique property, 'mine eternal jewel', will be 'Given to the common Enemy of man' (3.1.67–8). Most frightening of all, in this respect, is the presence of other and rival sovereign bodies both now and in the future. To allow Banquo to live and become 'father to a line of kings' would be to 'wear our health but sickly in his life, / Which in his death were perfect' (3.1.59; 106–7). In a sense, it is better to be dead, because it is only in the condition of perfect invulnerability it grants, and enjoyed by Duncan, that the self passes beyond the reach of any hazard.

In one sense, the compulsions that manifest themselves in Macbeth and Lady Macbeth's pursuit of power over their own bodies and those of their subjects is symptomatic of tyranny. Yet, as Bradin Cormack has shown, 'at the core of Shakespeare's exploration of tyranny, there lies an analysis of sovereignty itself'.[25] Notably, Cormack demonstrates how Shakespeare's later romances, principally *The Winter's Tale*, counter exalted claims over the scope and indivisibility of sovereign power that circulated widely in Jacobean culture and derived primarily from the work of Jean Bodin. In Bodin's conception of the body politic, there is a single and indivisible source of sovereign power that cannot be distributed, a decisive locus of authority that has the power to make and rescind law. Yet if Bodin argued that 'the mark of sovereignty is the mark that is *uncommon*, not shared, not derivable', then, according to Cormack, Shakespeare's work is both critical of and explores alternatives to 'sovereignty's connection to its own uniqueness'.[26] There is much in this approach that corresponds to Shakespeare's earlier preoccupations in *Macbeth*. We might also note that Bodin's *The Six Bookes of a Commonweale* (1606) was translated into English in the same year identified for the play's composition and, in addition, how drastically the implications of sovereignty that inhered in the vernacular term 'commonweale' were redefined in this work. Bodin advanced a comprehensive attack on the ethos of interdependence and mutuality that was intrinsic to commonwealth thought – in particular, its understanding of the sovereign as an interrelated part of the body politic. The latter way of thinking stressed the consonance between the individual and the corporate body: '[I]f men knew that when they look to common profit,' Thomas Starkey observed, '[...] they therewith also regard their own singular and private' interests. On this view, lawful sovereignty was always conceived of as limited because it was inseparable from the whole of which it was a part. Attempts to interfere or supersede this would only result in tragedy, as those who neglect the 'commonwealth never conceive how their own destruction is secretly coupled to their own acts and deeds; for if they did, surely they would not suffer themself so to err and so to run to their own ruin'.[27]

Bodin's formulations were strikingly different in emphasis. 'Soueraigntie is not limited either in power, charge, or time certaine', he asserts; it is 'an absolute power, not subject to any law' and 'it behoveth him that is a soveraigne not to be in any sort subject to the commaund of another'. Even if a sovereign has come to power by force, 'yet neverthelesse the tyrant is a soveraigne: as the violent possession of an intruder is in nature a possession'. The sovereign is exempt from the law of his predecessors or even the law he makes himself; he stands as one 'who may bind all his subjects, but cannot bind himselfe'. Indeed, this is the defining property of sovereign power: 'giving laws unto the subjects in generall, without their consent.'[28] Bodin's ideas helped bolster the insistence by a number of Jacobean thinkers, including James, that the king possessed unique prerogative powers. These were normally to be held in reserve but could be exercised if the circumstances demanded it because of 'that special Power, Preminence, or

Privilege which the King hath over and above other Persons, and above the ordinary course of the Common Law'.[29]

Macbeth absorbs these ideas most notably by portraying those who pursue sovereignty as having in common an insistence on both the singularity of the body and its potential for reserve and secrecy. This is integral to the play's tragic situation, and *Macbeth* invites a sharply critical view of such a concept of the body and its repercussions for the body politic. I have already discussed the harm Macbeth and Lady Macbeth inflict upon themselves and the world around them by beginning to conceive of their own bodies and its capacities in this way. Yet the play is even more daring in refusing to draw a contrast between those characterized by such habits of mind and virtuous kingship. Indeed, it reveals how Macbeth's opponents share his understanding of sovereign power even as they wish to dispossess him of it.

This issue becomes most pressing during the lengthy, unsettling – and seemingly extraneous – dialogue on the nature of kingship between Malcolm and Macduff. The former begins by quizzing Macduff on his decision to abandon his wife and children and join with the rebels in England (a family whom we have just witnessed being slaughtered by Macbeth's forces). He continues to engage in a protracted testing of Macduff's loyalty, for reasons that remain enigmatic, by convincing him that his rule will compound rather than cure Scotland's afflictions. Malcolm affirms his utter disregard for the commonwealth: he will relinquish all the 'king-becoming graces' and exploit the country for his private interests. In this manner, the play's best hope for the restoration of rightful authority echoes and repeats the language used by the tyrant: 'had I power, I should / Pour the sweet milk of concord into Hell / Uproar the universal peace, confound / All unity on earth.' (4.3.97–100). On hearing these sentiments, Macduff acknowledges that, in such circumstances, he too would kill the king (103).

The implications of this puzzling scene can be grasped more fully when it is understood as exploring further the consequences of a (future) sovereign who determines to sunder himself from the ethos of the commonwealth. The latter insisted that word and thought should be consonant with each other: 'even as the common weal is in everyman's mouth, so also it should be fixed in their hearts.'[30] Malcolm claims that his provocative statements were simply acts of 'false speaking' designed to test Macduff's loyalty and that his true nature is entirely other to his misrepresentation of it. In fact, he is chaste, truthful and dedicated to the service of his people: 'What I am truly, / Is thine, and my poor country's, to command' (131–2). Yet as Macduff states, it is difficult now to distinguish between truth and falsehood, and it might also be noted that Malcolm has succeeded in eliciting a telling admission from his follower that he would, in the last instance, be willing to commit regicide. What is crucial about this ambiguous scene is that it reveals Malcolm's understanding of sovereignty to be commensurate with his own person and will. Throughout, Malcolm directs attention inwards to what he is and what he will become. This is troubling, because it is difficult to assess his nature, especially when we recollect his own mordant acknowledgement of the mutability that follows from the achievement of power: 'A good and virtuous nature may recoil, / In an imperial charge' (19–20). Yet it also implicates him in a practice of sovereignty that is concentrated on self-preservation and the advancement of his own interests. Indeed, the exposure of this results from an immediately manipulative and instrumental dialogue with one of his future subjects. The disturbance this creates is renewed by the alacrity with which Malcolm insists on his personal authority at the conclusion of the play. This is marked both by his notable use of the royal 'we' and by a further chilling echo of the language used by Lady Macbeth: 'this, and what needful else / That calls upon us, by the grace of Grace, / *We will perform* in measure, time and place.' (5.9.37–9, emphasis added; cf. 1.7.70–1).

This is one of many moments, of course, when the play's restorers or defenders of rightful sovereignty are caught sharing words and ideas with their opponents. The extremity of Macbeth's rejection of all claims upon him virtually precludes him from acknowledging the death of his wife (5.5.17–18). Yet this refusal to recognize commonalty with others, even those closest to us, extends beyond him. Macduff is badly compromised by the abandonment of his wife and children that follows from his decision to join with Malcolm in England. This is exposed to searing criticism by Lady Macduff in the moments before her annihilation and that of her children: 'His flight was madness ... He wants the natural touch' (4.2.3; 9). Malcolm's English ally Siward is also shown to be deficient in this respect. He accepts the death of his son at Macbeth's hands in accordance with the principle of honour and as the price of restoring Malcolm's authority: 'Why then, God's soldier be he!' When Malcolm attempts to remind Siward of the value of his son's life and the depth of his sacrifice, his reply is terse: 'He's worth no more; / They say he parted well and paid his score: / And so, God be with him!' (5.9.13; 17–19)

One of the most compelling aspects of *Macbeth*'s engagement with political ideas lies, therefore, in its unfolding of the consequences of asserting bodily autonomy over commonalty of being. The alarm caused by the play arises from the manner in which this also involves the ascendancy of a thesis of sovereignty which appears to be spreading, entering different levels and kinds of relationships and depleting the distinctions between political opponents. Yet *Macbeth* provides the resources to think critically about this process not only by its tragic ramifications but also because of its constant reminders of an alternative way of conceiving the body. Indeed, the residual awareness of this perspective, even in the moment of its vanishing, informs many of the play's most equivocal and unsettling moments. Other ways of thinking about the body and of holding and exercising power can still be perceived. In his flawed way, Duncan points towards this possibility even in the troubling moment of bestowing the succession upon Malcolm. He conceives this, however misguidedly, in the public interest and in terms of a corporate or distributive understanding of kingship: 'which honour must / Not unaccompanied invest him only, / But signs of nobleness, like stars, shall shine / On all deservers' (1.4.39–42). This is a complex moment, because Duncan's action defines sovereignty as solely defined by his prerogative in the very moment he seeks to share its benefits. Still, the language itself reaches out beyond his own will and desires and this gesture, at least, shadows Macbeth's immediate response (in an aside) which uses the same analogy to concentrate relentlessly on his own covert impulses: 'Stars, hide your fires! / Let not light see my black and deep desires; / The eye wink at the hand' (1.4.50–52).

Yet it is perhaps even more disconcerting that one of the places in the play where an alternative understanding of the body and its interrelationship with others persists is in Macbeth's own stricken awareness of the values he has defied and destroyed. It is the latter who recollects the transfiguring role of civil governance: 'in th' olden time, / Ere humane statute purg'd the gentle weal' (3.4.74–5). This perception is made equally evident in his famous, if idealized, testimony to the virtues of Duncan's kingship and, more simply, in his moving acknowledgement of his status as kin and as a guest (1.7.12–25). It is Macbeth too who acknowledges the self-rewarding quality of the obligation he owes to Duncan, 'The service and the loyalty I owe, / In doing it, pays itself', as well as the mutual responsibilities they share: 'Your Highness' part / Is to receive our duties: and our duties / Are to your throne and state, children and servants' (1.4.22–5). As in Holinshed, Duncan's kingship is also evaluated and, at times, found wanting by these principles, but they survive within Macbeth's awareness of how his achievement of sovereignty has involved repealing the principles of reciprocity and exchange that would have sustained his authority:

> honour, love, obedience, troops of friends,
> I must not look to have; but in their stead,

Curses, not loud, but deep, mouth-honour, breath,
Which the poor heart would fain deny, and dare not.

(5.3.25–8)

This realization of the absurdity and emptiness that attend his success accords with one of the play's presiding ironies: that the sovereignty Macbeth and Lady Macbeth pursue as a singular possession is a desire that is shared between them; it is already doubled and distributed despite their insistence on an autonomy that leads only to 'experiences of displacement, doubleness, and agential confusion'.[31]

This reading of *Macbeth* has proposed that the play has an argument to make over the political implications of corporeal experience rather than staging an equivocal debate about this issue. On the one hand, others can be regarded as if they were members of one's own body; on the other, the body can be perceived as self-sufficient. The disturbing consequences of the latter are revealed as political agents divorce themselves from commonwealth principles; this perspective also dominates the understanding of Scottish history presented by Holinshed. Indeed, as Nicholas McDowell has suggested, this aspect of Shakespeare's play may explain the interest it commanded among seventeenth-century parliamentarians and republicans both during the civil war and into the commonwealth period itself.[32] This might give us pause before accepting accounts of *Macbeth* where the protagonist's alienation is taken as revealing 'the weakness of human praxis' which lies at 'the core of political life'.[33] In contrast, seventeenth-century responses remind us of the play's productive role not only in deciphering a political crisis but identifying alternatives to its emergence.

Shakespeare's attitude towards commonwealth principles was undoubtedly a restless and sometimes sceptical one.[34] Yet his work is everywhere alert to the power and potential of these ideas and his political theatre is defined by its concern with these values and the threats they confront. It is telling that within months of James' accession, Shakespeare presented such a forbidding account of a society where all of its monarchs, Duncan, Macbeth and Malcolm, found their sovereignty in ways that remove it from a corporate conception of the body politic. Viewing its implications in this way provides an alternative to some of the categories conventionally used to define not only this play but the broader standpoint of Shakespeare's work as being either monarchist, republican, pragmatic or, more recently, as a harbinger of a liberal ethos of individualism.[35] Consequently, the tragic experience undergone by the politic bodies of *Macbeth* suggests another way of understanding the convictions that shaped Shakespeare's political interests.

Notes

1 All quotations are to 'Macbeth', ed. Kenneth Muir, in *The Arden Shakespeare Complete Works*, Richard Proudfoot, Ann Thompson and David Scott Kastan (eds) (Walton-on-Thames, 1998), 2.1.49–60.

2 David Norbrook comments that the outcomes of the play reveal that 'the principles of monarchy and hierarchy were too deeply implanted in the body to be overcome'. In '*Macbeth* and the Politics of Historiography', in *Politics of Discourse: The Literature and History of Seventeenth-Century England*, Kevin Sharpe and Steven N. Zwicker (eds) (Berkeley, 1987), pp. 78–116, 113.

3 See, for example, David Scott Kastan, '*Macbeth* and the Name of King', in *Shakespeare After Theory* (London and New York, 1999), pp. 165–82.

4 See Kent Cartwright, 'Scepticism and Theatre in *Macbeth*', *Shakespeare Survey*, 55 (2002), pp. 219–36.

5 Stephen Greenblatt, *Shakespeare's Freedom* (Chicago, 2010), p. 79.

6 Thomas Starkey, *A Dialogue Between Reginald Pole and Thomas Lupset* (c. 1533–6), ed. Kathleen M. Burton (London, 1948), p. 62.

7   Kent Cartwright, 'Scepticism and Theatre in *Macbeth*', p. 224.

8   Phil Withington, *Society in Early Modern England: The Vernacular Origins of Some Powerful Ideas* (Cambridge, 2010), p. 140.

9   Early Modern Research Group, 'Commonwealth: The Social, Cultural, and Conceptual Contexts of an Early Modern Keyword', *The Historical Journal*, 54 (2011), pp. 659–87, 666.

10 See Sally Mapstone, 'Shakespeare and Scottish Kingship: a Case History', in *The Rose and the Thistle: Essays on the Culture of Late Medieval and Renaissance Scotland*, Sally Mapstone and Juliette Wood (eds) (East Linton, 1998), pp. 158–89.

11 Holinshed, *The first and second volumes of Chronicles* (1587), sig. N3r; cf. *The Chronicles of Scotland, compiled by Hector Boece, translated into Scots by John Bellenden 1531*, R. W. Chambers, E. C. Batho and H. Winifred Husbands (eds), Scottish Text Society, 2 vols. (Edinburgh, 1938–41), II, 94.

12 Cf. Boece, *The Chronicles of Scotland*, II, pp. 101–5.

13 J. H. Burns, *The True Law of Kingship: Concepts of Monarchy in Early Modern Scotland* (Oxford, 1996), p. 91. Roger A. Mason notes Bellenden's crucial role as a translator in determining the significance of Boece's work, especially 'the immense weight which Bellenden attached to the idea of the "commonweal" in his version of the chronicles ... the community whose welfare was at stake'. In *Kingship and the Commonweal: Political Thought in Renaissance and Reformation Scotland* (East Linton, 1998), p. 97. Mason calculates that Bellenden's translation uses the term 'commonweal' about 150 times, see ibid., n. 63.

14 Holinshed, *Chronicles*, sig. O2r. In a recent essay, Roger Mason notes that Boece saw the institution of primogeniture as a welcome development that led, eventually, to a 'more stable and enduring system'. See 'Scotland', in *The Oxford Handbook of Holinshed's Chronicles*, Paulina Kewes, Ian W. Archer and Felicity Heal (eds) (Oxford, 2013), pp. 647–62, 651.

15 For analysis of the political ideas informing Holinshed, see 'Part IV: Politics, Society, and Religion', *The Oxford Handbook of Holinshed's Chronicles*, pp. 375–490; see also Annabel Patterson, *Reading Holinshed's Chronicles* (Chicago, 1994), esp. Ch. 6.

16 Shakespeare's theatrical colleague, Edward Alleyn, owned a copy of Buchanan's *Rerum Scoticarum Historia* (1582). See A. R. Braunmuller, 'Introduction', *Macbeth*, 2nd edn (Cambridge, 2008), pp. 14–15. For Thynne's use of Buchanan, see Patterson, *Reading Holinshed's Chronicles*, pp. 36–7.

17 George Buchanan, *A Dialogue on the Law of Kingship among the Scots* (1579), ed. and trans. Roger A. Mason and Martin S. Smith (Aldershot, 2004), pp. 99, 57, 67. In the second citation, Buchanan is quoting Cicero, *De Legibus,* III, iii, 8.

18 For example, David Norbrook, in '*Macbeth* and the Politics of Historiography', sees the play as 'an attempt to revise the more radical views implicit in its sources' (p. 98).

19 See Roger A. Mason, *Kingship and the Commonweal*, pp. 215–41.

20 See, for example, Henry N. Paul, *The Royal Play of Macbeth* (New York, 1950); Alvin Kernan, *Shakespeare, the King's Playwright: Theater in the Stuart Court, 1603–1613* (New Haven, 1995).

21 'The Trew Lawe of Free Monarchies', in *King James VI and I: Political Writings*, ed. Johann P. Sommerville (Cambridge, 1994), pp. 62–84, 63.

22 For an economical account of James' political ideas see J. P. Sommerville, 'James I and the divine right of kings: English politics and continental theory', in *The Mental World of the Jacobean Court*, ed. Linda Levy Peck (Cambridge, 1991), pp. 55–70.

23 Peter C. Herman, '*Macbeth*: Absolutism, the Ancient Constitution, and the Aporia of Politics', in *The Law in Shakespeare*, Constance Jordan and Karen Cunningham (eds) (Basingstoke, 2007), pp. 208–32, 212.

24 Alan Sinfield, '*Macbeth*: History, Ideology and Intellectuals', in *Faultlines: Cultural Materialism and the Politics of Dissident Reading* (Oxford, 1992), pp. 95–108.

25 Bradin Cormack, 'Shakespeare's Other Sovereignty: On Particularity and Violence in *The Winter's Tale* and the Sonnets', *Shakespeare Quarterly*, 62 (2011), pp. 485–513.

26 Ibid., pp. 490, 485.

27 Starkey, *A Dialogue Between Reginald Pole and Thomas Lupset*, p. 70.

28 Jean Bodin, *The Six Bookes of a Commonweale*, trans. Richard Knolles (1606), ed. Kenneth Douglas McRae (Cambridge, MA, 1962), pp. 85, 88, 91, 87, 93, 98. James VI's political ideas had been influenced by Bodin and his library contained the *Six Livres de la République* (1576); see G. F. Warner, ed., 'The Library of James VI 1573–83', *Scottish History Society Miscellany I* (Edinburgh, 1893), pp. xi–lxxv, xlii.

29 John Cowell, *The Interpreter* (1607), cited in Francis Oakley, 'Jacobean Political Theology: The Absolute and Ordinary Powers of the King', *Journal of the History of Ideas*, 29 (1968): pp. 323–46, 325. Compare the claim made in Edward Forset's *Comparative Discourse of the Bodies Naturall and Politic*, also published in 1606, that the monarch was the 'Politicall soule of the State in his full royaltie and amplitude', the force that constituted and bound the commonwealth (sig. C3v).

30 Starkey, *A Dialogue Between Reginald Pole and Thomas Lupset*, p. 70.

31 Bryan Lowrance, '"Modern Ecstasy": *Macbeth* and the Meaning of the Political', *ELH*, 79 (2012): pp. 823–49, 832.

32 Nicholas McDowell, 'Milton's Regicide Tracts and the Uses of Shakespeare', in *The Oxford Handbook of Milton*, Nicholas McDowell and Nigel Smith (eds) (Oxford, 2009), pp. 252–71, 266. See also Martin Dzelzainis, 'Milton, Macbeth, and Buchanan', *Seventeenth Century*, 4 (1989): pp. 55–66.

33 Lowrance, 'Modern Ecstasy', p. 842.

34 Dermot Cavanagh, 'Sovereignty and Commonwealth in Shakespeare's *Henry VI, Part 2*', in *The Oxford Handbook of Tudor Drama*, Thomas Betteridge and Greg Walker (eds) (Oxford, 2012), pp. 619–34.

35 See, for example, Andrew Hadfield, *Shakespeare and Republicanism* (Cambridge, 2005); Peter Holbrook, *Shakespeare's Individualism* (Cambridge, 2010).

4

'To crown my thoughts with acts': Prophecy and Prescription in *Macbeth*

Debapriya Sarkar

Often perceived as the most topical of Shakespeare's tragedies, *Macbeth* repeatedly turns to questions of time as it imports on stage the sections of Holinshed's *Chronicles* that were particularly relevant to the new English monarch, James, who traced his lineage to Banquo.[1] *Macbeth* scholarship, too, has frequently returned to issues of temporality, history and genealogy to explore the play's ruminations on time.[2] From the witches' opening query, 'When shall we three meet again?' (1.1.1), to Lady Macbeth's claim that she 'feel[s] now / The future in the instant' (1.5.55–6), to Macbeth's musings on time's passage: 'To-morrow, and to-morrow, and to-morrow / Creeps in this petty pace from day to day' (5.5.19–20),[3] *Macbeth* enacts what David Scott Kastan has identified as the 'play's very insistence upon its future' and its refusal to 'stop'.[4] As political events including Duncan's naming Malcolm 'The Prince of Cumberland' (1.4.39) and

Macbeth's worries about his 'barren sceptre' (3.1.61) become inseparable from questions about future rule, Macbeth acutely feels the necessity of *knowing* the future, repeatedly asking *how* potential events – contingent and unknowable – might be understood and manipulated to authorize kingship. To demonstrate how this very unknowability of the future might serve as its authorizing principle and resolve these eruptions of contingency, *Macbeth* appeals to the form of esoteric knowledge that promised certainty about approaching times: prophecy becomes the thematic and formal vehicle that reveals the 'future in the instant'.

The topicality and transgressiveness of the prophetic mode, its popularity in contemporary writing, and its associations with political genealogy make prophecy an ideal instrument for examining concerns about sovereignty that lie at the heart of *Macbeth*. Unsurprisingly, scholars have noticed the role that prophecy plays in *Macbeth,* but they usually mark the political content of the prophecies rather than the processes of knowing that govern the visionary mode.[5] An examination of the epistemology of prophecy – the theories of knowledge underlying such predictive utterances – reveals how vatic discourse uses contemporary ideas of action and prescription to shape the audience's understanding of political futurity in the play. As such, *Macbeth*'s prophecies are not merely instances of 'hindsight masquerading as foresight', which Marjorie Garber identifies as the condition of all dramatic prophecies, units of certainty of a completed pastness:[6] 'the audience knows that these "impossible" things will prove true, and it can do nothing with that knowledge but wait for the fulfilment of the future anterior – the future that is already inscribed'.[7] Such a reading forecloses the possibility that the interpretation of prophecy *is* action, in which the futuristic promise of prophetic epistemology shapes theatrical action and invites spectators imaginatively to project from what they see onstage. To adopt but also to adapt Garber's terms, *Macbeth*, I argue, is about 'foresight' rather than 'hindsight': its open-ended prophecies stage their states of contingency and invite interpretations from characters, demanding that the play's intended audiences – characters and the external spectators – react experientially to them. Prophecy in *Macbeth* produces neither fact nor a predestined future before the fact but augurs forms of interpretation that shape our understanding of how characters simultaneously earn places in history and on the stage, or in the future and in the present.

Coupling predictive surety with the unknown future, *Macbeth* grapples with a major epistemic shift occurring in the early seventeenth century, which scholars such as William Eamon and Elizabeth Spiller mark as the movement from knowing to doing, or from *gnosis* to *praxis*;[8] various forms of occult knowledge become associated with natural philosophy and transform the practical value of predictive epistemologies.[9] Moreover, influential works on poetics such as Philip Sidney's *Defence of Poetry* claim that even poetry, which 'nothing affirms', aims towards *praxis* or 'well-doing' over *gnosis* or 'well-knowing'.[10] At a moment when action and uncertainty intersect in a variety of discourses about imaginary and natural worlds, *Macbeth's* ambiguous sources of esoteric knowledge and the play's exploration of the complexity of prophecies serve as crucial examples of the changing concerns over access to, use of and scope of the 'occult forces' of 'nature'.[11] In this essay, I focus on the characters' encounters with the 'Weïrd Sisters' (2.1.20), who enter the play as 'instruments' (1.3.124) of occult knowledge; their futuristic predictions animate characters to perform interpretative projections and serve as the signal examples of how prophetic utterances influence theatrical action. By conjoining the contingent future with vatic revelations that promise certainty, *Macbeth* asks *how* the witches' enigmatic prophecies come true, and more specifically, how they are actualized within a dramatic form. *Macbeth's* prophecies forcefully reveal gaps between the dramatic present and the historical future. By inviting characters to interpret, understand and act on the witches' equivocal prophecies, *Macbeth* transforms prophetic revelations into transgressive recipes for political, and theatrical, action.

Prophetic epistemology

Prophecy had a complex status in Elizabethan and Jacobean England, where the prophet was defined in two different ways: 'either for a shewer, or foreteller of things to come', in the words of John Harvey, or as 'a preacher, or interpreter of the scripture'.[12] Prophecy signified not a single concept but ranged from proceedings in astrology to mathematics to church practices.[13] The contingent endings associated with all predictive arts were countered by claims that prophets had divine inspiration or unmediated access to privileged, esoteric knowledge which enabled them to foretell the truth. Prophetic revelations were both appealing and threatening because they disseminated elite knowledge to commoners and promised that revelations would certainly be realized in future history. In 'Of Prophecies', even a sceptical Francis Bacon acknowledges that people give prophecies 'grace, and some credit' because some have *proved* true: 'men mark when they hit, and never mark when they miss.'[14]

Prophecies represented an amalgamation of occult, practical and poetical epistemologies, and realizing prophecy in history entailed reconciling theories of *praxis* or 'doing' with the productive aspects of *poiesis* or 'making'.[15] Since a prediction *became* a prophecy only in moments of historical fulfilment, the end-oriented activity of *poiesis* was inextricable from the act of vatic utterance: prophecy was, then, both action and product. Prophetic expressions were also poetic in the sense that poetry 'nothing affirms', purports to direct readers towards future action and invites audiences to interpret figurative modes of representation.[16] Naturalists often classified prophecies under the category of *secreta*. Unlike Aristotelian *scientia*, where only regularities or unchanging elements of nature were worthy of philosophical inquiry, '*secreta*' encapsulated diverse phenomena from the 'manifestation of occult qualities' to 'events that occur unexpectedly or idiosyncratically' to events for which one 'can observe effects, but not causes, because they are particulars; phenomena; not demonstrable'.[17] *Secreta* manifest themselves in the form of wonders, marvels and accidents, and they find expression in diverse practices and media, including natural magic, practical arts, alchemical experiments, recipe books and prophetic utterances.[18]

Prophecy's promises of certain knowledge, achievable in the future, led to the scrutiny of its epistemic claims. Works such as Henry Howard's *A Defensatiue Against the Poyson of Supposed Prophesies* (1583) and John Harvey's *A Discoursiue Probleme Concerning Prophesies* (1588) underline the contingency involved in the mode. Prophecy, Harvey argues, had become an 'vncertaine collection of mans inuention, without any further diuine instinct, angelicall illumination, or propheticall gift of foreknowledge, either mediate, or immediate, either sensible, or intellectuall'.[19] Howard too stresses the uncertain underpinnings of the vatic voice: 'We know that men are images of God, but no Gods indeed; that our wits may deeme, but not diuine, forcast vpon occasion, but not prefigure without certainty.'[20] Both writers stress the uncertainty of human understanding and argue that divine intervention might not be accessible to all. There might be some 'true' prophets, but the majority of prophecies were false. Claims of access to, and the desire for, certainty could lead to folly, since men and women seek 'deeper knowledge, after future causes' and are stung by 'Curiosity' when 'God pleaseth to make [these things] knowne by ordinarie meanes'.[21] Exceeding the limits imposed by God, human beings try to appropriate God's unique knowledge: '[o]f declaring future things before they come to passé, it belongeth only to the wisedome divine.'[22] What false prophets claim as divine calling is actually learning gained by 'the light of long experience' and 'signes of observation'.[23]

Howard and Harvey underscore how grandiose claims of prophetic knowledge lead to multiplying predictions, which run counter to the promise of the mode that history would fulfil one true prophecy. As prophecies multiply, or – in Keith

Thomas' terms – with the increase in the 'counter-prophecy', possible *true* futures also multiply.[24] The proliferation of prophecies and diverse interpretations of individual prophecies undermine the promise of singular, certain knowledge, but they also suggest that one potential future could be *made* to come true; revelations held within them the capacity to shape historical ends. As esoteric knowledge was being popularized through the dissemination of practical 'how to' books, audiences could read futuristic promises, including prophecies, as recipes for action.[25] The term 'recipe' refers to a technical category – a 'list of ingredients' and a 'set of instructions describing how they were to be employed' – in which the 'accumulated experiences of practitioners [was] boiled down to a rule'.[26] More broadly, however, recipe signifies 'a prescription for an experiment, a "trying out"'.[27] Derived from the Latin imperative 'take', it 'prescribes an action' where 'the recipe's "completion" is the trial itself'.[28] Until they are actualized through a trial, recipes are incomplete and imperfect. As such, they instantiate the *active fulfilment* of futuristic knowledge.

The witches' trials with 'ingredience' (4.1.34) provide the clearest examples of the recipe in *Macbeth*.[29] These recipes, however, lack instructions or goals and *Macbeth* downplays their prescriptive value to dramatize the pervasive effects of disseminating secret knowledge. Encountering the witches trying out recipes, Macbeth asks: 'How now, you secret, black, and midnight hags! / What is't you do?' The witches only reveal they perform 'A deed without a name' (4.1.48–9). Instead of divulging the meanings or purpose of this 'Enchanting' (4.1.43), they point to the impossibility of explicating their task, of boiling it down to a 'rule', of even giving it a 'name'. The technical recipe remains insufficient to capture the actualization of occult forces because it cannot fully account for or transform the contingency of the future. Instead, the play transfers the logic of the prescription – a performative and futuristic way of knowing – onto the unactualized prophecies that exist as future possibilities. The witches' prophecies emerge as recipes – they implicitly '[prescribe] an action' – and invite characters to fulfil the predictions. They intimate that the potential political futures they reveal will become *true* when characters employ contingent means – here theatrical action – to realize them and in the process, *Macbeth* asks what constitutes proper *praxis* in the play's created world.

Macbeth and Banquo learn their futures – Banquo's descendents and Macbeth will be kings – from the witches' dissembling verbal prophecies that simultaneously obfuscate meaning and invite interpretation. They reveal possible futures that will retroactively *become* 'prophecies' if they are fulfilled in historical time. They 'hail' Macbeth as 'Thane of Glamis!', 'Thane of Cawdor' and declare '[thou] shalt be King hereafter' (1.3.48–50), revealing his present status and predicting his future rule. Only Banquo's demand that they reveal his future makes them prognosticate again. Their initial predictions for him –'Lesser than Macbeth, and greater', 'Not so happy, yet much happier' (1.3.65–6) – are, like a lot of their utterances, *enigmas*, which according to George Puttenham, is the figure through which ' [w]e dissemble again under covert and dark speeches'.[30] The riddle or enigma obscures the evidentiary quality of language: it 'is pretty but that it holds too much of the *cachemphaton,* or foul speech and may be drawn to a reprobate sense'.[31] The *enigma* might approach 'foul speech' but by dissembling, makes it 'pretty'– or 'fair', to borrow a term from the witches (1.1.11). This ambiguity demands the constant work of interpretation, since 'the sense can hardly be picked out but by the party's own assoil'.[32] The witches' final promise to Banquo, 'Thou shalt get kings, though thou be none' (1.3.67), augurs future possibilities and transports him into a distant future through the revelation of his descendants' fates even as the phrase 'though thou be none' shuts *him* out; it directs audiences to a future beyond Macbeth's individual one, towards the specific moment in the historical present when James claims to be the living fulfilment of this lineage.

The different temporal and genealogical concentrations of the two prophecies create tensions between multiple possibilities and singular certainty and shape Macbeth's and Banquo's responses. The prophecies directed to Banquo are futuristic, while the witches' predictions for Macbeth are limited to and realized in moments of presentness. During this first encounter, the two characters model opposing ways of interpreting prophecies, and their acts of interpretation lead audiences to different models of dramatic action and character. While Macbeth repeatedly turns to denotative language and reads prophecies conclusively, and subsequently as prescriptions, Banquo's implicative or poetic reading, in which he marks ambiguities and gaps among seeming, being and knowing, positions him as the character most clearly able to decipher the possibilities of dissembling language.[33] The play formalizes these responses in temporal terms: Banquo's character must disappear from the stage in order to emerge as the figure of futurity and history, while Macbeth's actions forcefully embed him as a tragic character in the performative present.

Macbeth's initial question, 'Speak, if you can: – what are you?' (1.3.47), attempts unsuccessfully to designate what the witches *are,* an effort he variously repeats in this scene. He seeks literal answers to the question 'what are you' and posits zero-sum conclusions. He oscillates between declaring the prognostications as completely true or false, beyond 'prospect of belief' (1.3.74). Macbeth tries to define the ontological status of the witches and uncover the meaning of their riddles but separates the two issues. In his desire to establish the truthfulness of their prophecies, he does not consider whether what they *are* might serve as evidence of their credibility. Macbeth's increasing curiosity manifests in his wish for more information: 'Stay, you imperfect speakers, tell me more / ... Say from whence / You owe this strange intelligence? or why / Upon this blasted heath you stop our way / With such prophetic greeting?' (1.3.70–8). He demands specific answers – 'whence', 'tell me more', 'why' – in order to literalize this riddling language and insist they perfect their 'imperfect' predictions. Their imperfection, suggests Macbeth, lies in their inability to reveal all, but the adjective implicitly answers his question of what they 'are' and serves as a warning. Yet he subverts his desire to explain their meaning and piles up interrogatives and imperatives fully to divine the 'prophetic greeting'. Macbeth's separation of knowledge and being – his distinction of what the witches know from what they *are* – leads him to focus on his own existence, and subsequently on *how* he must actualize their prophecies.

Banquo, by contrast, elaborates on their ambiguous ontology from the beginning:

> What are these,
> So wither'd, and so wild in their attire,
> That look not like th'inhabitants o'th'earth,
> And yet are on't? Live you? or are you aught
> That man may question? You seem to understand me,
> By each at once her choppy finger laying
> Upon her skinny lips: you should be women,
> And yet your beards forbid me to interpret
> That you are so.
>
> (1.3.39–46)

Although Banquo's initial question ('What are these') is designative, he immediately recognizes the inadequacy of this query. The 'yet[s]' and 'or' capture the proliferating possibilities that arise from attempts to name them or to identify their meaning; as linguistic and logical operators of possibility, these terms underscore the impossibility of singular signification. Interlocutors cannot conclusively 'interpret' what they *are*, because of the absence of classifying markers: Banquo wonders whether they are terrestrial or living, men or women? The multiple, contradictory markers of identity establish their ambiguous ontology. Their complex forms, like their riddled language, 'forbid' us from 'understand[ing]' them and concluding 'what' they 'are', and remain irreconcilable with the multiple things they 'seem'.

Banquo associates their capacity to produce veiled knowledge – their ability to 'dissemble again under covert and dark speeches' – with their states of being; unlike Macbeth, he intimately links epistemology to ontology. Banquo couples their unique cognitive capacity to prognosticate from multiple possibilities – 'If you can look into the seeds of time, / And say which grain will grow and which will not, / Speak then to me' (1.3.58–60) – to speculations about the potential significations of their marvellous states of being: 'Are ye fantastical, or that indeed / Which outwardly ye show' (1.3.53–4). Banquo's conditional appeal to the witches that they '[s]peak' to him is predicated on the belief that their ambiguous ontology signals their unique ability to interact differently with time, look into its 'seeds' and divulge one secret from various possibilities. Their revealed secrets to Macbeth of 'present grace, and great prediction / Of noble having, and of royal hope' (1.3.55–6) mark potentialities that can divulge the future from various options ('which grain will grow and which will not'). As fitting responses to his recognition of their ontological and linguistic ambiguities, and his refusal to draw conclusions from the riddling evidence produced by their esoteric pronouncements, the witches present Banquo with *enigmas*.

Even after the prophecies are partially fulfilled, Banquo keeps reiterating that one should not dissociate what the witches know from what they are. He cautions Macbeth that since 'oftentimes, to win us to our harm, / The instruments of Darkness tell us truths' (1.3.123–4), one must not accept the predictions as already fulfilled knowledge. He sees what Macbeth cannot, that even *true* prophecies might have 'reprobate sense' hidden in their 'pretty' language; the witches are 'imperfect', to transport Macbeth's word, *because* their being cannot serve as evidence of the truth. Their ontology and predictions invite suspicion and scepticism, rather than an impulse to act out the predicted futures. Banquo sees these prophecies as verbal promises that '[m]ight yet' (1.3.121) come to fruition. Although the 'instruments of Darkness' use words to incite exigent means, Banquo suggests that interpretation is a sufficient form of action. As Macbeth and Banquo gain access to secret knowledge, the play uses their opposing responses to dramatize the conflicting possibilities of action available to characters.

Macbeth's unawareness of the multiple roles he *presently* occupies converts epistemic lack into ontological doubt. The witches' revelations of Macbeth's present and future titles initially contrast with his incomplete knowledge that 'the Thane of Cawdor lives' and his yet-unshaken conviction that 'to be King / Stands not within the prospect of belief' (1.3.72–4). The revelations, instead of making him question the witches' ontology, produce imperfection in him and split *his* unified self: 'Shakes so my single state of man / That function is smother'd in surmise / And nothing is, but what is not' (1.3.140–2). His knowledge of his current titles remains dissociated from the past events of the battle that have altered his roles. These predictions direct attention to past occurrences – of which he is still unaware – and to his possible future roles, and they propel him to wonder and doubt the 'truths' of their claims. From this moment, Macbeth's agency is increasingly predicated on prophecy. The utterances define the present more than the future, as the uncertainty of the prognostications splits his subjectivity and leads to self-construction and self-doubt.

Macbeth accepts the 'affirmed' status of the prophecies, however, as soon as he learns that the Thane of Cawdor has been 'overthrown' (1.3.116) and substitutes a linear associative logic for the witches' unaffirmed, poetic language. Immediately after his encounter with the witches, he receives reports of his new titles from Ross and Angus that entail a shift of attitude toward the witches. Since 'Two truths are told, / As happy prologues to the swelling act / Of the imperial theme', therefore 'This supernatural soliciting' has 'given [him] earnest of success, / Commencing in a truth' (1.3.127–33). He now imagines the translation of prophecy into historical fact. Constructing an associative relationship between what has happened and what *should* happen, he imposes his own linear chronology upon the play's polychronous temporality – after all, what he now perceives as the witches' predictions of a contingent future are reports of past events in preceding scenes from the battle and Duncan's decision to reward him.[34] He therefore reads his *present* titles of Glamis and Cawdor as precursors to future rule: 'The greatest is behind' (1.3.117). Macbeth extracts himself from this polychronous moment and maps the contours of his sure future; he sees an unknown past – the displacement of Thane of Cawdor – actualizing itself in *this* moment in Ross's speech act.

Theatrical action: Realizing possibility

Yet, in his unequivocal acceptance of the unknown future lies an undercurrent of uncertainty and the impossibility of knowing the future except as a performed act. Macbeth associatively projects this knowledge towards the predicted future and asks Banquo a question that will haunt him for the rest of the play: 'Do you not hope your children shall be kings, / When those that gave the Thane of Cawdor to me / Promis'd no less to them?' (1.3.118–20). He performs yet another analogical process of reasoning that highlights the active nature of the prophecies: since the sisters 'gave' him the 'Thane of Cawdor' they will bestow the 'Promis'd' to Banquo. The speculation on positions *given* to them leads Macbeth to consider if he might *take* them through performed action. His acceptance that the 'prophetic greeting' has been partially fulfilled makes him wonder if the rest are practical prescriptions, and by extension, if all prophetic discourse demands action. He does consider the various ways in which he might become king, but his reasoning always resolves into a binary division: to act or not to act. He ultimately relies on the logic of prescription – a performative and anticipatory mode that enables one to learn by enacting what is prescribed – to interpret the import of the predictions. Macbeth, then, defines the witches' prophecies as operative knowledge and substitutes 'recipe', we could say, for 'poetic' epistemology as the basis of prophetic discourse.

After this encounter with the witches, *Macbeth* explores how the political future becomes a product of prescription and conclusive interpretation. From the time he learns that he is the Thane of Cawdor, Macbeth believes he has certain knowledge of the future, and with Lady Macbeth's encouragement, increasingly rationalizes the necessity of 'deed' (1.7.24) in order to actualize the prophecies. In the time leading up to Duncan's murder, his mind is filled with images of potential action, 'suggestion' of 'horrid image' and thoughts of 'murther' (1.3.134–9). He oscillates between the position of not acting ('If Chance will have me King, why, Chance may crown me, / Without my stir' [1.3.144–5]) and the necessity of doing so, especially when Duncan chooses his son Malcolm as his heir: Malcolm's title of 'Prince of Cumberland' becomes an obstacle on which Macbeth must 'fall down, or else o'erleap' (1.4.49).

Although he continues to equivocate on 'trying' to fulfil the prophecies, by the time Duncan's party visits Inverness, Macbeth is no more focused on 'interpretation' as an end in itself, but on the goal he must realize. Through Lady Macbeth's insistence on 'deeds', and her urging that Macbeth privilege his 'own act and valour' over mere 'desire' (1.7.40–1), he comes to see *acting* as the only way to eliminate other possible futures:

> If it were done when 'tis done, then 'twere well
> It were done quickly: if th'assassination
> Could trammel up the consequence, and catch
> With his surcease success; that but this blow
> Might be the be-all and the end-all.

> (1.7.1–5)

In spite of the conditional 'If' with which he begins this soliloquy, Macbeth primarily concerns himself with questions of action and performance: 'th'assassination' must be 'done' as a 'blow' to his desired end (the 'end-all'). Instead of waiting for the prophecies to resolve themselves in the future, he believes that immediate fulfilment, their being 'done quickly', will provide an ideal resolution ("twere well'). Rejecting his faith in 'Chance' and focusing solely on the promised ending, Macbeth seeks *means*, or a course of action in a prophecy that does not prescribe one, convincing himself that acting on predictions is necessary to reintegrate his split self and ensure his future rule.

Thus, Macbeth identifies the 'nearest way' to the throne that Lady Macbeth thinks he cannot 'catch' because he is 'too full o'th' milk of human kindness' (1.5.16–17): the murder of the king. Expedient action emerges as the *only* way to remake the future and convert what he, in Banquo's words, might 'yet' be, into the actuality the witches have promised. To find the most expedient means to the throne, the Macbeths revise the signification of prophecy: instead of asking *what* a prophecy means, as Banquo repeatedly does, one must strategize *how* it can be actualized. Seeking the 'nearest way' becomes the sole solution that can resolve the contradictions in Macbeth's being. Erasing the wandering thoughts that simultaneously direct and prevent him from regicide because 'they shake his single state', Macbeth must undertake sure action, '[boil] down to a rule' the prophecy and catalyze the future from the predictive to the prescriptive to the active.[35] This translation of prophecies into prescriptions leads Macbeth to regicide, to the throne and to further speculations.

'The greatest is behind': Making the future visible

After Macbeth follows the 'nearest way' and becomes King, he returns to the predicament of the original prophecies. Having ensured that the prophecies are partially true, he grapples with his temporary role in history: his story ends, whereas the 'happier' Banquo's future is potentially endless. Contrasting his limited reign with Banquo's projected continual futurity, Macbeth meditates on the latter's transgressive role:

> under him,
> My Genius is rebuk'd; as, it is said,
> Mark Antony's was by Caesar. He chid the Sisters,
> When first they put the name of King upon me,
> And bade them speak to him; then prophet-like,
> They hail'd him father to a line of kings:
> Upon my head they plac'd a fruitless crown,
> And put a barren sceptre in my grip,
> Thence to be wrench'd with an unlineal hand,
> No son of mine succeeding. If't be so,
> For Banquo's issue have I filed my mind;
> For them the gracious Duncan have I murther'd;
> Put rancours in the vessel of my peace.
>
> (3.1.54–66)

Macbeth identifies Banquo as an oppositional figure and realizes his deeds, including regicide, serve Banquo's descendants. Banquo himself emerges as a 'prophet-like' actualizing force. Macbeth suggests that Banquo generates, perhaps *creates,* his own prophecies: because *he* 'chid' the sisters and 'bade them speak', they prophesied his future. Macbeth's knowledge 'filed [his] mind' and led him to '[murther]' only to secure another's political future. While the play initially separates Macbeth and Banquo through their opposing modes of interpretation, Macbeth's rumination exposes the formal effects of these interpretative differences. Macbeth's conclusive stance makes him act to secure a crown that permanently delimits him to perform actions in the present, while Banquo's implicative attitude facilitates his emergence as a figure of history.

This distinction between Macbeth as a figure with an end and the projected endlessness of Banquo's line is formalized in the primarily visual revelations produced in Macbeth's

second meeting with the witches in which they reiterate their
status as dissimulators of the occult by refusing affirmatively
to announce what they know. When Macbeth appeals to
the process and source of their knowledge ('I conjure you,
by that which you profess / Howe'er you come to know
it, answer me' (4.1.50–1)), he receives a series of visual
and aural cues from three apparitions: '*an armed head*',
'*a bloody child*' and '*a child crowned, with a tree in his
hand*'. The first warns directly: 'beware Macduff; / Beware
the Thane of Fife' (4.1.71–2). The others speak in riddles.
The second prescribes limited inaction but also advises him
to occupy various states of mind – 'Be bloody, bold, and
resolute: laugh to scorn / The power of man, for none of
woman born / Shall harm Macbeth' (4.1.79–81) – and the
third warns him to refrain for a certain time from active
intervention: 'Be lion-mettled, proud, and take no care [...]
Macbeth shall never vanquish'd be, until / Great Birnam
Wood to high Dunsinane hill / Shall come against him'
(4.1.90–4). The apparitions *prescribe* attitudes, virtues and
mental states of being.

Macbeth heeds the first warning but responds ambiguously to the second: 'live, Macduff: what need I fear of
thee? / But yet I'll make assurance double sure, / And take
a bond of Fate: thou shalt not live' (4.1.82–4). His diminishing worry coincides with his failure yet again to mark the
figurative nature of prophecies. Focusing on 'paraphrases',[36]
he discounts both equivocal and direct warnings and rejects
the final prediction as an impossibility: 'That will never be'
(4.1.94). Before he mistook prophecies for prescription. Here,
he misinterprets prescribed states of being as unequivocal
truths and immediately proposes action: 'The very firstlings
of my heart shall be / The firstlings of my hand' (4.1.147–8).
Earlier he had equivocated on the relation of prophetic
utterance to action. Now the 'hand' works simultaneously
with the 'heart', collapsing gaps between cognition and action:
Macbeth will immediately 'crown [his] thoughts with acts'
(4.1.149).

The witches reciprocate Macbeth's conclusive stance with their most transparent prophecy. As he seeks resolution to the one question that cannot be completely answered within the play's compressed temporality ('shall Banquo's issue ever / Reign in this kingdom?' [4.1.102–3]), they '[s]how' (4.1.108) the approaching times. In a scene that Peter Stallybrass identifies as *Macbeth*'s 'emblematic centre',[37] the play enacts the 'future in the instant'. The visual spectacle makes present the ambiguous verbal prophecies and shuts Macbeth out of anticipated futures, instead of reinserting him into history:

A *show of eight kings, the last with a glass in his hand;*
BANQUO *following.*

MACBETH
Thou art too like the spirit of Banquo: down!
Thy crown does sear mine eye-balls: – and thy hair,
Thou other gold-bound brow, is like the first: –
A third is like the former: – filthy hags!
Why do you show me this? – A fourth? – Start, eyes!
What! will the line stretch out to th'crack of doom?
Another yet? – A seventh? – I'll see no more –
And yet the eighth appears, who bears a glass
Which shows me many more; and some I see
That two-fold balls and treble sceptres carry.
Horrible sight!

(4.1.112–22)

The glass functions as a perspective device that takes Macbeth into a theatrical future in which he witnesses the culmination of the line in James, alerting him of a time from which his lineage has been erased.[38] By marking his lack of descendants, this '[s]how' visually and symbolically shuts Macbeth out of continuing narratives of futurity. Macbeth's earlier imagination that the future is 'behind' had produced a visual epistemology of time: unknown futures cannot be deciphered because they remain visually obstructed or 'behind'. This scene makes visible such a future by transforming what was 'behind' into an immediately observable theatrical scene.

The procession, moreover, completes a process of abstraction that fixes Macbeth's roles within the dramatic framework. Macbeth's encounters with the complex temporality of prophecy spur his obsession with his own future but paradoxically transform him into an emblem – or evidence – of anomalous misrule. This scene visually culminates the verbal process of emblematic erasure that began when characters like Macduff and Malcolm refused to acknowledge Macbeth's particular identity; instead of using his name, they employ general terms including 'tyrant' (4.3.178) or 'usurper' (5.9.21) to define him.[39] His position shifts from the particular 'brave Macbeth (well he deserves that name)' (1.2.16) to the titular figure of 'Thane' and 'King', to the general category of 'tyrant'. Malcolm's refusal to name Macbeth ('This tyrant, whose sole name blisters our tongues' [4.3.12]) suggests how the act of naming indexes an individual. Macbeth's individuality, encapsulated in his 'name', disappears with its gradual erasure. The spectacle does not merely 'split' Macbeth's 'single state', it underscores his emblematic status and ensures his disappearance from future history.

Yet *Macbeth*'s prophetic interpretations also enact how a character earns himself or herself a place on the stage and in the present. Banquo's emergence as a figure who augurs the future begins only when his character disappears from the theatrical present. In contrast to Banquo's potential endless futurity, Macbeth's rule is transformed into a singular event where the titular character interprets and acts out the conditions for his own present existence. Macbeth's exigency, the product of his conclusive interpretations and misinterpretations, negates the continuation of his line, but it also inaugurates an occasion for *experiencing* how a notion of theatrical presentness emerges. Macbeth's current actions onstage repeatedly unsettle the play's dramatization of the past as future as well as its aim to prescribe, in the line of kings, the audience's political present. As Macbeth turns interpretative strategies on their head, his execution of prophetic utterance produces the action in which 'thoughts' repeatedly become 'acts'. Through Macbeth's staged immediacy, then, the play offers one model of actualizing prophecy: the theatrical action that makes present different temporalities as well as fabricated states of being.

But the play also suggests that the act of interpretation might itself actualize prophecies and take audiences beyond the staged action. As Macbeth's place in a continuing future gives way to the procession seen through the glass, the audience implicitly gains entry into this polychronous moment when the theatrical future intersects with the historical present. The visual clarity of this emblematic scene, ending in the representation of James, overcompensates for the enigmatic language and propels audiences to recognize their own moment as an actualized future projected from the play. In this moment, the theatrical future translates into the historical present and serves to perpetuate sovereign lineage. *Macbeth* privileges possibility – enacted by Banquo – as *the* way of knowing uncertain futures, and the play's promise of continuity transports audiences, with Banquo, to their futures beyond the spectacle of an 'instant'. The visual prophecy offers a prescription, but not the one Macbeth grasps: audiences must perform a simultaneously reassuring and unnerving prospective *act*. The spectacle provides them both 'ingredients' and 'instructions', in the shape of the figures and in the form of the projected line. Instead of ending on conclusive evidence, *Macbeth* demands its audiences project implicatively from what they witness onstage – Macbeth's head on a stand, the spectacle of Banquo's lineage, the image of James – to the implicit promise of their own futures extending beyond the boundaries of the dramatic form. They must adopt the play's implicative and poetic interpretative strategies, which will lead them to the certainty of the historical present and subsequently towards the imagination of *their* possible futures. Such a projection, which is of course a strategy of legitimizing political rule and lineage, will enable them to extend this vision towards the real futures that might come into being after James' reign itself expires. *Macbeth,* then, prophesies to its audiences that their imaginative acts of projection, when 'tried' out, will exceed the exigencies of the fictional present and even go beyond their singular, historical moment of interpretation; it teaches them *how* one imagines a future 'in the instant'.[40]

Notes

1   Scholars trace the topicality of *Macbeth* by focusing on politics, sovereignty and witchcraft. For representative works, see David Scott Kastan, *Shakespeare After Theory* (New York, 1999), pp. 165–82; Stephen Greenblatt, 'Shakespeare Bewitched', in *New Historical Literary Study: Essays on Reproducing Texts, Representing History,* Jeffrey N. Cox and Larry J. Reynolds (eds) (Princeton, 1993), pp. 108–35; Peter Stallybrass, 'Macbeth and Witchcraft', in *Focus on Macbeth,* ed. John Russell (Boston, 1982), pp. 189–209. On how the witches serve as signifiers of ethnography and environment, see Mary Floyd-Wilson, 'English Epicures and Scottish Witches', *Shakespeare Quarterly* 57.2 (2006), pp. 131–61.

2   See Jonathan Gil Harris, *Untimely Matter in the Time of Shakespeare* (Philadelphia, 2009), pp. 119–39; David Scott Kastan, *Shakespeare and the Shapes of Time* (Hanover, 1982), pp. 91–101; Garrett A. Sullivan, Jr., 'Coda: "Wrought with things forgetting"', in *Memory and Forgetting in English Renaissance Drama* (Cambridge, 2005), pp. 132–6; Donald W. Foster, 'Macbeth's War on Time', *English Literary Renaissance* 16.2 (1986), pp. 319–42; Jonathan Goldberg, 'Speculations: Macbeth and Source', in *Shakespeare Reproduced: The Text in History and Ideology,* Jean E. Howard, Marion F. O'Connor (eds) (New York, 1987), pp. 242–64, 242.

3   William Shakespeare, *The Arden Shakespeare Complete Works,* Richard Proudfoot, Ann Thompson and David Scott Kastan (eds) (London, 2011).

4   Kastan (1982), pp. 100, 87.

5   For example, see Sharon L. Jansen Jaech, 'Political Prophecy
    and Macbeth's "Sweet Bodements"', *Shakespeare Quarterly*
    34.3 (1983), pp. 290–7.

6   Marjorie Garber, '"What's Past is Prologue": Temporality
    and Prophecy in Shakespeare's History Plays', in *Renaissance
    Genres: Essays on Theory, History, and Interpretation*, ed.
    Barbara Kiefer Lewalski (Cambridge, MA, 1986), pp. 301–31,
    308.

7   Ibid., p. 318.

8   William Eamon, *Science and the Secrets of Nature: Books of
    Secrets in Medieval and Early Modern Culture* (Princeton,
    1994); Elizabeth Spiller, *Science, Reading, and Renaissance
    Literature: The Art of Making Knowledge, 1580–1670*
    (Cambridge, 2004), esp. pp. 1–23. For a study of maker's
    knowledge, see Antonio Pérez-Ramos, *Francis Bacon's Idea
    of Science and the Maker's Knowledge Tradition* (New York,
    1988). For the relationship between practical arts and drama,
    see Henry S. Turner, *The English Renaissance Stage: Geometry,
    Poetics, and the Practical Spatial Arts 1580–1630* (Oxford,
    2006).

9   See Eamon, pp. 267–360.

10 Sir Philip Sidney, *A Defence of Poetry*, ed. Jan Van Dorsten
    (Oxford, 1966), pp. 53, 29. *Macbeth*'s use of equivocal
    language also refers to Henry Garnet's *A Treatise of
    Equivocation*, explicitly dramatized in the porter's claim 'Here's
    an equivocator' (2.3.8). See Kastan (1999) for doubling in
    Macbeth, especially of the figures of the king and the tyrant,
    which hinders unequivocal understanding of events or complete
    restoration of order.

11 Eamon, p. 4.

12 John Harvey, *A Discoursiue Probleme Concerning Prophesies*
    (London, 1588), p. 37. James' ascension to the English throne
    was interpreted as the realization of ancient prophecies. Garber
    (1986) notes: 'King James was popularly supposed to be the
    fulfilment of a "Merlin prophecy" about the restoration of
    Britain under a new Arthurian king' (p. 311). In *Religion
    and the Decline of Magic* (New York, 1971), Keith Thomas
    elaborates on James' use of 'the Brutus myth' and related

ancient prophecies to 'consolidate his ascension to the English throne' (p. 417).

13 For the relationship between astrology and prophecy, see Patrick Curry, *Prophecy and Power: Astrology in Early Modern England* (Cambridge, 1989). For the relationship between political prophecy and preaching, see Howard Dobin, *Merlin's Disciples: Prophecy, Poetry, and Power in Renaissance England* (Stanford, 1990). Thomas' modernizing narrative, that diminishing faith in prophecy led to the decline of magic, has been challenged by works like Tim Thornton's *Prophecy, Politics and the People in Early Modern England* (Rochester, 2006).

14 Francis Bacon, *Essays or Counsels, Civil and Moral* in *Francis Bacon: The Major Works*, ed. Brian Vickers (Oxford, 2008), p. 414.

15 *Praxis* signifies 'practical knowledge' in which 'action contains its end in itself', while *poiesis* is 'productive knowledge' where 'making finds its ends in its object' (Turner, pp. 46–7). For an example of the breakdown between *praxis* and *poiesis* in Shakespearean drama, see Richard Halpern, 'Eclipse of Action: Hamlet and the Political Economy of Playing', *Shakespeare Quarterly* 59:4 (2008), pp. 450–82.

16 For the close associations between poetry and prophecy, see Roger E. Moore, 'Sir Philip Sidney's Defense of Prophesying', *SEL Studies in English Literature 1500–1900* 50.1 (2010), pp. 35–62.

17 Eamon, p. 54. *Praxis* and *poiesis* dealt with variable or changing entities (Turner, p. 46). For distinctions between certain and probable knowledge, see Peter Dear, *Revolutionizing the Sciences: European Knowledge and its Ambitions, 1500–1700* (Princeton, 2001), esp. pp. 1–48; Barbara J. Shapiro, *Probability and Certainty in Seventeenth-Century England: A Study of the Relationships between Natural Science, Religion, History, Law, and Literature* (Princeton, 1983), esp. pp. 3–14.

18 For changing values of objects of study in the period, see Lorraine Daston and Katharine Park, *Wonders and the Order of Nature, 1150–1750* (New York and Cambridge, MA, 1998).

19 Harvey, p. 16.

20 Howard, Henry, *A Defensatiue Against the Poyson of Supposed Prophesies* (London, 1583), p. 32.

21 Ibid., p. 191.

22 Ibid., p. 271.

23 Ibid., p. 27.

24 Thomas, p. 139.

25 Eamon, p. 10.

26 Ibid., pp. 131, 7.

27 Ibid., p. 131.

28 Ibid., 131.

29 For the various recipes, see Act 4.1. For textual history and the possible spuriousness of 4.1, see *Arden Shakespeare*, p. 773. Also see Shakespeare, William, *The Norton Shakespeare,* Stephen Greenblatt et al. (eds) (New York, 2008), p. 2563.

30 George Puttenham, *The Art of English Poesy*, Frank Whigham and Wayne A. Rebhorn (eds) (Ithaca, 2007), p. 272. See Steven Mullaney, 'Lying Like Truth: Riddle, Representation and Treason in Renaissance England', *ELH* 47.1 (1980), pp. 32–47, for the use of the poetic figure 'ambiguita' in *Macbeth*. John Frow, *Genre* (New York, 2006) links *Macbeth's* prophecies to riddles.

31 Puttenham, p. 273.

32 Ibid., p. 272

33 I borrow the terms 'implicative' and 'conclusive' from Andrew H. Miller, *The Burdens of Perfection: On Ethics and Reading in Nineteenth-Century British Literature* (Ithaca, 2008). Miller distinguishes 'implicative' and 'conclusive' criticism: while the latter works to 'establish facts, convey information, and make judgments, …[and] ask for no continuation from its readers', implicative criticism is 'generative', 'thinking', asks readers to 'elaborate' (p. 30) on writers' cognitive processes and is 'marked first of all by the display of thinking, [as] writers unfold the implications of their ideas rather than convey their conclusions' (pp. 221–2).

34 I borrow the term 'polychronous' from Harris, who defines

the 'untimeliness' of matter, or how '[i]n its polychronicity, an object can prompt many different understandings and experiences of temporality – that is, of the relations between now and then, old and new, before and after' (pp. 3–4).

35 Eamon, p. 7.

36 Emma Smith, *The Cambridge Introduction to Shakespeare* (Cambridge, 2007), p. 71.

37 Stallybrass, p. 200. For the 'problematics of vision' (p. 191) in *Macbeth,* see Huston Diehl, 'Horrid Image, Sorry Sight, Fatal Vision: The Visual Rhetoric of *Macbeth*', *Shakespeare Studies* 16 (1983), pp. 191–203.

38 For multiple connotations of the 'two-fold balls' and 'treble scepters' in relation to James' rule, see E. B. Lyle, 'The "Twofold Balls And Treble Scepters" in *Macbeth*', *Shakespeare Quarterly* 28.4 (1977), pp. 516–19.

39 See Marjorie Garber, *Shakespeare's Ghost Writers: Literature as Uncanny Causality* (New York, 1987) for Macbeth's transformation into 'an object lesson, a spectacle, a warning against tyranny, a figure for theater and for art' (p. 114).

40 I would like to thank Henry Turner, Ann Thompson, Scott Trudell, Colleen Rosenfeld, Sarah Novacich, Katherine Williams, Ann Coiro, Jacqueline Miller, and the members of the Rutgers Medieval-Renaissance Colloquium for their insightful responses to this essay.

5

Lady Macbeth, First Ladies and the Arab Spring: The Performance of Power on the Twenty-First Century Stage

Kevin A. Quarmby

LADY MACBETH: Only look up clear;
To alter favour ever is to fear.
Leave all the rest to me. (1.5.71–3)

MACDUFF: Each new morn,
New widows howl, new orphans cry; new sorrows
Strike heaven on the face, that it resounds
As if it felt with Scotland, and yell'd out
Like syllable of dolour. (4.3.4–8)

Macbeth's tyrannical rule over Scotland grows ever more violent as he suffers each successive setback. The equivocatory prophecies of the Witches, misinterpreted by king and queen alike, fuel the self-destructiveness of a regime founded on fear and oppression. Lady Macbeth is driven insane with guilt. Macbeth fights on, only to suffer defeat at the hands of that revenging husband and father, Macduff, whose entry into the world involved no less pain and incisive violence. Shakespeare's tragic narrative traces the downfall of Scotland's 'butcher and his fiend-like queen', the one beheaded, the other, 'by self and violent hands', taking her own life (5.9.35–7). Bloody as this Jacobean tragedy is, its plot still resonates congruously with twenty-first-century Middle East events. The political unrest of 2011, labelled locally and by Western media as the Arab Spring, brought many changes to a region long dominated by dictatorial regimes. Most gruesome of these events was the death of Colonel Gaddafi at the hands of his subjects. Dragged from a drainpipe and filmed on multiple handheld personal devices, Gaddafi suffered the brutal revenge of the nation he had ruled for forty-two years.

The significance for Shakespeare scholars of this moment of revenge killing was twofold. Unsurprisingly, newspapers and online commentators embraced the analogous potential of Gaddafi's end with Shakespearean *Schadenfreude*. Robert F. Worth of the *New York Times*, for instance, likened Gaddafi to Macbeth, whereby the colonel 'understood that he had gone "so far in blood" that there was no turning back'.[1] Worth concluded that Gaddafi's whole 'reign seemed to follow an inexorable arc toward ruin', with the 'handsome young revolutionary […] transformed into the drugged, puffy-faced madman howling for slaughter in the streets of his own cities'. Macbeth's bloody decline was apparently paralleled in Gaddafi's drug-fuelled violence. Even *Macbeth*'s witches made their implicit appearance, with Worth reporting how Libyans 'believed [G]addafi used black magic to keep himself in power for so long'. As a journalist, Worth was 'almost tempted to believe' this supernatural association, since he 'found Chadian witchcraft amulets in some of the weapons depots abandoned by [Gaddafi's] loyalists'. Although most Libyans were unlikely to associate their leader with his Shakespearean counterpart, one American journalist and international commentator, steeped in the traditions of a Western literary education, made full use of Macbethian imagery to describe the drama of Gaddafi's downfall.

In the UK, similar Shakespearean imagery tinctured British media descriptions of Libya's Arab Spring. Richard Spencer of the right-wing broadsheet newspaper the *Telegraph*, for example, when triumphantly declaring 'Col Gaddafi killed', misquoted Polonius to describe a certain 'method in [Gaddafi's] madness'.[2] The colonel's deadly clowning, so Spencer argued, masked the bitter reality of his dictatorial regime: 'its brutality, its unbending belief in the ruler's destiny, its clarity that in the end, survival is worth any number of deaths.' Most significant for Spencer, however, was Gaddafi's 'zenga zenga' ['alley by alley'] speech of 22 February 2011, a tirade made internationally and ironically famous by its musical remix as a YouTube viral hit.[3] Describing the 'narcissism' of this 'true dictator', Spencer observed that Gaddafi's 'lonely and impregnable' rant – 'I and the millions will march in order to cleanse Libya, inch by inch, house by house, home by home, alley by alley, individual by individual, so that the country is purified from the unclean' – showed an 'obsession with cleanliness worthy of Lady Macbeth's "Out damned spot"' speech. Similarly, the anonymous and ungendered Wordpress blogger SkyeNoor, uncomfortable about the perceived abuse of Gaddafi's 'lifeless body' following the colonel's capture and death, offered her/his equally Shakespearean analogy. Describing how Gaddafi's 'life has come full circle', SkyeNoor noted that, '[i]n the words of Lady Macbeth, what's done cannot be undone'.[4] Both these political commentators – the by-lined Spencer and the anonymous SkyeNoor – easily associate a four-hundred-year-old tragic character with a recently murdered Middle East dictator. Most noticeable, however, is the fact that, in Gaddafi's case, the analogue is not restricted to the Scottish tyrant king, but includes his queen as well. It is Lady Macbeth who epitomizes the destructive power of Gaddafi's regime, and who thus defines the fateful inevitability of the obsessive colonel's downfall. The downtrodden Libyan leader is seemingly emasculated and regendered by triumphalist and apologist alike.

What might such analogous associations tell us about the reception of other political leaders in the twenty-first century, and what is the relevance of incorporating Lady Macbeth in the weaponry of such negativistic political discourse? As is clear, Gaddafi's call for national purification prompted at least one strangely feminized 'Lady Macbeth' analogy at the end of his regime. The Libyan leader's contentious status in international affairs had, however, provoked earlier 'Lady Macbeth' commentary, long before his disgrace and downfall. In 2009, for example, two-and-a-half years before Gaddafi's fall from favour, the UK-based journalist and self-proclaimed 'libertarian conservative', James Delingpole, wrote an online news report, yet again for readers of the *Telegraph*.[5] Delingpole posed the question, 'Was "Lady Macbeth" behind Barack Obama's snub of Gordon Brown?'.[6] This provocative headline was in response to reports that President Obama had ordered the removal (and repatriation to the UK) of a bronze bust of Britain's wartime hero, Sir Winston Churchill.[7] The bust, by Sir Jacob Epstein, was no longer to grace the Oval Office at the White House. Delingpole's report also highlighted Obama's refusal to offer bilateral talks with the then UK Prime Minister, Gordon Brown. Not only did President Obama apparently snub Gordon Brown, but he also offered the primetime speech slot at New York's G20 Summit to none other than the Libyan leader, Colonel Gaddafi.

For several decades treated as a pariah by Western leaders because of his tacit acceptance of terrorist training camps that operated on Libyan soil, Gaddafi was now courted as a strategic ally in Middle East affairs by the US political hierarchy. This potentially divisive preferential treatment appeared doubly offensive because of Brown's Scottish nationality and Libya's association with the Lockerbie bomb atrocity. The Pan Am Flight 103 terrorist attack killed 259 passengers and crew, and eleven other innocent citizens on the ground residing in or visiting the Scottish town of Lockerbie.[8] At the time of the 'snub', Scotland even held imprisoned the convicted Lockerbie bomber, Abdelbaset al-Megrahi, whose 2010 release on compassionate grounds was as yet undecided. The snub of Brown and favouring of Gaddafi appeared, therefore, the ultimate national insult. Who was responsible for such political manoeuvring? As is obvious, one 'conservative' UK journalist had no doubt about 'Lady Macbeth's' identity: Michelle Obama, wife of the President of the United States. It was not Gaddafi, but America's First Lady who had transmogrified into the 'fiend-like queen' of the White House (5.9.35).

Delingpole's political (and personal) insult led to heated debate on both sides of the Atlantic. The Washington correspondent for the *Telegraph*, Alex Spillius, denounced his colleague's argument as 'flimsy' and motivated by self-publicity.[9] Kevin Wicks of BBC America likewise branded Delingpole as one of a group of 'nattering old scolds' pushing an agenda of 'easy racism and sexism'.[10] The *New York Times* 'Opinion' columnist, Maureen Dowd, described how Delingpole 'snipped', and the British tabloid press 'carped', at a First Lady whose willingness to display the 'biceps' on her 'well-disciplined body', and her apparent 'complete confidence in her skin', were being seized on by right-wing detractors as unseemly and socially unacceptable.[11] Undeterred by these rebukes, Delingpole continued to refer to Michelle Obama as 'Lady Macbeth'. When later in 2009 she appeared on the international political stage, Michelle Obama's refusal publicly to embrace the Italian Prime Minister, Silvio Berlusconi, added fuel to Delingpole's analogous fire. Supposedly expecting a far more intimate kiss on both cheeks, Berlusconi was, according to Delingpole, seemingly 'unimpressed by Lady Macbeth's exquisitely toned arm', especially when America's First Lady proffered the Italian premier not an embrace, but a firm though distant handshake.[12] Obviously no fan of Berlusconi, Delingpole nevertheless reprises his Lady Macbeth jibe (and its attendant paranoia over masculinized physical strength) to insinuate the Italian Prime Minister as another male victim of aggressive First Lady behaviour.

No more offensive than the overtly racist satirical 'spoof' US news sites that offer scandalous descriptions of Macbethian witchcraft, Afro-Caribbean voodoo and wild satanic rituals in the Obaman White House, Delingpole's comments nevertheless pander to a political class for whom race, gender and female Machiavellianism remain bugbears that threaten the stability of the patriarchal state machine.[13] His comments also confirm that 'First Ladies' are not immune from scrutiny when accompanying their presidential husbands. In the context of similar assaults against First Ladies in international politics, Delingpole's analogous association, although unpleasant and derogatory, is not necessarily surprising. Indeed, the image of Lady Macbeth as weapon in the arsenal of political character assassination taps into a cultural commonplace recognizable the world over: that of a leader's wife as manipulative Lady Macbeth, the malevolent *dea ex machina* puppet-master urging her husband to follow a decidedly private, female agenda. This cultural commonplace, invariably accompanied by home-grown animosity towards the wives of powerful leaders, has flourished since the fall of Communism. In the closing decade of the twentieth century, the soubriquet was applied easily to Elena Ceauşescu, wife of the disgraced Romanian dictator Nicolai, who was executed alongside her husband in 1989.[14]

In the twenty-first century, the Arab Spring foregrounded similar analogies between Lady Macbeth and the wives of brutal Middle East leaders. As the British journalist Angelique Crisafis reports in her 2012 *Guardian* article, which describes her conversation with 'one Middle East expert in Paris' who commented how '[e]very revolution has its Lady Macbeth', there are several 'first ladies of oppression' in the Arab world who fit the Shakespearean analogy.[15] These include the exiled and detested 'Lady Macbeth of Carthage' Leila Trabelsi (wife of Tunisia's Zine El-Abidine Ben Ali), 'Egypt's Lady Macbeth'

Suzanne Mubarak (wife of Egypt's Hosni Mubarak), the 'cold, calculating' Asma al-Assad (wife of the Syrian leader Bashar al-Assad), as well as Safia Farkash, the second wife of Colonel Gaddafi, who fled to Algeria when troubles flared in Libya.[16] So strong is this association that the Tunisian-born Paris-based director Lofti Achour staged his own adaptation, called *Macbeth: Leila and Ben – A Bloody History*, for the UK's 2012 World Shakespeare Festival.[17] As Achour explained to a United Arab Emirates newspaper prior to the play's first performance, *Macbeth: Leila and Ben* represents a 'mockumentary' of Tunisia's disgraced leader and his wife.[18] More significantly, Achour stresses the challenge he set his collaborator, the Franco-Italo-Tunisian actress Anissa Daoud playing 'Leila Macbeth', to 'bring to the stage a living person with a public persona that still provokes the hatred and bitterness that [Leila Trabelsi] does'.[19] Claiming to 'relate' *Macbeth* to 'power struggles not just in Tunisia, but also the wider Arab world', Achour mockingly juxtaposes the 'Lady Macbeth of Carthage' with his own 'Leila Macbeth' construct, thus demonstrating the continuing relevance of such Macbethian imagery in an Arab Spring context.[20]

The wealth of newfound First Lady comparisons is not, however, restricted to British journalistic analysis or Franco-Tunisian mocking drama. Elsewhere, reporters are equally willing to adopt such imagery, as confirmed by Melinda Liu's almost apologetic headline, 'Does China really have its own Lady Macbeth?'.[21] Liu's article, published on the American news website *The Daily Beast*, describes how Gu Kailai, wife of the Politburo Secretary Bo Xila, became a suspect in the 2011 death of the British businessman Neil Heywood. Written four months before Kailai's one-day trial, conviction, and surprisingly lenient two-year suspended death sentence, Liu's response to the initial accusation demonstrates the ease with which the First Lady/Lady Macbeth analogue can apply to any woman whose power stems, by association, from the status of her husband, and whose actions are deemed unsuited to her sex. Surprisingly, even the First Lady of Australian politics, the 2010 elected Prime Minister Julia Gillard, was not immune from the analogous attacks of male counter-parts. In a heated 2011 debate on carbon pricing, Australia's Leader of the Opposition, Tony Abbott, accused Gillard of being a 'latter day Lady Macbeth' because of her determi-nation to tax high-polluting industries.[22] Political discord, cross-party disagreement, or even an accusation of murderous complicity are sufficient to ensure Shakespeare's infamous female character rears her 'fiendlike' head in news reports, newspapers and online commentary worldwide.

This international list of 'Lady Macbeth' hopefuls demon-strates how Delingpole's First Lady analogy accords with similar expressions of political animosity, as articulated by commentators who recognize the headline-grabbing value of Shakespeare's infamous female character. Even so, the comparison of Michelle Obama with Macbeth's dangerous queen is by no means a new phenomenon in US politics. In fact, the Lady Macbeth/First Lady analogue has a lengthy and discernible history tracing back to the opening years of the nineteenth century. Consequently, First Lady 'Lady Macbeths' have been accused of exerting undue influence over their powerful husbands ever since the White House was first occupied in 1800.[23] The history of this specific analogy, and its correlation to the actual performance of Lady Macbeth on the American stage, is the subject of Gay Smith's 2010 book, *Lady Macbeth in America: From the Stage to the White House*.[24] In it, Smith argues that 'Shakespeare's Lady Macbeth has haunted America from the founding of the United States to the present'.[25] Lady Macbeth is, as Smith observes, perceived as so 'iconic' in the United States that she has been elevated from fictive character to 'mythic type', which is permanently ingrained in 'America's cultural memory'.[26] Lady Macbeth's 'iconic' and 'mythic' cultural status might thus account for the Western media's readiness to adopt, or more rightly adapt, aspects of this character's personality to describe Colonel Gaddafi and other Arab Spring political protagonists.

Smith traces the earliest manifestation of such 'iconic' Lady

Macbeth/First Lady negativity to disquiet about President John Adams' wife Abigail, presidential First Lady between 1797 and 1801. Abigail Adams became infamous for using the theatre, and most specifically productions of *Macbeth*, 'to propagandize support for her husband and [for] mongering for war against the French'.[27] Likewise, Woodrow Wilson's second wife Edith Galt was accused of Lady Macbeth skulduggery for her suspected running of the executive single-handedly after her husband's stroke, while Eleanor Roosevelt represented a no less formidable or potentially insidious force in her husband's presidency.[28]

The First Lady/Lady Macbeth analogue continued to hold sway in post-Second World War America, even spawning a raft of 'alternative' *Macbeths* that made unsubtle wordplay on the names of the White House occupants. As Todd Landon Barnes traces in his 2008 article, 'George W. Bush's "Three Shakespeares": *Macbeth*, *Macbush*, and the Theater of War', as early as 1965, Texan President Lyndon Johnson and his wife Lady Bird were cast as principal protagonists in Barbara Garson's fifteen-minute comic skit, *Macbird*.[29] Described likewise by Smith as a satire that 'surpasses most others in both length and quality', Garson's drama sought to 'warn how the country was in danger of being led into an even more deadly war, first by Jack Kennedy and then by Lyndon Johnson'.[30] In the aftermath of John F. Kennedy's assassination in 1962, the staged assassination of the fictive 'President Ken O'Dunc' would seem particularly incendiary and insensitive.[31] It must also have appeared uncomfortably prescient in the light of Bobby Kennedy's equally tragic murder in 1968. For Barnes, however, a more recent equivalent to Garson's satirical conflation of *Macbeth* and US politics is Michael Hettinger's 2003 production of *The Tragedy of Macbush*, a play that also spawned several *Macbush*-style satires.[32] *The Tragedy of Macbush*, and the *Macbush* satires that followed its lead, were noticeably less concerned with First Lady involvement in political affairs and more with the perceived hawkishness of President George W. Bush.

They also demonstrate how, contrary to Michelle Obama's supposed stance, George W.'s First Lady, Laura Bush, was hailed as a model of political non-involvement. Unlike her predecessors – Barbara Bush, Nancy Reagan and Rosalynn Carter – Laura Bush was considered *not* to have embraced the archetypal 'Lady Macbeth' role to manipulate her husband.[33] Instead, George W. was left to occupy the metaphorical throne of Macbeth in isolated splendour.

If Laura Bush escaped relatively unscathed from Lady Macbeth comparison, the same could not be said for her predecessor, Hillary Clinton.[34] As early as 1992, a year before Bill Clinton's occupation of the White House, *American Spectator* contributor Daniel Wattenberg famously coined the phrase, 'The Lady Macbeth of Little Rock'.[35] Wattenberg's soubriquet for Hillary Clinton struck a political sketch-writing chord, and spawned a host of similar analogous commentaries. In consequence, only six years later and following the Monica Lewinsky affair, *TIME* could report that 'the Lady Macbeth view of Hillary' had become a commonplace of 'conservative' opinion.[36] Rather than being the victim of an unpleasant 'witch-hunt', Hillary Clinton was, at least by 'conservative' commentators, accused of consciously adopting her 'Lady Macbeth' persona as part of some personal reconstruction, and to maximize her political powerbase.[37] In her new 'role' – as forbearing and merciful First Lady 'guardian' – Hillary Clinton personified Lady Macbeth to right-wing Americans. Traditionally left-wing women intellectuals, however, seeing Hillary Clinton's incarnation as a supportive and forgiving wife as a betrayal of her feminist principles, likewise condemned her 'Lady Macbethian' qualities. 'Conservative' and 'liberal' opinion seemed strangely united in their negative associativity.

A decade later, during Hillary Clinton's 2007 campaign as candidate for the Democratic Party presidential nomination, Rupert Murdoch's right-wing British newspaper *The Times* revived the Lady Macbeth association. Gerard Baker's contentious headline, 'The vaulting ambition of America's Lady Macbeth: Hillary Clinton's shameless political reconstructive surgery', proved that the First Lady of 1990s US politics was still seen as a threat to 'conservative' political order by one UK correspondent.[38] The vitriolic bile of 'Lady Macbeth Hillary Clinton' rhetoric was likewise evident in the anonymous 'Washington-based British journalist and political observer', known enigmatically as 'Dateline D.C.', who pilloried 'Hillary & her "Weird Sisters"' in the *Pittsburgh Tribune-Review*.[39] Describing *Macbeth* as a play that 'reveals the tragedy of a woman's lust for power and betrayal of friends', this unknown 'journalist' offers her/his overly simplified and textually selective representation of Hillary Clinton as 'Lady Macbeth [being] aided in her purpose by three aged creatures, the Weird Sisters'. Taking several liberties with the act 4 scene 1 text, 'Dateline D.C.' describes how the 'three hags [...] call up "snakes, newts and the toes of frogs" to conjure a "hell's broth" of "furies" to plague man as they hobble and prance around a steaming cauldron on a wind-swept heath'.[40] Hillary Clinton's 'three hags' were themselves 'three very respected elderly ladies' who 'vowed [...] to defend and promote Sen. Clinton's candidacy': Geraldine Ferraro, Madeleine Albright and Billie Jean King. Joining forces behind their Lady Macbeth, these 'three hags' instilled 'fear' in the voting public that their nation would falter without Hillary Clinton's steadying hand. For this 'Washington-based British journalist', Hillary Clinton and her entourage personify all that is evil in Shakespeare's drama, their combined malevolent weight seeking to promote the candidacy of a woman president whose lust for power and betraying tendencies are overshadowed by the scare tactics of their policies.

Although Hillary Clinton failed to secure her party's nomination for the presidency, her status remained that of manipulative wife whose support for her husband furthered her own political ambitions. As Gay Smith observes, Clinton's status among US political satirists accords with over two hundred years of Lady Macbeth analogizing, which offered a decidedly misogynistic political image with which to compare the wives of America's most powerful male figure. At the end of her study, Smith also suggests that the First Lady/

Lady Macbeth analogue owes its ubiquity entirely to the stage history of US drama. For generation after generation, powerful female actors have demonstrated the subversive topicality of Lady Macbeth to American theatregoers. In consequence, Smith concludes, it is this specific Shakespeare play that has, 'by virtue of strong actors in the role of Lady Macbeth, provided America with a fictive figure analogous to First Ladies in the White House, for better, for worse'.[41] A fictive figure 'for worse' seems understandable. A fictive figure 'for better', however, seems far more problematic. Certainly, in Smith's opinion, First Lady/Lady Macbeth politicking might not be as bad for the stability of the nation as such 'iconic' and 'mythic' comparisons need necessarily imply.

Obviously written in the run-up to, and during the early heady months following, Barack Obama's Presidential Inauguration in December 2008, Smith's book can only comment on the 'many voices' of Obama and the skill of his political rhetoric.[42] Eventually printed and published in 2010, a matter of months after the 'Michelle Obama/Lady Macbeth' controversy, the book's production schedule ensured that its appearance came too soon for this specific First Lady to gain a single mention within its pages. In consequence, Smith offers a concise history of American First Ladies as 'Lady Macbeths' without the benefit of Obaman political hindsight. The varying fortunes of Obama's presidency and equally opportunistic 'Lady Macbeth' jibes made against his wife are understandably missing from Smith's book. In addition, and although it represents a full analysis of the First Ladies of the United States, Smith's study understandably neglects to consider Lady Macbeth's role as a journalistic commonplace for political sketch-writers elsewhere in the world. As the 2011 Arab Spring showed, the Lady Macbeth analogue could apply to any number of Middle Eastern First Ladies. US-centric in its analysis, Smith's work might not appreciate the global extent of such an analogy, but it nevertheless offers a fascinating point of departure for similar First Lady/Lady Macbeth investigation of productions from both sides of the Atlantic.

Such is the transatlantic power of the American presidency as a potent image of wifely manipulation that the veteran actor Sir Ian McKellen still recalls its relevance for his 1976 RSC production of *Macbeth*, directed by Trevor Nunn.[43] With the Lady Macbeth of Dame Judi Dench representing the 'perfect hostess', McKellen reminisces how, during rehearsals and 'not long after Watergate', he remarked to his director, 'Well, of course, they're the Nixons, aren't they?':

> And Trevor Nunn said 'No, no, they're not the Nixons, they're the Kennedys.' They're the golden couple, the couple everybody wants to visit, including the King. A couple we all admire. (Curry, *Shakespeare On Stage*, p. 152)

If in 1976 the Nixons and the Kennedys are discussed as potent images in the rehearsal room of Britain's Royal Shakespeare Company, it should not be surprising that, less than thirty years later, the same First Lady/Lady Macbeth negativity continues to influence British theatre. There is, however, a distinctive localization to Britain's First Lady imagery that focuses on home-grown instances of political paranoia about underhand female practice in the corridors of power.

As Delingpole's and Dateline D.C.'s contentious remarks about Michelle Obama confirm, the vocabulary of First Lady/Lady Macbeth negativity is not confined to the US. Neither are the objects of such attacks only American. In Britain, during the opening months of the twenty-first century, opposition politicians and pundits also referred to the equivalent First Lady of British politics, Cherie Booth, in the same derogatory manner.[44] As early as 2000, politicians were accused of 'jousting' to apply the Lady Macbeth name because of Cherie Booth's overt though unelected support of her husband, Prime Minister Tony Blair.[45] This negativity stemmed initially from comments by the 'Tory [Conservative] attack-dog John Bercow', a politician later elected to the important post of Speaker of the House of Commons.[46] Stephen Dodd, writing in 2000 in the British tabloid the *Independent* (a newspaper

that, at the time, prided itself on its non-partisan stance),
regaled how Bercow chanced 'his luck with a side-swipe at
[this] far from vulnerable target':

> Professionally outraged that Cherie had the audacity to
> champion the British government's Human Rights Bill in a
> newspaper article, [Bercow] suggested she had become 'an
> unacceptable cross between First Lady and Lady Macbeth'.
> (Dodd, 'Knifing')

As is obvious, the First Lady/Lady Macbeth analogue was
as identifiable to a British political audience as it had been
to its American counterpart. Indeed, Cherie Booth's status
as an analogous First Lady/Lady Macbeth soon entered the
mainstream of popular culture. Reviewing a 2009 collected
edition of work by the British writer and broadcaster Miles
Kington, Jonathan Sale described the most 'spectacular'
example of the late humorist's work to be 'his cod-Shakespeare
series "History of King Tony", with Cherie Blair as Lady
Macbeth and the Three Witches as Fleet Street hacks'.[47] The
name 'Blair' added to the punning potential of such attacks,
with 'Lady Macbeth' regularly cited alongside the 1999
psychological horror movie *The Blair Witch Project* for comic
effect.[48]

The Blair name and regime offered its own version of
the First Lady/Lady Macbeth scenario. Indeed, two major
examples of British *Macbeth* in performance point at least to
the perception of decidedly Blairite First Lady analogy: the
2004 RSC version directed by Dominic Cooke with Gregory
Hicks and Sian Thomas, and the 2007 Chichester Festival
Theatre production directed by Rupert Goold, with Patrick
Stewart and Kate Fleetwood. In both these twenty-first-
century productions, the imagery of their respective Lady
Macbeths accommodated topical comparison with the British
First Lady. In his theatre review for the RSC *Macbeth* in
Britain's *Daily Mail*, for instance, Michael Coveney describes
Sian Thomas as 'strangely resembling Cherie Blair with

a better hairstyle'.[49] In her guise as the nation's Prime Ministerial First Lady, Thomas's Lady Macbeth becomes the 'vivid partner in [her husband's] ambitious crime', leaving one 'only [to] wonder slightly about their sex life'.[50] For Coveney, the strength and ambition displayed in Sian Thomas' performance hinted at a political agenda for Dominic Cooke's production. Its appearance in Stratford-upon-Avon almost precisely a year after the March 2003 allied invasion of Iraq imposed its own topicality on this Edwardian-dress 'Slavic' production.

As reviewer for the *Rogues and Vagabonds* theatre website, the author of this chapter also noted the topicality of its staging, with Greg Hicks playing a tyrannical force that was '[n]ot so much Saddam Hussein, more Tony Blair'.[51] When asked in private conversation whether the company were aware that commentators might recognize the Prime Minister and his wife in their portrayals, Greg Hicks replied sardonically: 'no we didn't explore that theme […] in fact as I recall we didn't explore very much […] it was not my favourite or finest hour.'[52] Similarly, Sian Thomas confirmed that there was 'no conscious idea of presenting [her] Lady Macbeth as Cherie Blair or any other "real life" political wife':[53]

Dominic Cooke the director and myself tried to make her as real and believable a woman as possible, with human vulnerabilities and nuances – so as to try and get away from the accepted cliché of her as an evil scheming bitch. But the production was set loosely in a *fin de siècle*, late 19th century period, and there was certainly no conscious allusion to the Blairs. (Sian Thomas, private email)

Despite the fact that Thomas admitted 'rarely' to reading the reviews, and so being 'unaware that some critics had thought [she] had made that choice' – 'they are', she wryly describes, 'a power unto themselves!' – she nevertheless agreed that 'one cannot escape (and wouldn't want to) the desperate ambition and need that drives the woman'.[54] In her 2006 published

'Actor's Perspective', which claims Sarah Siddons rather than Cherie Booth as the 'actress from the past' who influenced her performance, Thomas even describes the 'fiend-like queen' soubriquet as no more than 'propaganda of the regime that supplants her'.[55] Whether, as Thomas claims, Lady Macbeth is truly 'vulnerable, and [...] also incredibly brave', with a 'willpower' that, 'considering she is not naturally as hard as nails', is undoubtedly 'extraordinary', it is noteworthy that this post-invasion production offered a female protagonist whose perceived similarity with Britain's First Lady guaranteed at least one mention in the national press of Cherie Booth as the play's analogous political influence.[56]

Three years later, Rupert Goold directed his wife, Kate Fleetwood, in a far more contentious and internationally applauded production of *Macbeth*. Originating in the Chichester Festival Theatre on England's south coast in May 2007, the play transferred to London's Gielgud Theatre in September of the same year. This production, which starred Patrick Stewart in the title role, was greeted with reviews that proclaimed it the 'best *Macbeth* [ever] seen', the '*Macbeth* of a lifetime' and 'a difficult play [...] magnificently realised'.[57] Transferring again to Broadway in February 2008, it received similar, if somewhat more muted critical acclaim. Ben Brantley, theatre critic of the *New York Times*, when noting its arrival at the Harvey Theater of the Brooklyn Academy of Music, commented that 'Rupert Goold's good and nasty interpretation', full of 'sound and fury', would 'signify, if not nothing, then not much more than yet another politically minded evening of Shakespeare in period drag were it not for the brilliant performance' of Stewart.[58] As for Fleetwood's 'vulpine' Lady Macbeth, Brantley described her as someone who 'has coarsened herself to be a player in this dangerous world':

> She would appear to be half her husband's age, and she has the hard-boiled aspect – not uncommon on Park Avenue these days – of the trophy wife who has married up and

is not about to relinquish her perch. (Brantley, *New York Times*, 15 February 2008)

A 'trophy wife' perhaps, but, in a private interview with this chapter's author, Fleetwood described the political and cultural significance of her performance with candour and humour.[59] Admitting that the play's 'strong interpretation' – its 'Stalinist approach' – was 'very much aimed politically', Fleetwood acknowledged that Elena Ceaușescu, wife of the disgraced president of Romania, 'was certainly referenced in rehearsals'. Even so, this analogous association was 'born out of [Rupert Goold's] discussion' with Patrick Stewart 'way before [she] was on board'. Fleetwood decided consciously not to 'linger on' or 'ape' the Ceaușescan analogy, electing instead to base her character on a beloved British television cookery personality, the journalist and author Nigella Lawson.[60] Celebrated in the UK for her overt onscreen sensuality and seductive fetishization of the cooking process, Lawson famously catered for the Blairs' 2003 Downing Street luncheon in honour of President George Bush and his First Lady, Laura.[61] Despite this obvious political association, Fleetwood did not consider this lunch meeting in her own characterization, even though the more generalized 'bake-off', with regard to 'political wives and their catering responsibilities and prowess', was mentioned in rehearsals.[62] Instead (and employing similarly fetishized culinary metaphors to explain her decision to adopt less a 'hard-boiled aspect' and more the 'sensual approach [...] to catch the king'), Fleetwood described her Lady Macbeth as embarking on 'seduction through the belly' as the benign mask for her 'hunger for power'.[63] Nigella Lawson's TV personality imposed its sexualized style on Fleetwood's performance without ever suggesting a politicized history for this character choice.

For an American Broadway audience, the influence of an eroticized British TV cookery expert on Fleetwood's Lady Macbeth would be less than obvious, despite any presidential familiarity with Lawson's culinary expertise. Indeed, when Gay Smith discusses in a brief paragraph at the end of her book the significance of the play's New York manifestation, she seems unaware of the gastronomic associations of Fleetwood's performance. Instead, Smith describes Goold's Broadway production as appearing 'late in the Bush/Cheney second term', and focuses especially on how it 'reflected, as in a mirror darkly, the administration's actions' vis-à-vis Iraq.[64] Stewart and Fleetwood's Macbeth and Lady Macbeth were obviously, according to Smith, making a decidedly political statement about contemporary events. According to Fleetwood, this association is not without some merit, at least as far as one aspect of her performance was concerned. Reflecting on her husband's specific direction that he wanted her Lady Macbeth to seem 'distracted' after she returned from Duncan's bloody body, Fleetwood describes Goold offering his wife a directorial 'note' to assist with her performance. Reminding her of the televised moment when President George W. Bush received news of the 9/11 bombings, Goold asked Fleetwood to consider how Bush 'carried on reading to the children about the goat'. It was, therefore, Bush's subsequent 'glassy distraction' that Goold wanted his wife to emulate, an expression which haunted political analysts in the aftermath of the horror. From this moment on, Fleetwood's Lady Macbeth became not First Lady, but decidedly 'presidential' in its performative analogy. For Smith, such an association was understandably impossible to discern, especially since she was unaware of the rehearsal process and very specific character note offered to Fleetwood by her husband. Smith did, however, suggest an alternative analogy, not with George W. and Laura Bush, but with Vice President Dick Cheney and his wife, Lynne Ann.[65] Accordingly, Fleetwood was deemed to have created a Lady Macbeth who was not the First Lady of the United States, but the nation's Second Lady instead.

It is no surprise that this very British production should be seen, by Smith and by the play's Broadway reviewers, through the prism of American politics. Eighteen months after the New York production closed, Fleetwood and Stewart were reunited to record Goold's *Macbeth*, now re-envisioned for the screen. Shot in an aristocratic recluse's subterranean palace at Welbeck Abbey in Nottinghamshire in a mere three weeks, this filmed version offered even more opportunities for Fleetwood to develop her 'great hostess' role in the caricaturish style of a quintessentially British 'culinary goddess'.[66] When broadcast on UK terrestrial television in December 2010, Goold's dangerous stage version, adapted to include Stalinist propaganda film montages that segue militarily between the scenes, achieved a far wider British audience. For television viewers in the UK, the gash of Fleetwood's red-lipsticked mouth conjured images not of America's First or Second Lady, nor of a seductive television cook. Instead, Fleetwood's appearance suggested Tony Blair's wife, Cherie, that iconic figure whose pronounced mouth was so beloved of British political cartoonists. Continuing in her career as a highly respected Queen's Counsel barrister, Cherie Booth was now no longer First Lady to a Prime Minister, but the spouse of a Middle East Peace Envoy. Nevertheless – and despite the protracted period since first stage rehearsals in 2007 to television film première in 2010 – Fleetwood acknowledges that Cherie Booth was indeed considered as a model for Lady Macbeth in the original rehearsals, although this association was not developed beyond the discussion stage. For the 2010 UK television viewer, the ghost of an infamous British First Lady might still be discernible in Fleetwood's appearance, but her relevance to contemporary political events seemed as distant as the fascistic pseudo-communist imagery that underpinned the self-destructive tyranny of Stewart's Macbeth.

In America, the press and politicians might condemn foreign (i.e. British) correspondents like Delingpole who continued to represent Michelle Obama in Lady Macbeth guise. Nevertheless, a *Macbeth* staged far closer to the US homeland only highlights the power of this 'iconic' image in American politics. As the Canadian theatre reviewer J. Kelly Nestruck confirms, for the 2009 Stratford Ontario season *Macbeth* was 'transposed to a "mythic mid-20th-century Africa"', complete with 'messy postcolonial power' struggle.[67] The unique topicality of this 'postcolonial' production stemmed from its very specific casting, with the white Macbeth of Colm Feore in league with the black Lady Macbeth of Yanna McIntosh. Apart from the obvious racial nuances of this acting partnership for a play relocated to a white-dominated African country, there appeared for Nestruck a more pressing analogy waiting to be drawn. The *Globe and Mail* critic opined that the relocation of the drama, and Feore's politicized interpretation of Macbeth's character, immediately brought 'to mind none other than Barack Obama'. Of far greater significance, however, was that Nestruck claimed to notice this association long before Yanna McIntosh's Lady Macbeth had arrived onstage. The Obama allusion was further reinforced, however, by McIntosh's almost caricaturish adoption of 'the hairdo, composure and sculpted biceps of Michelle Obama'. Despite the actors 'lack[ing] the chemistry of America's first couple', there seemed little doubt in Nestruck's mind that the play's director, Des McAnuff was aware of his First Lady/Lady Macbeth imagery and its significance when transposed to its 'mythic' postcolonial African locus.

As the productions of *Macbeth* in the UK and Canada confirm, Lady Macbeth as First Lady imagery regularly inspires the performance of power on the twenty-first-century stage. Ongoing political events and characters regularly resurface in the theatrical medium, thus adding a topical nuance to contemporary stagings that will be lost to future generations unschooled in such subtle analogous reading. With American First Ladies since 1800 being associated with Lady Macbeth, Michelle Obama is merely joining a long line, not of kings that 'stretch out to th'crack of doom' (4.1.117), but of manipulative First Ladies, all suspected of exerting undue influence on their husbands. Elsewhere in the world, the wives of powerful male politicians are just as suscep-tible to First Lady/Lady Macbeth negativity. The onstage portrayal of these First Ladies might owe much to the cultural and ethnic backgrounds of their respective actors. Lady Macbeth portrayals might also unwittingly invite reviewers and commentators to conceive a political allegory where none was originally intended. Regardless of intentionality, these subtle instances of analogous portraiture remain worthy of continued study. In view of the potential volatility of such 'iconic' imagery, it would be fascinating to know if the royal First Lady, Queen Anne of Denmark, was likewise perceived – or even portrayed – as Lady Macbeth when the King's Men first presented *Macbeth* to its Globe (and possible court) audience over four hundred years ago.

Notes

1   Robert F. Worth, 'Qadaffi's Faustian Bargain', The 6th Floor: Eavesdropping on The Times Magazine (Blog), *New York Times Magazine*, 21 October 2011 http://6thfloor.blogs.nytimes.com/2011/10/21/qaddafis-faustian-bargain/ [accessed 11 April 2012].

2   Richard Spencer, 'Col Gaddafi killed: a clown with a deadly intent at heart', *Telegraph* (20 October 2011) http://www.telegraph.co.uk/news/worldnews/africaandindianocean/libya/8839910/Col-Gaddafi-killed-a-clown-with-a-deadly-intent-at-heart.html [accessed 11 April 2012].

3   Noy Alooshe, 'Muammar Gaddafi – Zenga Zenga Song', YouTube Video (22 February 2011) http://www.youtube.com/watch?v=cBY-0n4esNY [accessed 11 April 2012].

4   SkyeNoor, 'Somebody's Got to Say It: Where Is the Sanctity of Gaddafi's Body?', *SkyeNoor: A Personal Perspective*, Blog (24 October 2011) skyenoor.wordpress.com/tag/colonel-gaddafi/ [accessed 11 April 2012].

5   James Delingpole, 'WordPress "About" Page' (2011) http://jamesdelingpole.com/wordpress/about/ [accessed 12 June 2012].

6   James Delingpole, 'Was "Lady Macbeth" behind Barack Obama's snub of Gordon Brown?', *Telegraph*, 5 March 2009 http://blogs.telegraph.co.uk/news/jamesdelingpole/9095137/was_lady_macbeth_behind_barack_obamas_snub_of_gordon_brown/ [accessed 1 December 2010].

7   Tim Shipman, 'Barack Obama sends bust of Winston Churchill on its way back to Britain', *Telegraph*, 14 February 2009 http://www.telegraph.co.uk/news/worldnews/barackobama/4623148/Barack-Obama-sends-bust-of-Winston-Churchill-on-its-way-back-to-Britain.html [accessed 19 April 2012].

8   Anna Sabasteanski, *Patterns of Global Terrorism 1985–2005: U.S. Department of State Reports with Supplementary Documents and Statistics, Volume 1* (Great Barrington, MA: Berkshire Publishing Group, 2005), pp. 89–90.

9   Alex Spillius, 'Michelle Obama is no Lady Macbeth', *Telegraph*, 5 March 2009 http://blogs.telegraph.co.uk/news/alexspillius/9098097/Michelle_Obama_is_no_Lady_Macbeth/ [accessed 12 June 2012].

10 Kevin Wicks, 'The British press is up in arms over "Obamagate"', *BBC America*, 'Anglophenia' http://www.bbcamerica.com/anglophenia/2009/03/the-british-press-is-up-in-arms-over-obamagate/ [accessed 12 June 2012].

11 Maureen Dowd, 'Should Michelle cover up?', *New York Times* 'Opinion', 7 March 2009 http://www.nytimes.com/2009/03/08/opinion/08dowd.html [accessed 12 June 2012].

12 James Delingpole, 'Lady Macbeth sticks it to Berlusconi', *Telegraph*, 25 September 2009 http://blogs.telegraph.co.uk/news/jamesdelingpole/100011370/lady-macbeth-sticks-it-to-berlusconi/ [accessed 18 January 2011].

13 Sarah Baxter, 'Right plays "Kill the Witch" with Barack Obama's wife', *Sunday Times*, 15 June 2008 http://www.timesonline.co.uk/tol/news/world/us_and_americas/us_elections/article4138123.ece [accessed 29 January 2011]; 'Michelle Obama Plants Witch's Herbs On Vernal Equinox', The Spoof, 21 March 2009. http://www.thespoof.com/news/spoof.cfm?headline=s2i49919 [accessed 29 January 2011].

14 Gale Stokes, *The Walls Came Tumbling Down: The Collapse of Communism in Eastern Europe* (Oxford: Oxford University Press, 1993), p. 54.

15 Angelique Crisafis, 'The Arab world's first ladies of oppression', *Guardian*, 28 February 2012 http://www.guardian.co.uk/world/2012/feb/28/arab-first-ladies-of-oppression [accessed 12 June 2012].

16 Ibid. See also: Kim Willsher, 'Leila Trabelsi: The Lady Macbeth of Tunisia', *Guardian: ShortCuts Blog*, 18 January 2011 http://www.guardian.co.uk/world/2011/jan/18/leila-trabelsi-tunisia-lady-macbeth [accessed 12 June 2012]; Henry Samuels, 'Tunisian deposed leader dominated by "Lady Macbeth"', *Telegraph*, 10 February 2011 http://www.telegraph.co.uk/news/worldnews/africaandindianocean/tunisia/8316771/Tunisian-deposed-leader-dominated-by-Lady-Macbeth.html [accessed 12 June 2012]; Elizabeth Rubin, 'The Feminists in Tahrir Square', *Newsweek*, 14 March 2011 http://www.thedailybeast.com/newsweek/2011/03/06/the-feminists-in-the-middle-of-tahrir-square.html [accessed 12 June 2012]; Rana Moussaoui, 'Syria's First Lady falling from grace', *Your Middle East*, 14 January 2012 http://www.yourmiddleeast.com/features/syrias-first-lady-falling-from-grace_4115 [accessed 12 June 2012].

17 Royal Shakespeare Company, '*Macbeth: Leila and Ben – A Bloody History*', World Shakespeare Festival 2012 http://www.worldshakespearefestival.org.uk/london/riverside-studios/macbeth.aspx [accessed 29 June 2012].

18 Rebecca McLaughlin-Duane, 'Tunisian director adapts *Macbeth* for the World Shakespeare Festival', *The National* [UAE], 23 April 2012 http://www.thenational.ae/arts-culture/on-stage/tunisian-director-adapts-macbeth-for-the-world-shakespeare-festival#full [accessed 29 June 2012].

19 Ibid.

20 Ibid.

21 Melinda Liu, 'China's Jackie Kennedy: Gu Kailai and the Bo Xilai's Scandal', *The Daily Beast: Women in the World*, 12 April 2012 http://www.thedailybeast.com/articles/2012/04/12/china-s-jackie-kennedy-gu-kailai-and-the-bo-xilai-s-scandal.html [accessed 12 June 2012].

22 Australian Broadcasting Corporation, 'Setting a fixed price on carbon', *Insiders*, 27 February 2011 http://www.abc.net.au/insiders/content/2011/s3149979.htm [accessed 12 June 2012].

23 Kenneth Weisbrobe, 'Is Michelle Obama the Ultimate Insider?', *History News Service*, 20 February 2010 http://www.h-net.org/~hns/articles/2010/021010a.html [accessed 30 January 2011].

24 Gay Smith, *Lady Macbeth in America: From the Stage to the White House* (Basingstoke: Palgrave Macmillan, 2010).

25 Ibid., p. 183.

26 Ibid., p. 2.

27 Ibid., p. 2.

28 Ibid., pp. 3–4; Weisbrobe, 'Ultimate Outsider'.

29 Todd Landon Barnes, 'George W. Bush's "Three Shakespeares": *Macbeth, Macbush,* and the Theater of War', *Shakespeare Bulletin*, 26.3 (2008): pp. 1–29 (18). Smith, *Lady Macbeth*, pp. 7–9, 183.

30 Smith, *Lady Macbeth*, p. 9.

31 Ibid., p. 8.

32 Barnes, *Macbush*, p. 3.

33 Gil Troy, 'Looking Back: Lessons for the First Lady – and her Husband – From History', in Robert P. Watson, ed., *Laura Bush: The Report of the First Lady, 2005* (New York: Nova Science Publishers, 2005), pp. 99–102.

34 Smith, *Lady Macbeth*, pp. 9–16.

35 Daniel Wattenberg, 'The Lady Macbeth of Little Rock; Hillary Clinton's hard-left past and present', *American Spectator*, 25:8 (1992), pp. 25–32.

36 Karen Tumulty, Nancy Gibbs, Jay Branegan, Margaret Carlson and Priscilla Painton, 'Hillary Clinton: The Better Half', *TIME*, 28 December 1998. http://www.time.com/time/magazine/article/0,9171,989909-4,00.html [accessed 29 January 2011].

37 Ibid.

38 Gerard Baker, 'The vaulting ambition of America's Lady Macbeth: Hillary Clinton's shameless political reconstructive surgery', *The Times*, 26 January 2007. http://www.timesonline.co.uk/tol/comment/article1296179.ece [accessed 29 February 2011].

39 'Dateline D.C.', 'Hillary & her "Weird Sisters"', *Pittsburgh Tribune-Review*, 15 April 2007. http://www.pittsburghlive.com/x/pittsburghtrib/opinion/columnists/datelinedc/s_502753.html [accessed 29 January 2011].

40 Ibid.

41 Smith, *Lady Macbeth*, p. 186.

42 Ibid., pp. 184–5.

43 Julian Curry, *Shakespeare On Stage: Thirteen Leading Actors on Thirteen Key Roles* (London: Nick Hern, 2010).

44 My thanks to Ann Thompson for reminding me of Cherie Booth's unusual genealogical connection with American politics. Daughter of the British actor Tony Booth, Cherie is the first cousin four times removed of the notorious nineteenth-century actor and pro-slavery political activist, John Wilkes Booth. See Earl Aaron Reitan, *The Thatcher Revolution: John Major, Tony Blair, and the Transformation of Modern Britain, 1979–2001* (Lanham MD: Rowman and Littlefield, 2003), p. 69. John Wilkes Booth, Cherie Booth's great-great-great-grandfather's brother's son, assassinated President Abraham Lincoln at Ford's Theatre, Washington DC, 14 April 1865. It is ironic that the play being performed that night was Tom Taylor's 1858 British farce, *Our American Cousin*.

45 Paul Waugh, 'Cherie Blair is the "Lady Macbeth" of British politics', *Independent On Sunday*, 8 August 2000. http://www. independent.co.uk/news/uk/politics/cherie-blair-is-the-lady-macbeth-of-british-politics-711023.html [accessed 30 January 2011].

46 Stephen Dodd, 'Knifing New Labour's "Lady Macbeth"', *Independent*, 13 August 2000. http://www.independent.ie/ world-news/knifing-new-labours--lady-macbeth-515623.html [accessed 30 January 2011].

47 Jonathan Sale, 'Review of *The Best by Miles*, by Miles Kington', *Independent*, 1 December 2009. http://www.independent.co.uk/ arts-entertainment/books/reviews/the-best--by-miles-by-miles-kington-1831620.html [accessed 30 January 2011].

48 Cahal Milmo, 'Witchcraft and nail clippings: the weird world of Cherie Blair?', *Independent On Sunday*, 20 September 2005. http://www.independent.co.uk/news/uk/politics/witchcraft-and-nail-clippings-the-weird-world-of-cherie-blair-507546.html [accessed 30 January 2011].

49 Michael Coveney, 'Hicks Brings Out the Beast in *Macbeth*', *Daily Mail*, 26 March 2004. http://webcache.googleusercontent. com/search?q=cache:zSgz-Td72ZsJ:findarticles.com/p/

news-articles/daily-mail-london-england-the/mi_8002/is_2004_
March_26/bravura-bullets-friday-theatre/ai_n37173056/pg_2
[accessed 28 January 2011].

50 Ibid.

51 Kevin Quarmby, 'Theatre Review, *Macbeth*, Royal Shakespeare
Theatre', *Rogues and Vagabonds*, 18 March 2004. http://
www.quarmby.biz/reviews/review_Macbeth.htm [accessed 2
September 2012].

52 Gregory Hicks to Kevin Quarmby, Private 'Facebook'
Correspondence, 9 January 2011.

53 Sian Thomas to Kevin Quarmby, Private Email
Correspondence, 30 June 2012.

54 Ibid.

55 Sian Thomas, 'Lady Macbeth', in *Performing Shakespeare's
Tragedies Today: The Actor's Perspective*, ed. Michael Dobson
(Cambridge: Cambridge University Press, 2006), pp. 95–7.

56 Ibid., p. 97.

57 Chris Wiegand, 'Reviews Roundup: *Macbeth*', *Guardian*, 28
September 2007. http://www.guardian.co.uk/stage/2007/sep/28/
theatre3 [accessed 30 January 2011].

58 Ben Brantley, 'Something Wicked This Way Comes', *New
York Times*, 15 February 2008. http://theater.nytimes.
com/2008/02/15/theater/reviews/ 15macb.html?pagewanted=1
[accessed 30 January 2011.

59 Kate Fleetwood, Private Interview with Kevin Quarmby, 8 May
2012.

60 Nigella Lawson is the daughter of the Conservative politician
Nigel Lawson, who achieved 'rising star' status as Chancellor
of the Exchequer in Margaret Thatcher's re-elected 1983
government; see Reitan, *Thatcher Revolution*, p. 54.

61 See 'TV chef Nigella Lawson' being greeted by George Bush,
'In Pictures: Bush visit day 2', *BBC News*, 20 November 2003.
http://news.bbc.co.uk/2/hi/in_depth/photo_gallery/3223156.stm
[accessed 3 September 2012].

62 Kate Fleetwood, private text message to Kevin Quarmby, 3
September 2012.

63 Fleetwood, interview, 8 May 2012.

64 Smith, *Lady Macbeth*, p. 184.

65 Ibid., p. 184.

66 For the history of this palace, see Tom Freeman-Keel and Andrew Crofts, *The Disappearing Duke: The Intriguing Tale of an Eccentric English Family – The Story of the Mysterious 5th Duke of Portland*, 2nd edn (Craven Arms: Seek Publishing, 2005).

67 J. Kelly Nestruck, 'A Macbeth neither fair nor foul', *Globe and Mail*, 2 June 2009. http://www.theglobeandmail.com/news/arts/a-macbeth-neither-fair-nor-foul/article1165470/ [accessed 2 January 2011].

PART THREE

Critical Approaches and Close Reading

6

'A walking shadow': Place, Perception and Disorientation in *Macbeth*

Darlene Farabee

When Lady Macbeth publicly hears of Duncan's murder, her response is 'Woe, alas! / What! in our house?'.[1] Critics have found this response baffling; she has had time to think of something better to say. Eighteenth-century editors generally see this as a blunder on the part of Lady Macbeth, a mistaken lack of preparation for an inevitable discovery.[2] George Lyman Kittredge claims it is '[a] natural expression for an innocent hostess, horrified at the thought that such a thing has happened to one of her own guests'.[3] More likely, and more sensibly, her comment relates to the facts of location. It may be a hostess' concern that cloaks the commentary, but the audience already has knowledge of Lady Macbeth's involvement with the murder; an audience can only see this comment as some attempt to appear innocent to the other characters. Macbeth, offstage for Lady Macbeth's reception of the news, does not respond directly to her commentary. On the difference between their public responses to the news, William Warburton remarks that, 'on the contrary', Macbeth 'now labouring under the horrors of a recent murder, in his exclamation, gives all the marks of sorrow for the fact itself'.[4] However Banquo's immediate response to Lady Macbeth's outcry emphasizes the oddity of her concern about place: 'Too cruel, anywhere' (2.3.86).

In the midst of the confused revelation of Duncan's murder, Lady Macbeth's comment rings an odd note both for the characters onstage and for the audience. This and other moments that similarly emphasize location point to a larger concern of the play – a constant notion of location, both in mention of place and the attempts to perceive one's own whereabouts. The characters, particularly Macbeth, consistently comment upon and wonder about location and movement. In the larger frame of the play, the emphasis on location and the related confusion of sensory perception produce similar effects on the audience and develop the narrative movement of the play. Macbeth's moral and psychological deterioration manifests itself through his inability accurately to perceive his location and direction. Other characters' experiences and reiterated comments about location exacerbate Macbeth's deterioration.

Characters' locations

The first appearance of Macbeth onstage shows him entering with Banquo as they travel into a location already occupied by the witches. Macbeth's first line echoes the witches' words, saying 'So foul and fair a day I have not seen' (1.3.38), and shows his immersion in circumstances beyond his control.[5] In response, Banquo asks a traveller's common question for information about the distance to their destination: 'How far is't call'd to Forres?' (1.3.39). This unanswered are-we-there-yet question gets lost in the surprise of seeing the witches; worry about exact location disintegrates into questions about and exclamations on the witches' appearance. Macbeth, after hearing the first of the witches' proclamations, attempts to stop their movement; his imperative 'Stay' both halts them in their chanting and presumably from moving on to some other place (1.3.70). His emphasis on a directional orientation of their information ('Say from whence / You owe this strange intelligence') matches his concern that the witches 'stop our way' or course of travel (1.3.75–6; 77). When the witches disappear, Banquo appropriately asks: 'Whither are they vanish'd?' (1.3.80). Macbeth's immediate response links 'whither' to a failure of perception: 'what seem'd corporal melted' (1.3.81). To 'seem', in Shakespeare's plays, nearly always implies false perceptions and Macbeth's comment encourages Banquo to voice the possibility that they have 'eaten on the insane root / That takes the reason prisoner' (1.3.84–5). In this instance, as in so many that follow, inchoate location leads to sensory confusion.

Macbeth's first soliloquy in 1.7 begins the conflations of time and location that increase over the course of the play. Macbeth is separated in this scene from the main action taking place offstage. The Folio stage direction reads: '*Ho-boyes. Torches. Enter a sewer, and divers Servants with Dishes and Service over the Stage. Then enter Macbeth.*'[6] Interrupting his soliloquy, Lady Macbeth enters twenty-eight lines later and remarks: 'He has almost supp'd. Why have you left the chamber?' (1.7.29). Macbeth must have been in the chamber with Duncan and the other guests and left.[7] In other words, Macbeth leaves the place where most of the other characters are gathered and seeks this emptied place for his soliloquy, in contrast to many characters who are often left alone onstage as other characters exit.[8]

Macbeth's first soliloquy noticeably emphasizes the location of the events he contemplates – despite his own dislocation from events happening offstage. In this soliloquy he uses 'here' in a variety of ways important for both this particular speech and for larger questions in the play:

If it were done, when 'tis done, then 'twere well
It were done quickly: if th'assassination

> Could trammel up the consequence, and catch
> With his surcease success; that but this blow
> Might be the be-all and the end-all – *here,*
> But *here,* upon this bank and shoal of time,
> We'd jump the life to come. – But in these cases,
> We still have judgment *here*; that we but teach
> Bloody instructions, which, being taught, return
> To plague th'inventor: this even-handed Justice
> Commends th'ingredience of our poison'd chalice
> To our own lips. He's *here* in double trust[.]
>   (1.7.1–12 emphasis added)

Initially then, 'here' is 'upon this bank and shoal of time', a marker of chronology; this temporal notation has oddly geographical realities. After the rhetorical reversal of 'But', Macbeth's assertion that 'We still have judgment here' complicates matters considerably. Is it 'here' in this emptied location Macbeth occupies in that moment? Or is it 'here' in Macbeth's own mind? Kittredge explains that this 'here' refers to 'in this world', presumably as the contrary location to 'the life to come' from the previous line.[9] Kenneth Muir notes without clarification that 'judgment here' refers back to both earlier uses of 'here'. In line 12, Macbeth uses 'here' to denote location in his description of Duncan's stay. In this speech, 'here' initially refers to the chronological moments, shifts through a more complex notion of the location of choice, and rests in the questions raised by Duncan's immediate physical location in the Macbeths' household.

Angus Fletcher's description of the function of soliloquy offers some useful ways of thinking about how this particular soliloquy of Macbeth's works:

> In a soliloquy, the speaker enhances the role of separation from the self, to increase incorporation into the self, through a liminal loosening of all conventional stereotypes. The soliloquy is defenseless. [...] In the great dramatic

soliloquies of Renaissance drama, there is thus a special poignancy in that the audience is made fully aware of the vulnerability of such a speaker, who is in a single speech enacting a much larger social drama.[10]

Macbeth's soliloquy separates him from himself insofar as it allows the audience to experience the wanderings of his mind. The defencelessness of the speech increases with Macbeth's awareness that he ought to be elsewhere. This moment separates him from the duties he ought to be performing as a host, even as he simultaneously ponders the ultimate inhospitable act.[11] Macbeth's vulnerabilities – perceptual incapacities, the possibilities for inhumane actions, uncontrollable locations, and erratic movements – all appear in this soliloquy.

When Macbeth is next alone onstage, he asks: 'Is this a dagger, which I see before me[?]' (2.1.33). Again, the soliloquy is framed by other characters' earlier participation with the scene's space. That Banquo and Fleance already occupied the place before Macbeth's entrance emphasizes the liminal nature of the place; it is one that must be guarded, and Banquo throws out the demanding question of a guard to a stranger: 'Who's there?' (2.1.10). Macbeth takes control of the place by ordering the others to leave, and he remains in a location both inexact and unguarded. When he sees the dagger before him ('I have thee not, and yet I see thee still'), he likely grasps and clutches at empty air as most productions stage it (2.1.35). As an object of comparison or protection, he draws his own dagger and says: 'Thou marshal'st me the way that I was going' (2.1.41). His confusions over locating the nonexistent dagger encourage him to accept direction from either the phantom dagger or the dagger he draws. He links his attempt to disregard that direction to the confusion of his perception: 'Mine eyes are made the fools o' th' other senses / Or else worth all the rest' (2.1.44–5). Despite these problems of perception, Macbeth continues the description of his choices and actions as a pathway when he describes his own and 'Murther's' possible movement through the night:

[...] wither'd Murther,
Alarum'd by his sentinel, the wolf,
Whose howl's his watch, thus with his stealthy pace,
With Tarquin's ravishing strides,[12] towards his design
Moves like a ghost.

                                                    (2.1.52–6)

His vision leads him to movement and the movement has a direction determined by the dagger. He immediately begins to describe his movement, although he most likely remains in one area of the stage to deliver this speech.[13] Macbeth hopes that the 'firm-set earth' will 'Hear not my steps, which way they walk, for fear / The very stones prate of my where-about' (2.1.56; 57–8). 'Hear' and 'here' are confounded in this instance; his 'where-about' becomes an indefinable location.

Macbeth's deteriorating spatial orientation appears even more clearly after Duncan's murder. After Lady Macbeth leaves to return the daggers to their 'proper' place, Macbeth hears knocking: 'Whence is that knocking?' (2.2.56). He claims that 'every noise appals' him, (2.2.57), but the real problem here seems to be that he cannot tell from where it comes. When Lady Macbeth returns, she does not have this same problem; she remarks quite specifically the location of the knocking: 'I hear a knocking / At the south entry' (2.2.64–5). Lady Macbeth has no difficulties locating the source of the sound that Macbeth finds so frightening. Evelyn Tribble, in the context of a comparison with Kurosawa's film adaptation, discusses the effects of the 'soundscape' (to use Bruce R. Smith's term) of *Macbeth*. Tribble's descriptions of the instinctual 'startle' response are particularly useful for thinking about how the play depends on immediate sensory responses from the characters. Tribble explains that the association between 'sound and fear' includes 'the capacity of sound to startle, to stir a physical response and to prompt an orienting response, a search for the source of the sound'.[14] Lady Macbeth's awareness of the origin of the sound shows that Macbeth's startled responses inaccurately respond to the noise.

Macduff's horrified descriptions of Duncan's death continually assert that the event – and, more importantly, the perception of the event – disrupts normal perceptual function. Initially, it is unspeakable; neither 'tongue nor heart / Cannot conceive nor name thee' (2.3.63–4). He warns other characters that to see it will 'destroy your sight' (2.3.71). At Lady Macbeth's entrance, he urges deafness, since ''Tis not for you to hear' (2.3.85). If accurate perception leads to comprehension, he imagines that the reverse must hold; incomprehensible horror must make the organs of perception inaccurate. David Lucking links Macduff's descriptions of the 'unnameable' in 2.3 to Macduff's actions in his later confrontation with Macbeth, where Macduff 'discover[s] in effect that words are not after all entirely impotent even when they are obliged to grapple with the unspeakable'.[15] However, Macduff's incoherence in 2.3 depends more on the way the body functions. In other words, the problem in that moment rests in the organ of speech rather than in language.

Compared to Macduff's insistence on the incomprehensibility of the events, Macbeth and Lady Macbeth separately attempt the appearance of innocence. As we've already seen, Lady Macbeth's insistence on the location of these events 'in our house' sits oddly in the scene. And despite Macduff's predicted alteration in the organs of perception, Macbeth's active response returns to the possibilities of movement he emphasized so heavily in his earlier evocation of 'Murther'. Macbeth describes killing Duncan's chamber guards as a movement: 'Th' expedition of my violent love / Outrun the pauser, reason' (2.3.108–9). Although generally glossed as 'haste', the word 'expedition' also calls to mind a journey, movement toward a destination.[16] After the departure of the banquet guests in 3.4, Macbeth describes his plan as a forward movement:

> I am in blood
> Stepp'd in so far that, should I wade no more,

Returning were as tedious as go o'er.
Strange things I have in head, that will to hand,
Which must be acted ere they may be scann'd.

(3.4.135–9)

The distance he has travelled makes it useless to turn back;
only the corporeal experience will allow him to understand
his own actions. Since he describes the actions and decisions
as one long endeavour of wading, the continuation on his
journey implies not only the inevitability but also the bodily
aspects of the experience. These 'Strange things I have in head'
can only be comprehended after being experienced.

Means of perceiving space

Although early modern medical treatises and more general
texts of the period usually describe five senses (sight, touch,
taste, smell, hearing), the additional sense of locomotion
was described by Julius Caesar Scaliger in 1557.[17] A nearly
contemporaneous dramatic representation, Thomas Tomkis'
Lingua, personifies the five senses battling against speech (the
character Lingua) as she attempts (and fails) to gain standing
as one of the senses.[18] This representation of the various
senses combating one another may not have influenced the
construction of Macbeth's dilemmas. However, the discussions of the senses in the period had not settled completely the
questions of modes of perception functioning within the human
body. And to include Macbeth's heightened and disordered
sense of his own movement coincides with similar disorder
of his other senses. Additionally, early modern descriptions
of movement, even of objects other than one's own body,
depended in tangible ways upon human perception. In the
absence of readily available accurate devices, measurement of
distance, for example, still relied on the understanding that a
fathom was the length of a man's outstretched arms, a unit of

length and a measuring tactic that depended on the sense of touch and the corporeal realities of anatomy.

For Macbeth, Banquo's clarity of direction, and the physical and moral certitude it implies, becomes worrisome: 'He hath a wisdom that doth guide his valour' (3.1.52). That guidance and certitude of direction presents Macbeth with further dilemmas. When planning Banquo's murder, Macbeth recognizes that he might 'With bare-fac'd power sweep him from my sight' (3.1.118), a removal that might mean banishment or death. As a reigning monarch, Macbeth has control of the location of his subjects, since banishment offers the option of removal. Exile, a power mechanism not used in this play, has public elements that Macbeth cannot afford to use. The more stealthy elements he employs, the murderers, describe themselves in terms usually applied to directionless or wearied travellers. One claims he will be reckless because 'I am one, my liege, / Whom the vile blows and buffets of the world / Hath so incens'd' (3.1.107–9). The other describes himself as 'So weary with disasters, tugg'd with fortune' (3.1.111). Caroline Spurgeon relies on this last description to support her assertion that:

> [Shakespeare's] use of verbs of movement is a study in itself, and one of his outstanding characteristics is the way in which by introducing verbs of movement about things which are motionless, or rather which are abstractions and cannot have physical movement, he gives life to a whole phrase.[19]

In *Macbeth* particularly, verbs of movement are introduced in unexpected constructions. Despite (or perhaps because of) this rhetorical and physical movement, Macbeth introduces stasis as desirable certitude:

> [...] Better be with the dead,
> Whom we, to gain our peace, have sent to peace,
> Than on the torture of the mind to lie

In restless ecstasy. Duncan is in his grave;
After life's fitful fever he sleeps well.

(3.2.19–23)

Almost immediately, that previously desirable stasis turns into imposed restraint. After hearing that Fleance has escaped, Macbeth describes himself trapped: 'But now I am cabin'd, cribb'd, confin'd, bound in / To saucy doubts and fears. – But Banquo's safe?' (3.4.23–4). The indeterminate location of Fleance traps Macbeth in a motionless state of doubt and fear. The murderers understand Macbeth's real concern when he asks about Banquo. In fact, they remark his location – he is 'safe in a ditch' (3.4.25) – before describing the injuries inflicted upon him.

Macbeth's eventual response to the appearance of Banquo's ghost recalls his assurance to himself about Duncan's whereabouts: 'The time has been, / That when the brains were out, the man would die, / And there an end; but now they rise again' (3.4.77–9). Initially, the spatial anomaly alerts Macbeth to the existence of the ghost; what ought to be an empty space appears filled: 'The table's full' (3.4.45). This appearance of Banquo's ghost shakes Macbeth's remaining faculties for locating himself: 'if I stand *here*, I saw him' (3.4.73 emphasis added). The doubt rests in whether he can accurately locate himself and then extends to his senses. He questions how others 'can behold such sights' and remain unmoved (3.5.113). Macbeth's vision of the ghost muddles further his confidence in his perception accurately to perceive the realities around him.

Without confidence in his ability accurately to perceive his own surroundings, Macbeth offers up all faculties for organized movement in exchange for an answer from the witches:

answer me:
Though you untie the winds, and let them fight
Against the Churches; though the yesty waves

Confound and swallow navigation up;
Though bladed corn be lodg'd, and trees blown down;
[...]
Even till destruction sicken; answer me
To what I ask you.

(4.1.50–61)

Macbeth refuses to believe the possibility that Birnam Wood
can 'Unfix his earth-bound root' (4.1.95). The disorder and
doubleness of Nature in the play has been widely remarked.[20]
The movement of 'Great Birnam wood to high Dunsinane hill'
(as the apparition phrases it) seems to be a final disordering
of the possible natural markers of location (4.1.93–4). One
expects, either when moving through a landscape or when
remaining still, that geographical features of the landscape will
remain relatively fixed. Rather than an assertion of natural
order, this disorder presents the ultimate unnavigable terrain.

Other characters in the play similarly describe difficulties
negotiating their surroundings. Rosse, delivering his warning
to Lady Macduff, describes the quandary of Macbeth's subjects
who find they cannot know their own positions and have no
way to control their own directions.

I dare not speak much further,
But cruel are the times when we are traitors,
And do not know ourselves; when we hold rumour
From what we fear, yet know not what we fear,
But float upon a wild and violent sea
Each way, and move.

(4.2.17–22)

These moves depend on metaphorically unchartable waters.[21]
When Rosse delivers the news of the death of Macduff's family,
he attempts to halt the senses themselves from working. 'I have
words / That would be howl'd out in the desert air, / Where
hearing should not latch them' (4.3.193–5). These nameable
events must be articulated, but best done in an open empty

landscape where hearing cannot locate them. Rosse describes himself as someone who hopes his own words will be unable to navigate the only appropriate terrain for unleashing them. In turn, a recipient sense of hearing in a listener will be unable accurately to perceive them. The sleepwalking scene shows the most extreme case of a character losing control of the senses.

> *Doct.* You see, her eyes are open.
> *Gent.* Ay, but their sense are shut.
>
> (5.1.24–5)

The watchers can only conclude that Lady Macbeth's senses are useless and, after this point, Macbeth's disintegration soon follows.

Many commentators have remarked on the confusion of Macbeth's senses in the play. Macbeth's own sense of space and location is the awareness the play confuses and consistently undermines from the opening scenes. Macbeth's entrances in act 5 noticeably depart from the previous sections of the play; in the final act he does enter to an empty stage, but these entrances only happen once he is unable to separate time and space in any meaningful fashion. Macbeth describes the perceptual confusions and near dissolution of his senses:

> I have almost forgot the taste of fears.
> The time has been, my senses would have cool'd
> To hear a night-shriek; and my fell of hair
> Would at a dismal treatise rouse, and stir
> As life were in't.
>
> (5.5.9–13)

The disintegration of his ability to separate the two culminates in his response to the news of Lady Macbeth's death; his comment that 'She should have died hereafter' provides fodder for critics trying to make sense of his ambiguous speech. In this instance, when Macbeth uses 'hereafter', the English language aids him in the confusion of space and time;

we might say 'nowadays' but we do not (nor have we ever) used 'now-after'. The 'here' of 'hereafter' both connects and confuses spatial and temporal locations.

> She should have died hereafter;
> There would have been a time for such a word. –
> To-morrow, and to-morrow, and to-morrow,
> Creeps in this petty pace from day to day,
> To the last syllable of recorded time;
> And all our yesterdays have lighted fools
> The way to dusty death. Out, out, brief candle!
> Life's but a walking shadow; a poor player,
> That struts and frets his hour upon the stage,
> And then is heard no more: it is a tale
> Told by an idiot, full of sound and fury,
> Signifying nothing.
>
> (5.5.17–28)

His line following 'hereafter' again emphasizes the location of time: '*There* would have been a time for such a word' (5.5.18). The 'to-morrows' '*creep* [...] in this petty *pace*' – the movement of time appears as motion across areas that can be paced out. Time past offers direction to fools who are offered a lighted 'way' or pathway 'to dusty death'. Time and its movement are translated here into spatial relationships.

After this disintegration of spatial certainties and temporal existence, Macbeth has useless control of an empty stage space; this meaningless control throws into relief his trapped circumstances, and his description reveals his loss of control of time and space. When Macbeth enters in 5.7, he claims that 'They have tied me to a stake: I cannot fly, / But, bear-like, I must fight the course' (5.7. 1–2). 'Course' (as Muir and others gloss) is the 'bout or round between the bear and the dogs'; but 'course' is also 'path' or 'way'.[22] He claims he is 'tied to a stake' or fixed to a location, and that he knows his location. Yet a short battle – and only twelve lines – later, he leaves the stage. In the final act of the play, Macbeth operates in what Henri Lefebvre describes as a 'monumental space'. In Lefebvre's descriptions of the production of social space, he emphasizes ways particular activities – in conjunction with spatial realities – produce functions of space. 'Monumental space', one classification he offers of a social space, produces complexities that 'involve levels, layers and sedimentations of perception, representation, and spatial practice which presuppose one another, which proffer themselves to one another, and which are superimposed upon one another.'[23] Only in the final moments of the play can we reasonably describe Macbeth's actions taking place in a 'monumental space'. He is not a monarch who establishes his power through the convening of audiences and courtly functions; we see those practices in *King Lear* and by Claudius in *Hamlet*. Instead, Macbeth's power to command a 'monumental space' appears only once his other means of controlling or perceiving space disintegrate. The layers of 'perception, representation, and spatial practice' built into the play coalesce into Macbeth's experiences and decisions of the final act.

Macbeth's short victorious battle against Young Siward shows Macbeth functioning as he will in his final scene, where he rejects the possibility of dying 'On mine own sword' (5.8.2). Immediately after the battle with Young Siward, Macbeth exits and in quick succession two short vignettes increase the speed of the events of the play and finalize the difficulties of location that have plagued Macbeth throughout. In brief appearances, first Macduff and then Malcolm and Old Siward appear as they search for Macbeth in the mêleé of the battles. These characters emphasize their own awareness of their locations, and they depend on sounds to direct their movements.

Macduff has a clear direction and comments on his own knowledge of Macbeth's whereabouts. Fittingly, this speech is the only time Macduff appears onstage alone in the play – a minor soliloquy in the midst of the battles. He claims his 'wife and children's ghost will haunt' him if he fails to find Macbeth; he is drawn away by the awareness that 'There thou shouldst be; / By this great clatter, one of greatest note / Seems bruited' (5.7.16; 20–2). Macduff clearly knows which way he needs to go, and he knows this from correctly hearing and interpreting the noise around him. Malcolm and Old Siward are similarly directive in their descriptions of their own movements. Siward directs Malcolm, 'This way, my Lord' (5.7.24). The brevity of their appearance (fifteen lines) bolsters the impression that these movements are purposeful and direct. It is in the next scene, of course, that Macbeth is slain. Macbeth's disintegration, his dislocation from his own sense of time and place, has prepared the audience for his death.

Audience understanding of space

The audience experiences some of the same dislocations the characters experience. The careful control of places and locations in the play heightens the already controlled areas of the stage on which the actions take place. However, the audience, continually aware (particularly in this play) of offstage events, usually has more information and at different times than most of the characters. Michel de Certeau defines space as a 'practiced place' that 'takes into consideration vectors of direction, velocities, and time variables'.[24] Space, as he defines it, 'is in a sense actuated by the ensemble of movements deployed within it'.[25] The discussion of the play and characters so far has focused on places and locations as the characters experience them within the frame of the play. It remains to explore some of the ways the audience experiences the stage space as the play's events unfold through the narrative movement. Susanne Langer says that although '[i]t has been said repeatedly that the theater creates a perpetual present moment […], it is only a present filled with its own future that is really dramatic'.[26] The 'virtual future' (to use Langer's term) created by drama functions in a space as de Certeau defines it: a 'practiced place'. In the case of drama, that space includes the stage, the audience, the characters, offstage action, entrances and exits, and the inexorable constant temporal movement of the production. Although individual production choices vary widely, careful attention to some spatial aspects of the play and the effects on the audience illuminate some of the ways the play produces narrative movement.

The first two scenes of the play neither include Macbeth onstage nor establish his location, but they offer some directional markers about how we (as audience members) are meant to understand locations. The Captain in 1.2 describes how 'with his brandish'd steel' Macbeth 'carv'd out his passage' in the battle (1.2.17, 19). The Captain describes Macbeth as knowing how to make a path, a passage, with direction. This description seems to establish Macbeth as a character who knows where he is going. This scene with the Captain appears between two scenes with the witches. The opening scene with the witches' first appearance emphasizes location: 'Where the place?' (1.1.6), and the impending meeting at that location: 'There to meet with Macbeth' (1.1.7).

Early in the play, audience members hear constant iterations of means of location. The witches reappear (in 1.3) and with 'ports', 'quarters' and 'shipman's card' describe a soon-to-be 'tempest-tossed' sailor (15, 16, 17, 25). These are directional markers and descriptions that offer another version of some of the dislocations that Macbeth himself suffers later in the play. The witches describe themselves as being exceptionally mobile; they are 'Posters of the sea and land' (1.3.33). 'Posters' are not simply travellers, they deliver items or news in particularly expedient fashion. These portents of misunderstood direction prepare the audience for these concerns before Macbeth appears.[27]

Most of the scenes of act 1 establish the locations aurally – what Bruce Smith calls 'the establishment of the auditory field of the play'.[28] In the first six of the seven scenes in act 1, the Folio stage directions establish locations with sounds: in 1.1 and 1.3 thunder precedes the witches' appearances; in 1.2, 1.4

and 1.6 sounds associated with royal pageantry precede the entrance of the King and others.[29] In 1.5, however, no sound accompanies Lady Macbeth as she enters '*alone with a letter*' (1.5.0 SD). She herself provides the aural location by reading the letter to the audience. Alan Stewart has shown how Macbeth's letter in 1.5 brings Macbeth onstage with Lady Macbeth while emphasizing his absence. Stewart has pointed out that the use of the letter 'spatially figur[es]' 'the Macbeths as singular' and that the letter's 'textual content, uttered in Lady Macbeth's voice' helps to collapse the characters into one.[30] He asserts that '[b]eyond its spatial figuring of the Macbeths as singular (a representation not possible by any other means), the letter plays with time, collapsing present and future'.[31] The letter does effectively collapse the two characters into the one speaking voice of Lady Macbeth as she reads out his letter, his voice, onstage. The experience of collapse works for the audience, but it also has the effect of disembodying Macbeth. Appropriately, Lady Macbeth produces this disembodiment of a character who has not yet appeared with her. For the audience, it presents a contrasting version of someone who has already been described as overtly physical in his military activities. His voice presents itself onstage through his wife's ventriloquism in an early instance of his corporeal indeterminacy.

The effect on the audience of Macbeth's entrance in 1.7 depends on pageantry and aural cues and immediately removes those elements. We audience members have been located, but we are aware that the pageantry has moved on past this space of the stage, leaving it emptied when Macbeth enters. If Macbeth, through this device, appears at one remove from the other action, the audience appears at two removes. The pageantry and (presumably) offstage noise ensure that the audience must be aware of the events happening elsewhere, even if the noise doesn't continue through the scene. This double remove matches the incessant doubling of language in the play and confuses the perception of what events might be central to the narrative.

In some important ways the audience becomes complicit in the events onstage, even when those events happen offstage. Palmer argues that, in the case of Duncan's murder offstage and Lady Macbeth's awareness of events, 'instead of distancing the deed from us […] the effect is to intensify its sacrilegious horror'.[32] Likely the horror increases through the imagined rather than the represented. While we are protected from witnessing the image, that very protection maintains the possibility that the vision of it might 'destroy […] sight', as Macduff fears (2.3.71). In some instances, however, the play offers the audience double visions of events by reporting events already witnessed by the audience. Frequently noted cases include Macbeth's letter to Lady Macbeth detailing the witches' prophecies, Banquo's murderers' reports of their activities, and the reporting of the killing of Macduff's family. These events are peculiar in other ways too; the audience has prior knowledge of these events. The witches' specific prophecies may come as a surprise, but we know they await Macbeth with specific intent; we hear the planning of Banquo's murder; and we know Macbeth plans to surprise Macduff's household and 'give to th' edge o' th' sword / His wife, his babes' (4.1.151–2). The prior knowledge, view of the event, and presence at the delivery of the news of these last two events involve the audience in ways denied to, for example, Lady Macbeth. The audience awareness is greater than that of any of the characters. In some fashion, this awareness makes the audience complicit in the actions.

In the case of the murders of Macduff's household, not only is the audience aware of each segment of the series, but the audience also experiences it with the rapidity that Macbeth desires after complaining that 'Time, thou anticipat'st my dread exploits: / The flighty purpose never is o'ertook / Unless the deed go with it' (4.1.144–6). Macbeth claims: 'This deed I'll do before this purpose cool' (4.1.154) and exits after two more lines. In 4.2 at Macduff's castle, the murderers enter after a quick eighty lines of dialogue split between Lady Macduff and Rosse and Lady Macduff and her son. In 4.3 Macduff, safely in

England, receives Rosse and the news of his family's death. The rapidity and quick succession of these events show Macbeth's plan carried out exactly. It also presents a useful example of the discontinuities in the audience experience of the passage of narrative time. Importantly, our own sense of time as an audience – a sense that never functions perfectly with any play – experiences some of the same deterioration that Macbeth and other characters in the play experience. Macbeth offers to 'let the frame of things disjoint' in favour of having the stasis of death; the audience experiences a disjointed frame (3.2.16).

Banquo's death plays a particularly important role in the ways the audience can orient itself to the actions and dilemmas in the play. Frequently, Shakespeare's plays present a 'normalizing' character who is able either to transcend the circumstances or at least outlast them and present the audience with information or material which might be considered more reliable than other information available. Horatio in *Hamlet* offers an example of such a character.[33] In this play, the normalizing character seems at the beginning to be Banquo, Macbeth's original confidant. The murder of Banquo turns the action of the play beyond the irrevocable events, and the audience remains with no single character to maintain that function. The audience becomes unmoored from the normalizing elements of the narrative.

The audience also experiences the hallucinatory misperceptions that Macbeth experiences. When the witches appear at the beginning of the play, Banquo serves to verify for the audience that the witches are real. The audience must accept the world of the play as one with supernatural beings that have a corporeal existence. When the dagger appears to Macbeth, the audience does not see the dagger and no other characters verify its existence. The audience must conclude, as does Macbeth, that the dagger is a hallucination. This instance serves to separate the audience from Macbeth's experience while still involving the audience in that experience as Macbeth reveals his thoughts and perceptions. When Banquo's ghost appears at the banquet, we (the audience) and

Macbeth see the ghost; Lady Macbeth and the other guests do not. The characters onstage who might act as witnesses to establish reality do not. As Macbeth's perceptions have disintegrated into hallucination, our own have followed suit. The Folio stage directions read: '*Enter the Ghost of Banquo and sits in Macbeths place*' (1298 TLN). The text specifically calls for the entrance of an actor here, a corporeal embodiment invisible to the other characters.[34] The audience can no longer trust characters to act as witnesses, a dislocation made all the more disconcerting by the fact that the murdered Banquo earlier acts as the normalizing character. We are trapped in Macbeth's interiority in the banquet scene because we do know what his disordered senses perceive; we deny the reality of the other characters despite needing to accept these other versions to make sense of the events of the play.

The audience awareness becomes attached in important ways to Macbeth's awareness; in this play replete with tellings and retellings of events, we only learn of the death of Lady Macbeth at the same time Macbeth does. We have known of most other events in the play at the moment of their happening; in this instance we are aligned with Macbeth's experience when his senses become most confused. The ultimate disjointing of Macbeth's perceptions comes with his death and decapitation. The Folio stage directions note: '*Enter Macduffe, with Macbeths head*' (2504 TLN). No more clearly could the space of the stage make visual the complete dissolution of Macbeth's perceptions.

The concentrations of spatial constructions in the narrative, the audience awareness of certain events, the changing and dislocating descriptions of location, and the consistent return to questions of place, all contribute to the narrative movement in the play. The construction of space through these intersections includes Lady Macbeth's outcry at the news of Duncan's death and alters how we might see place and location functioning. When Macduff offers Macbeth's head to Malcolm, he says: 'I see thee compassed with thy kingdom's pearl' (5.9.23). Macduff confirms Malcolm's kingship and metaphorically refers to a kingdom in order. 'Compassed' or encircled offers the closure the narrative demands even as it opens out to the wider locating questions of the play. The structural frames of the space of the play may provide a way of reading the spatial intricacies of the narrative movement of not only *Macbeth* but also the wider structures of early modern drama.

Notes

1   William Shakespeare, *Macbeth*, ed. Kenneth Muir (London: Thomson, 1951), 2.3.85–6; subsequent in-text citations refer to this edition unless otherwise noted. Through line numbers (TLN) refer to Charlton Hinman, ed., *The First Folio of Shakespeare* (New York: Norton, 1968).

2   For example, Warburton offers this explanation. William Warburton ed., *Macbeth* in *The works of Shakespear in eight volumes* Vol. 6 (London: J. & P. Napton, 1747).

3   George Lyman Kittredge ed., *Macbeth* (Boston: Ginn and Co, 1939), p. 144.

4   I include Warburton's note here since many eighteenth-century editors followed suit; Warburton, p. 367. Samuel Johnson, for example, quotes Warburton's note in full and without commentary. Samuel Johnson, ed., *Macbeth* in *The plays of William Shakespeare in eight volumes, with the corrections and illustrations of various commentators; to which are added notes by Sam Johnson* (London: J. and R. Tonson, 1755), pp. 367–484.

5   David Kranz, in his discussion of the verbal patterning of the play, points out rhetorical and rhythmic elements that make this line particularly memorable in its repetition: 'Fricative alliteration reinforces the repetition, and the completely monosyllabic nature of the line crisply highlights its iambic meter' (p. 346). David Kranz, 'The Sounds of Supernatural Soliciting in *Macbeth*', *Studies in Philology* 100, no. 3 (2003), pp. 346–83.

6   Hinman, 1.7.0 SD.

7   Most likely then Macbeth enters from the same door the servants have recently exited.

8   Hamlet's first soliloquy presents such an example. Ann Thompson and Neil Taylor (eds), *Hamlet* (London: Thomson, 2006): 1.2.129.

9   Kittredge, p. 171. William Carroll similarly notes 'in this world' for the use; A. R. Braunmuller does not comment on the use of 'here' in this passage. William Carroll ed., *Macbeth* (Boston: Bedford, 1999); A. R. Braunmuller ed., *Macbeth* (Cambridge: Cambridge University Press, 1997).

10 Angus Fletcher, *Time, Space, and Motion in the Age of Shakespeare* (Cambridge: Harvard University Press, 2007), p. 92.

11 Geraldo de Sousa, in his exploration of boundaries, architecture and the Macbeths' perceived safety gained from walls, notes that the Macbeths' house 'becomes a deadly trap for unsuspecting guests'. Geraldo de Sousa, *At Home in Shakespeare's Tragedies* (Farnham: Ashgate, 2010), p. 154.

12 The Folio text reads 'sides' here and the textual debate offers 'slides' and the now more popular 'strides' as optional readings for what appears to have been a misprinting. Either way, 'slides' and 'strides' both convey the movement important to the speech. Hinman, *Macbeth*, TLN 635.

13 Macbeth's reiterated vision of the dagger does not note that the dagger might be appearing in different positions. 'Thou marshal'st me the way I was going' has been read as the phantom dagger directing him toward Duncan's chamber; if this case informs production decisions, the imagined dagger would be fairly static. Macbeth gives the remainder of his speech in relation to that still point.

14 Evelyn Tribble, '"When Every Noise Appalls Me": Sound and Fear in *Macbeth* and Akira Kurosawa's *Throne of Blood*', *Shakespeare* 1, nos 1–2 (2005), pp. 75–90; 79.

15 David Lucking, 'Imperfect Speakers: Macbeth and the Name of King', *English Studies* 87 no. 4 (2006), pp. 415–25; 423.

16 The *OED* defines 'expedition' as 'speedy performance or

prompt execution' (1.a) and 'A journey, voyage, or excursion made for some definite purpose' (2.b). *The Oxford English Dictionary Online* (Oxford: Oxford University Press, 2010).

17 An example of a medical text that depends heavily on the division of five senses, Helkiah Crooke's *Mikrokosmographia* (London: William Jaggard, 1615) compiles and translates much of the anatomical material available in the period. Julius Caesar Scaliger, *Exotericarum Exercitationum Liber Qvintvs Decimvs, de Svbtilitate, ad Hieronymvm Cardanvm* (Lvtetiae [Paris]: Michaelis Vascosani, 1557).

18 Thomas Tompkis, *Lingua, or The Combat of the Tongue and the Five Senses for Superiority* (London: N. Okes, c. 1607). *Macbeth* is usually dated to 1606, although Alfred Harbage lists 1606–11 as limits; for Tomkis' *Lingua*, Harbage offers limits of 1602–7. Alfred Harbage, *Annals of English Drama 975–1700*, revised S. Schoenbaum (Philadelphia: University of Pennsylvania Press, 1964). In his introduction, Kenneth Muir suggests that *Lingua* echoes *Macbeth* rather than the reverse (p. xvii).

19 Caroline Spurgeon, *Shakespeare's Imagery and What It Tells Us* (Cambridge: Cambridge University Press, 1965), p. 51.

20 See, for example, Mary McCarthy, 'General Macbeth', *Harper's Magazine* (June 1962), pp. 35–9; reprinted in *Macbeth*, ed. Sylvan Barnet, 2nd revd edn (New York: Signet, 1998), pp. 157–67.

21 The desire to hold 'rumour' or loose speech away from articulation of feared events fits into a pattern explored by Arthur Kinney of a culture of surveillance, both in this play and in the wider culture of Jacobean politics. Arthur Kinney, 'Macbeth's Knowledge', *Shakespeare Survey 57*, no. 1 (2004), pp. 11–26.

22 See *OED*, 'course' n. 2.a and 11.a. The nautical term in this period means 'the direction in which, or point of the compass towards which, a ship sails' (*OED* 'course' n. 12.a).

23 Henri Lefebvre, *The Production of Space*, trans. Donald Nicholson-Smith (Oxford: Blackwell, 1991), p. 226.

24 Michel de Certeau, *The Practice of Everyday Life*, trans. Steven Rendall (Berkeley: University of California Press, 1984), p. 117.

25 de Certau, p. 117.

26 Susanne Langer, *Feeling and Form* (Upper Saddle River, NJ: Prentice-Hall, 1977), p. 307.

27 D. J. Palmer explores the visual impact of the play and stresses the importance and frequency in *Macbeth* of visual expressions prescribed through commentary by other characters. For example, Palmer points out that Banquo's commentary on Macbeth's initially physical reaction to the witches and their prophecies 'draws the attention of the audience to Macbeth, who is silent himself'. D. J. Palmer, '"A new Gorgon": Visual Effects in *Macbeth*', in *Focus on Macbeth*, ed. John Russell Brown (London: Routlege & Kegan Paul, 1982), pp. 54–69, 58.

28 Bruce R. Smith, *The Acoustic World of Early Modern England: Attending to the O Factor* (Chicago: University of Chicago Press, 1999), p. 276.

29 The stage directions in the Folio are: '*Alarum within* [...]'; '*Flourish*'; and '*Hoboyes and torches*' (1.2, 1.4 and 1.6 respectively).

30 Alan Stewart, *Shakespeare's Letters* (Oxford: Oxford University Press, 2009), p. 33.

31 Stewart, p. 33.

32 Palmer, p. 67.

33 Horatio sees the ghost of Old Hamlet which helps convince an audience that the ghost exists; likewise, Banquo confirms the existence of the witches in *Macbeth*.

34 In the dagger scene, the Folio does not include stage directions for any dagger as stage property. While this absence does not prove the dagger's absence, it makes it likely, given the stage business necessary to make it present.

7

Cookery and Witchcraft in *Macbeth*

Geraldo U. de Sousa

Now, good digestion wait on appetite,
  And health on both! (3.4.37–8)

Petruchio in *The Antiquary* (1634–6), a play by Shackerly
Marmion (1603–39), eagerly anticipates the presentation of
the dishes that the cook has prepared for a banquet. He knows
that food preparation and presentation require the cook's
'imagination', skills with his 'fingers', and 'curiosity'; indeed,
he knows 'gluttoning delights to be ingenious'.[1] He is so
impressed that he wonders: 'Who will now deny that cookery
is a mystery?', and adds an 'invention' of his own: 'I will have
all these descend from the top of my roof in a throne, as you
see Cupid or Mercury in a play' (490–1). The cook has, in
fact, provided a feast 'of twelve dishes, whereof each of them
is an emblem of one of the twelve signs of the Zodiac' (489).
Early cookery books make clear that cooks were expected,
among other skills, to be able to 'breake that Deare, leach
that sparrow, teare that Goose, lift that Swanne, sauce that
Capon, spoyle that hen, unbrace that Mallard, unlace that

Connie, dismember that Heron'.[2] In *Macbeth*, cookery serves
divers purposes: to entertain guests at banquets and dinner
parties; to prepare potions; to mix salves for transvection or
night flight; to drug food or drinks; to induce sleep; and even
to alter states of mind. Cookery intensely engages the perverse
imagination of the central characters. It also serves to link
the castle – the hearth as the emblem of home life – and the
outdoors – the witches' cauldron.

Early in *Macbeth*, the Captain refers to how Macbeth
'unseam'd' Macdonwald 'from the nave [navel] to th'chops /
And fix'd his head upon our battlements' (1.2.22–3);[3] on the
battlefield, Macbeth behaved like a savage butcher carving
the carcass of an animal. The Captain's praise intertwines
Macbeth's skills as a soldier and, tellingly, as a butcher. In his
1578 *The historie of man*, John Banister (1540–1610) writes
that the navel 'occupyeth the middle part of the body, since
whilest we are in the wombe of our mother we are nourished
thereby, and by the same also put fourth our excrementes';
through the navel and the arteries to which it is connected, the
foetus 'is replenished with insited heat & vitall spirite'.[4] On
a symbolical level, Macbeth prefigures Lady Macbeth's own
anti-maternal instinct to pluck her nipple from the feeding
baby's 'boneless gums' and dash its brain out (1.7.54–90); or
when Macbeth realizes later that he has drawn 'the wine of
life' from Duncan (2.3.93). In the context of Shakespeare's
play, this is the first instance in which the domestic realm
– and by extension, the house, household, and home life –
borders on and intermingles with something wild. In fact, as I
have argued elsewhere, the house repeatedly fails to establish
boundaries and to separate inside from outside; instead, the
house creates adjacency, juxtaposition and contiguity.[5] In this
ambiguous boundary, daily domestic activity abuts a fantastical, savage, wild world.[6] Cookery and witchcraft become
intimately intertwined. Outdoors, associated with the witches,
and the indoors, associated with the Macbeths, remain
contiguous, invading and pervading each other's domain.

Shakespeare's Scotland combines a complex cluster of

popular images and associations from travellers' experiences, chronicle history, geographical descriptions and news reports. In a letter dated 25 July 1498, Don Pedro de Ayala, the ambassador of Ferdinand and Isabella to the court of James IV, refers to 'savages' who dwell in remote parts of Scotland and have a distinct language of their own (i.e. Gaelic).[7] He points out the bellicose nature of the Scots: 'They spend all their time in wars, and when there is no war they fight with one another' (p. 43). John Major (c. 1467–1550), Scottish historian, philosopher and theologian, notes that Scotland is a country divided between the 'householding Scots' and the 'Wild Scots' of the Highlands, born in the mountains and dwelling in forests, who are by nature 'more combative'.[8] Nicander Nucius, a native of Kérkira (Corfu), remarks in 1545 that '[t]he Scotch are a more barbarous people in their manner of living than the English'; he blames the people rather than the lack of natural resources and fertile soil for the miserable living conditions he observed during his visit.[9]

Various other early travellers remark on the appalling state of poverty of the general population of Scotland.[10] Jean Froissart (c. 1337–c. 1405) visited Scotland in 1365, during the reign of David II. He notes that, when travelling or waging war, the Scots use no carriages, because of the mountainous terrain; carry no provisions of bread and wine; drink river water rather than water mixed with wine; and have no need for pots because they do not prepare meals. They presumably eat raw or inadequately cooked beef.[11] To 'warm their stomachs' – that is, to counter their poor, unsophisticated diet – the Scots eat oatmeal baked into 'cracknel or biscuit'; therefore, he adds, they can 'perform a longer day's march than other soldiers'.[12] His Chronicle, as well as his romance *Meliador*, has many references to the Southern Uplands and the Highlands, what he calls 'la sauvage Escoce' [Scotland the Wild].[13] According to Froissart, the French barons, knights and squires, led by Jean de Vienne, who landed at Leith in 1385, being used to the comforts of their homeland, such as 'handsome hotels, ornamented apartments, and castles with good soft beds to repose on', were struck by the poverty, wildness and discomforts they encountered in Scotland.[14] As Diverres points out, Froissart's 'reader conjures up a picture of the Scots as a wild and desperately poor people'.[15]

In the fifteenth century, Aeneas Sylvius Piccolomini (1405–64), future Pope Pius II, found in Scotland 'nothing but a rugged wilderness, unvisited by the genial sun'.[16] He was also struck by the 'state of nakedness' of the poor, whom he saw begging for alms at the church doors.[17] In Berwick, Northumberland, just four kilometres south of the Scottish border, however, he encountered an 'abundance of hens, geese, and various relishes, but no wine or bread', but fear of the Scots and similar primitive conditions were pervasive.[18] When he sat down for supper, 'the women from the surrounding houses flocked to look on as if they had never seen such a sight before'; when loaves of bread and wine, which he had obtained at a certain monastery, were laid on the table, 'the wonder of the barbarians was greater than ever, since wine and white bread were sights they had never seen before'.[19] He adds: 'Pregnant women and their husbands approaching the table handled the bread and smelt the wine, and prayed that a portion might be given to them' (p. 28). His meal did not end until two o'clock in the morning, when his hosts – the priest and the local landlord – rose from the table and unceremoniously departed, leaving their guest to fend for himself, 'among some hundred women, who, forming a circle round the fire, spent the night in cleansing hemp, and in lively conversation carried on through an interpreter' (p. 29). In the early seventeenth century, John Taylor, the Water Poet, found the Scottish roads exceedingly precarious: 'the way so uneven, stonie, and full of bogges, quagmires, and long heath, that a dogge with three legs will outrunne a horse with foure.'[20] At another point, he writes that he travelled in Scotland for twelve days 'before I saw neither house, corne field, or habitation of any creature, but deere, wilde horses, wolves, and such like creatures'.[21]

The cauldron, associated with Scotland in contemporary

literature,[22] specifically connects the witches to domesticity, and suggests, more generally, a rustic and crude method of food preparation, as distinguished from other methods such as 'hearth' and Dutch-oven cooking, which are similar to our slow-method of crockpot cooking.[23] Cookery in Scotland engages the imagination of numerous observers; it also invites harsh criticism. The witches' cauldron in *Macbeth* may have had its genesis in Medea's brew from John Studley's 1566 translation of Seneca's play;[24] or perhaps in misunderstandings of the Scottish diet, dependent on cauldrons of boiled food. Fynes Moryson reports that the Scots eat 'red Colewort and cabbage, but little fresh meate'. He writes that '[t]he Gentlemen recken their revenewes, not by rents of monie, but by chauldrons of victuals', but feed their servants and family on 'Corne and Rootes, not spending any great quantity on flesh'.[25] He writes of his experience as a dinner guest in a knight's house, where the knight's servants brought to the table 'great platters of porridge [pottage or broth], each having a little peece of sodden meate'.[26] 'Sodden meate'[27] seems to be a recurring theme in foreign accounts of Scottish eating habits. In his overall assessment, Moryson writes: 'And I observed no Art of Cookery, or furniture of Houshold stuffe, but rather rude neglect of both.'[28]

In the Scottish chronicles, food, drink and drugs play a significant role in various kinds of treachery. For example, when the king refuses to pardon certain rebels, Donwald harbours 'such an inward malice towards that king' that his own stomach becomes a cauldron: 'the same continued still boiling in his stomach.'[29] The stomach was believed to be not only 'a storehouse for the whole body, supplying provisions for all the organs' but also 'a cook, converting food into matter fit for each organ'.[30] Donwald and his wife prepare an elaborate feast to welcome the king and the royal entourage. After the king retires to his 'privie chamber', his two chamberlains return to the dinner hall and fall to 'banketting with Donwald and his wife, who had prepared diverse delicate dishes and sundrie sorts of drinks for their reare [late] supper or collation, whereat they staye up for long till they had charged their stomachs with such full gorges'. When they finally retire to their own chambers, 'a man might have removed the chamber over them, sooner than to have awaked them out their droonken sleep' (p. 482). Likewise, confronted with domestic rebellion and threat of foreign invasion by the Danes and Sueno of Norway, King Duncane, knowing that the enemies lacked sufficient provisions, 'offered to send foorth of the castle into the campe great provision of vittels to refresh the armie, which offer was gladly accepted of the Danes, for they had been in great penurie of sustenance manie daaies before' (p. 493). This offer, however, was the Scottish version of the Trojan horse:

> The Scots hereupon tooke the juice of mekilwoort berries, and mixed the same in their ale and bread, sending it thus spiced & confectioned, in great abundance unto their enimies. They rejoising fell to eating and drinking after such greedie wise, that it seemed they strove who might devoure and swallow up most, till the operation of the berries spread in such sort through all the parts of their bodies, that they were in the wend brought into a fast dead sleep, that in manner it was unpossible to awake them. (p. 498)

An Etymological Dictionary of the Scottish Language identifies 'mekilwort' [meckilwort] as the *Atropa belladonna*, the deadly nightshade, although in this passage the meckilwort works as a soporific rather than a poison.[31] Duncan sends Makbeth to the enemy camp first to kill the watch guards; 'aftwewards [Makbeth] entered the camp, and made such slaughter on all sides without anie resistance, that it was a woonderfull matter to behold, for the Danes were so heavie of sleepe, that the most part of them were slaine and never stirred' (p. 493). Only Sueno and ten others were able to escape. As a consequence of the defeat brought about by the ambush and indiscriminate and merciless slaughter, the Danes were forced to sign a peace treaty. In the Chronicle, shortly after this event, Banquo and Makbeth run into 'three women in strange and wild apparel' (p. 494), who foresee great things for both of them. In the Chronicle source, after Makbeth kills the king, he rules Scotland effectively, but eventually becomes fearful of Banquo, and to rid himself of his former ally, he invites Banquo and Fleance 'to come to a supper that he had prepared for them' (p. 498). Consumption of food advances an evil intent.

The first pamphlet on Scottish witchcraft, *Newes from Scotland*, was published in London in 1591, and, as Christina Larner notes, set a pattern for the association of Scotland in the English imagination with 'a place in which witch beliefs were maintained and accused witches pursued with a ferocity unknown south of the border'.[32] King James VI of Scotland investigated treasonable sorcery in 1590–91, and in 1597 he published his treatise, *Daemonology*, which inspired another peak of witch persecution.[33] One of the most notorious cases involved the use of a cauldron.[34] Early modern pictorial representations of witchcraft in Northern Europe often inverted seemingly routine, domestic scenes in which cooking utensils and the preparation and consumption of food and beverages were used for malefic purposes such as incantations, nocturnal flight or transvection, and black Sabbaths. For example, Hans Baldung Grien's seminal 1510 chiaroscuro woodcut of witchcraft depicts 'naked, female witches grouped around a cauldron and symbolically united by a triangle of cooking forks'.[35] As Zika notes, 'the women are engaged in a frenetic ritual that involves the preparation of food and drink, as well as an act of sacrifice'.[36] The cauldron between the legs of one of the women, along with other symbols, including the offering plate, the Hebraic inscription, and the cooking sticks, creates, as Zika remarks, 'the sense of uncontrolled forces' released – all of these images become associated with the women's gendered bodies.[37] He adds that, although the women seem to be 'engaged in the traditional female role of food preparation', 'the cultural meaning of food as nourishment is inverted', and transformed by other 'images of destruction such as the bones scattered on the ground, a child's skull in the bottom left corner, legs seen protruding from a pot carried by the witch riding through the sky'.[38] The cauldron, the female group, and women riding animals combine to form a visual code of witchcraft as a 'reversal and inversion of right order'.[39] In witchcraft, the sharing of food does not signal inclusion and trust; rather it introduces, as William Bradford Smith cogently argues, 'the potential for fraud and deception' 'into otherwise mundane social situations'.[40]

In his representation of the witches, Shakespeare combines materials from folklore, popular beliefs and classical literature. For example, Mary Floyd-Wilson argues that in *Macbeth,* 'Shakespeare depicts Scotland's environment as paradoxically fair and foul – climatologically temperate and authentically demonic'.[41] She notes, as well, that the play also presents 'a correspondence between witchcraft and weather'.[42] Witches were believed to be able to produce meteorological phenomena such as hail and storms. In a woodcut of c. 1493 in Ulrich Molitor's *Von den Unholden oder Hexen*, two witches add ingredients to a boiling cauldron to produce a storm.[43] Likewise, in Hans Baldung Grien's painting *The Weather Witches* (1523), two witches affect the weather. The witches' power, Zika notes, stems from an iconographical association of 'sexually available unmarried women or prostitutes' and 'the wild disturbances these women bring to nature, and the moral danger and disorder associated with their sexual attractions'.[44] At the beginning of the play, the witches enter, preceded by thunder and lightning; they make plans for their next meeting to take place 'In thunder, lightning, or in rain' (1.1.1–2). Indeed, *Macbeth* underscores the wild nature of the windswept Scottish landscapes, a topsy-turvy world, where 'Fair is foul, and foul is fair' (1.1.11), a perception echoed in Macbeth's first line: 'So foul and fair a day I have not seen' (1.2.38). Peter Stallybrass notes that the witches represent 'disorder in nature', have the customary evil 'familiars', and can foresee the future.[45] He adds that they bear 'features typical of the English village "witch"', yet remain mysterious and supernatural.[46] Frederick Kiefer raises the question of whether the witches are nymphs or fairies. He remarks that the old, lean, sexually ambiguous witches have 'the kind of bodies shaped by a hard life outdoors'; the witches 'manipulate, contaminate, and traverse' the air, with which they are especially associated.[47] They wear 'wild attire' and are 'shape-shifters'.[48]

The witches occupy a space between a supernatural world and a human one of household, family and community, with Lady Macbeth providing a bridge between them.[49] Frances Dolan argues that Lady Macbeth embodies 'the witch as a dangerous familiar and her witchcraft as "malice domestic"'; therefore, through Lady Macbeth the witches invade 'the household and its daily life'.[50] In Shakespeare's play, the witches never physically enter the bedchamber of the Macbeths; yet they, too, disturb the domestic in other ways. Macbeth's insomnia and Lady Macbeth's sleep-walking later in the play reveal the disruption that the witches initiated or brought about. The witches in the play thrive in the ambiguous 'hurly-burly' and chaos of the war, 'When the battle's lost and won' (1.1.3–4). They mirror and undermine the domestic. Naturally, they do what witches were believed to do. When the weird sisters appear in act 1, scene 3, having apparently flown from wherever they were in act 1, scene 1, they summarize their intervening activities, one of which must have been 'transvection' or flight. Transvection could be accomplished by means of a specially concocted salve applied to the sole of their feet.[51] One has been 'killing swine'; another tried to steal chestnuts from a sailor's wife, whose husband is off to Aleppo, 'master o'th'*Tiger*', to where the witch proposes to sail in a sieve. All three collude to derail the sailor's journey. Then in the First Witch's words, what they plan for the sailor may also apply to Macbeth: they plan to keep him awake for 'sev'n-nights nine times nine' and make him 'dwindle, peak, and pine', although not destroy his 'tempest-tossed' boat (1.3.19–25). By threatening to deprive both the sailor and

Macbeth of sleep, they seem to allude to a common method of torture, known as 'watching' the witch, or sleep deprivation, 'an almost routine method of extracting confession of the Demonic Pact', used in Scotland.[52] To underscore her malignant intent, the witch even produces 'a pilot's thumb / Wrack'd as homeward he did come' (1.3.28–9).

In this context, the witches bring together the domestic world of the sailor's wife, who is cracking and sorting her chestnuts, and forces of nature, represented by the turbulent sea, where many sailors meet their fate. In Shakespeare's Scotland, even domesticated animals threaten to revert to a wild state. Ross and the Old Man report that on the night of Duncan's assassination the king's horses 'Turn'd wild in nature, broke their stalls, flung out', and more tellingly, they ate each other (2.4.16–17, 18). Shakespeare's weird sisters disturb those homeward bound. They do so because they can affect the lives of voyagers who traverse their domain and come under their influence.

Macbeth and Banquo come under the influence of the weird sisters when they journey to Forres and from thence to Macbeth's home at Inverness. The journey home traverses a wild world (1.3.39–47). The hybrid, sexually ambiguous figures – withered and wild, not like humans yet treading upon the earth, female and yet bearded like males (1.3.45–7) – greet Macbeth with his familiar title, Thane of Glamis, and yet also with other titles that do not seem to belong to him: Thane of Cawdor and King. Banquo tries to calm the startled Macbeth, to whom he now refers as 'noble partner' (54); yet he must recognize that the apparition seems indeed 'fantastical' (53). The weird sisters vanish, as Macbeth describes, 'Into the air, and what seem'd corporal, Melted as breath into the wind. Would they had stay'd!' (81–2). The wheels of Macbeth's mind turn, as in a vortex of what he refers to as 'the imperial theme', which depends on a fantastical murder plan, yet in a realm where 'nothing is but what it is not' (1.3.128, 139, 142). The strange figures, mirroring the scraggy, desiccated, wind-swept surroundings, provide inspiration for the crime that Macbeth imagines and soon plans to carry out in the inner sanctum of his home.

Ordinary home cooking, criminality and sorcery seem connected in interesting ways. Wendy Wall argues that *Macbeth* offers a 'crossover between heath and hearth', whereby the weird sisters 'make household tasks into the uncanny' and invert everyday life; their 'grotesque brew' exaggerates and distorts 'the sinister nature' of contemporary medical remedies.[53] Contemporary cookery books contain instructions for such dishes as a 'chauldron for a swan' and how 'to bake a Pig like a Fawne',[54] but also home remedies such as 'A Caudle to comfort the stomacke good for an olde man'[55] and an ointment 'to provoke sleepe', which calls for 'a spoonefull of womans milke', rosewater, 'iuyce of Lettice' and nutmeg: 'lay it to your temples, and it wil provoke sleepe'.[56] The title page of the anonymous pamphlet, *The Araignement & burning of Margaret Ferne-seede* (London, 1608) blurs the boundary between cooking and murder, depicting Margaret preparing a poisoned broth in a large cauldron, which she used to poison her husband.[57] This woodcut seems to be directly based on the one used in James Carmichael's *Newes from Scotland, declaring the damnable life and death of Doctor Fian a notable sorcerer, who was burned at Edenbrough in Ianuary last. 1591.*[58] The witches in *Macbeth* boil almost anything in their cauldron of 'hell-broth', including juice of toad, oil of adder, ground mummy flesh, 'ravin'd salt-sea shark', 'gall of goat', 'finger of birth-strangled babe', 'liver of blaspheming Jew', 'nose of Turk, and Tartar's lip', 'baboon's blood', and so forth (4.1.1–38).[59] The witches apparently selected each ingredient to be thrown into the bubbling pot for its own distinctive, quintessential property, perhaps suggesting a parody of a general principle of distillation: 'dystyllynge is none other thynge but only a purfyenge of the grosse frome the subtyll & the subtill from the grosse, eche seperatly from other.'[60] Brunschwig provides recipes for such distillations as water of apples, walnuts, mushrooms, sage and rosemary, for example, but also unusual ones as 'water of grounde wormes' (p. 221). Together, these ingredients in the witches' cauldron create a powerful 'gruel'; indeed, cookery in this context blurs the boundaries between the edible and the inedible, medicine and poison, and human and animal.

Macbeth and Lady Macbeth dwell in three different castles.[61] As they move from Inverness to the royal castle at Forres, and then to the fortress at Dunsinane, food plays an important role in their concept of domestic space and of home. Food production, availability and consumption underwent a change in the Tudor and Stuart periods:

> Because of the growth and wealth of the middle classes, food throughout the century gradually moved steadily away from complication and grandeur, from food designed to impress and fill the spectator and diner with awe, towards food that was born out of a domestic kitchen from a small workforce.[62]

Shakespeare goes to great lengths to domesticate the castle at Inverness, by emphasizing concepts of home and home life through the rites of hospitality and the preparation of a feast for a royal guest. As the lady of the castle, Lady Macbeth plays a role which, as Daryl Palmer argues, 'gestures back at the old practice[s] of hospitality'.[63] Although Lady Macbeth at first trusts her husband to carry out the murder of Duncan, her words suggest that she manages the house and exercises control over their domestic space: 'Leave all the rest to me' (1.5.73). As we will see, this also involves the 'preparation' (32) of the house, as well as of food and drinks. Later, she makes a curious comment when her husband, disturbed by the vision of Banquo's ghost, fails to perform his duties as a host by giving the cheer:

> The feast is sold,
> That is not often vouch'd, while 'tis a-making,
> 'Tis given with welcome: to feed were best at home;
> From thence, the sauce to meat is ceremony:

Meeting were bare without it. (3.4.32–6)

In this passage, she underscores rules of hospitality, whereby the host freely provides food for the guest; but she also distinguishes 'feeding', the ordinary eating that one does at home, from 'solemn feasts', where even adding 'sauce' to meat acquires a ceremonial dimension. Eating and drinking preoccupy the imagination of the Macbeths and of other characters in the play. Husband and wife seem to be playing their expected parts as lord and lady of the castle; yet they imagine a different kind of role for themselves. As Palmer remarks: 'Like Lear, Duncan is blind to the possibility of such imagining because he believes completely in the security of hospitable decorums supported by the larger system of prestation.'[64]

Likewise, Macbeth and Lady Macbeth hide behind and exploit a tradition, quite apparent in early modern tragedy, which, in Palmer's words, 'evokes the split between private political aims and public duties of care'.[65] Although the banquet for Duncan occurs offstage, food imagery pervades his arrival at the castle at Inverness. Duncan says ambiguously to Macbeth and/or to Banquo that he has 'begun to plant thee and will labour / To make thee full of growing' (1.4.28–9), which Banquo assumes refers to himself: 'There if I grow, / The harvest is your own' (1.4.32–3). The extended metaphor continues with references to 'plenteous joys' (33); for Duncan, the apparent praise of Macbeth elicits the completing of the metaphor: 'True, worthy Banquo: he is full so valiant, / And in his commendations I am fed; / It is a banquet to me' (1.4.54–6). Harvest leads to the feast. The feast, however, occurs offstage, as the stage direction in act 1, scene 7 makes clear: '*Enter, and pass over the stage a Sewer, and divers Servants with dishes and service.*' References to the banquet occur here and there, as in Lady Macbeth's comment that Duncan has almost finished eating, and her surprise that Macbeth left the dining hall. Weariness from the long day's hard journey and wine drugged with sleep-inducing, mind-altering concoctions will

create the conditions for the assassination, as Lady Macbeth
points out:

> When in swinish sleep
> Their drenched natures lie, as in a death,
> What cannot you and I perform upon
> Th'unguarded Duncan? (1.7.68–71)

Suspense builds, as Lady Macbeth measures time in relation
to how far along Duncan is in his feasting: 'He has almost
supp'd' (1.7.29). Other reports suggest lack of temperance.
Banquo refers to the king's 'unusual pleasure' (2.1.13) at
the table; the Porter gives a fuller report to Macduff: 'Faith,
Sir, we were carousing till the second cock; and drink, sir, is
a great provoker of three things': 'nose-painting, sleep, and
urine' (2.3.24–5, 26). Even Duncan's horses turned wild in
their appetite, eating each other (2.4).

The second solemn banquet that the Macbeths host at
their castle at Forres shows not only the importance of
food and the rituals of hospitality in the play, but how the
host and hostess, as Palmer points out, want to 'remain at
the feast's center, a volatile nexus of authority', as they had
already done at Inverness.[66] In act 3, scene 1, our attention
focuses on the banquet. Banquo begs leave to absent himself
and Fleance until dinner time, to which Macbeth sinisterly
responds: 'Fail not our feast' (3.1.27), anticipating never
to see Banquo or Fleance again. The banquet provides a
cover, an alibi, or 'clearness' with 'no rubs nor botches
in the work' (3.1.132, 133). Later Macbeth divides his
attention between his duties as the host at the banquet
and his plan for the murder. The bright banquet hall seems
connected to the treacherous dark forest, where the hired
murderers await Banquo and Fleance. At the news of
Fleance's escape, Macbeth feels 'cabin'd, cribb'd, confin'd,
bound in / To saucy doubts and fears' (3.4.24–5). Lady
Macbeth chastises her husband for his failure to propose
the expected 'cheer', reminding him that the banquet entails

more than consumption of food. Banquo's ghost appears and sits on Macbeth's 'stool'. Macbeth finds himself displaced from his own banquet table: 'The table's full' (45). The domestic and the wild, genteel solemnity and savage feast, intertwine in a perverse imagination.

In the world of *Macbeth* the characters sometimes seem to become what they eat. At the apparition of the weird sisters, Banquo asks of Macbeth: 'Have we eaten on the insane root / That takes the reason prisoner?' (1.3.84–5). Lady Macbeth assumes that Macbeth's fearful nature comes from his mother's milk, the 'milk of human kindness' (1.5.16); in the unsexing of her body, she hopes that the 'murth'ring ministers' (1.5.48) will become a witch's familiars, coming to her 'woman's breasts' and taking her 'milk for gall' (1.5.46–7). Later Macbeth uses the occasion of his having his usual drink before bed to send a signal to his wife to 'strike upon the bell', a signal that all is ready for the murder of Duncan (2.1.31–2). Lady Macbeth drugs the 'possets' – drinks made from warm milk, spices and liquor: 'I have drugg'd their possets, / That Death and Nature do contend about them, / Whether they live, or die' (2.2.6–8). As Lennox later describes, some become 'the slaves of drink, and thralls of sleep' (3.6.13); but the same drugs have a different effect on Lady Macbeth: 'That which hath made them drunk hath made me bold' (2.2.1).

In this context, food becomes the emblem of intemperance. Like greed, appetite becomes a vulture that will devour anything, as Malcolm, pretending to be a tyrant to Macduff, points out: 'And my more-having would be as a sauce / To make me hunger more' (4.3.81–2). Caithness paints a picture of Macbeth's distempered nature, as someone who has eaten too much: 'He cannot buckle his distemper'd cause / Within the belt of rule' (5.2.15–16); and Menteith also recognizes Macbeth's 'pester'd senses' by 'all that is within him' (23–4). Even Macbeth wants to distance himself from his enemies, to whom he refers as 'the English epicures'; he shows resolve, so that 'The mind I sway by, and the heart

I bear, / Shall never sag with doubt, nor shake with fear'
(5.3.8, 9–10). In his desperate attempt to find peace, Macbeth
wishes the doctor could examine 'The water [urine] of my
land, find her disease, / And purge it to a sound and pristine
health' (5.3.51–2). He adds: 'What rhubarb, cyme [senna],
or what purgative drug, / Would scour these English hence?'
(5.3.55–6). But, as the end of the play makes clear, Scotland
needs to be purged of his tyranny, not of those he refers to
as English epicures.

The end of the play emphasizes starvation, scarcity, or food
unsuitable for human consumption. Macbeth realizes that his
'way of life / Is fall'n into the sere, the yellow leaf' (5.3.22–3),
that his life has been hollowed out and has become dry,
withered and desiccated. He also realizes that he has 'supp'd
full with horrors' (5.5.13). In fact, he had recognized this
earlier, when he states:

> But let the frame of things disjoint, both the worlds suffer,
> Ere we will eat our meal in fear, and sleep
> In the affliction of these terrible dreams
> That shake us nightly (3.2.16–19)

In a sense he has drunk of the weird sisters' 'hell-broth' and
Lady Macbeth's gall for milk. Likewise, Malcolm, promising
to summon home his 'exiled friends abroad', also recognizes
that a different kind of feast is possible now that the 'dead
butcher' and 'his fiendlike queen' are gone. A new kind of
eating will be possible, as a lord had pointed out earlier: 'Give
to our tables meat, sleep to our nights, / Free from our feasts
and banquets bloody knives' (3.6.34–5). Ironically, Macbeth
himself had recognized the role of 'good digestion' in fostering
a humoral balance in the body (3.4.37–8).

Notes

1   Marmion's play was first published in 1641. References to the
    play are to *A Selection of Old English Plays*, vol. 12, ed. W.
    Carew Hazlitt (London, 1875). See John Drakakis, 'Marmion,
    Shackerley (1603–1639)', *Oxford Dictionary of National
    Biography*, Oxford University Press, 2004. http://www.
    oxforddnb.com/view/article/18083 [accessed 30 October 2013].

2   *The booke of caruing* (London, 1613), sig. A2. See also the
    1508 and 1513 editions of this anonymous book, *The boke
    of keruynge* (London, 1508 and 1513), STC 3289, STC 3290.
    The book provides a detailed list of terms and a description
    of implements needed for 'carving' and preparation of food,
    in addition to various recipes and methods for the preparation
    of dishes and sauces, and the order in which the dishes are to
    be served. The woodcut on the title page depicts a king and
    queen and another couple being served a meal at the head
    table, as well as a court jester. Two other guests sit at a lower
    table.

3   William Shakespeare, *Macbeth*, ed. Kenneth Muir, Arden
    Shakespeare (London and New York, 1983). All quotations
    from the play are from this edition.

4   John Banister, *The historie of man* (London, 1578), STC 1359,
    Fol. 65. The instruments depicted in a woodcut, titled 'A Table
    of the Instruments seruying to Anathomicall dissection', bear, of
    course, a striking resemblance to the cook's implements and a
    carpenter's tools.

5   For a fuller discussion of the home and home life in the play,
    see Chapter 4, 'Boundaries of Home in *Macbeth*', in my book
    At Home in Shakespeare's Tragedies (Farnham and Burlington,
    VT: Ashgate, 2010), pp. 143–67. This essay veers off from the
    chapter's focus on the representation of home to explore the
    specific topic of the function of food in the play. This paper was
    originally written for a seminar, led by Ann Thompson, held at
    the Annual Meeting of the Shakespeare Association of America
    in Seattle in 2011. I am grateful to Laura Aydelotte, University
    of Chicago and Newberry Library, for her comments,
    suggestions and questions about my paper.

6 Sousa, *At Home*, p. 143.

7 P. Hume Brown ed., *Early Travellers in Scotland* (Edinburgh: D. Douglas, 1891), p. 39.

8 John Major, *History of Greater Britain, England and Scotland* [*Historia majoris Britanniae tam Angliae quam Scotiae* (1521)], as excerpted in P. Hume Brown ed., *Scotland Before 1700 from Contemporary Documents* (Edinburgh: D. Douglas, 1893), p. 60. See Sousa, *At Home*, p. 144.

9 Brown, *Early Travellers*, p. 60, and Nicander Nucius, *Second Book of the Travels of Nicander Nucius of Corcyra* (London, 1841).

10 Brown, *Early Travellers*, p. 43; Sousa, *At Home*, pp. 144–5.

11 A. H. Diverres, 'Jean Froissart's Journey to Scotland', *Forum for Modern Language Studies* 1.1 (1965), pp. 54–63; Brown, *Early Travellers*, pp. 8–9. Sousa, *At Home*, p. 144.

12 Brown, *Early Travellers*, pp. 8–9. 'Sodden' has a range of meanings: boiled, rotten, spoiled, or improperly cooked. Diverres suggests that this oft-quoted passage, which Froissart appropriated, came originally from Jean de Bel's account 'based on his experiences during Edward III's campaign against the Scots in 1327' (p. 63). Froissart, who often relies on his own first-hand experience and interviews, must have deemed this to be true.

13 Diverres, p. 59.

14 Brown, *Early Travellers*, p. 11; see also Diverres, p. 60; and Sousa, *At Home*, p. 144.

15 Diverres, p. 59.

16 Brown, *Early Travellers*, p. 29; Sousa, *At Home*, p. 144.

17 Brown, *Early Travellers*, p. 29.

18 Brown, *Early Travellers*, p. 28.

19 Brown, *Early Travellers*, p. 28.

20 John Taylor, *Travels through Stuart Britain: The Adventures of John Taylor, the Water Poet*, ed. John Chandler (Stroud, Gloucestershire, 1999), p. 39; Sousa, *At Home*, p. 145.

21 Taylor, *Travels*, p. 39.

22 See Joan Fitzpatrick, *Food in Shakespeare: Early Modern*

Dietaries and the Plays (Aldershot and Burlington, VT: Ashgate, 2007), p. 48. In *Shakespeare's Visual Theatre: Staging the Personified Characters* (Cambridge: Cambridge University Press, 2003), Frederick Kiefer writes that the bodies of the weird sisters evidence both 'sexual ambiguity' and the effects of 'a hard life outdoors' (p. 111).

23 I am grateful to our friends, John and Ardith Pierce, who introduced us to traditional Dutch-oven cooking, when David Bergeron and I visited them at their tranquil cabin near the Canadian border, in Sandpoint, Idaho, in August 2012.

24 See Geoffrey Bullough, *Narrative and Dramatic Sources* (London and New York: Routledge, 1973), 7: 521–2; and for an insightful discussion of Seneca's influence on the play, see Robert Miola, *Shakespeare and Classical Tragedy* (Oxford and New York, 1994), pp. 92–121, and the introduction to his edition of the play: *Macbeth*, a Norton Critical Edition (New York and London: W. W. Norton, 2004), pp. vii–xxi.

25 Brown, *Early Travellers*, p. 88.

26 Brown, *Early Travellers*, p. 88.

27 In this context, I take 'sodden' to mean 'boiled'.

28 Brown, *Early Travellers*, p. 89.

29 Bullough, 7: 481. All quotations from the *Chronicles* will be from Bullough.

30 Sujata Iyengar, *Shakespeare's Medical Language: A Dictionary* (London and New York: Continuum, 2011), pp. 318–19.

31 John Jamieson, *An Etymological Dictionary of the Scottish Language* (London, 1808), 2 vols. The *OED* traces the first usage of the word to John Bellenden's 1531 translation of Hector Boece's *Scotorum historia*: 'Þe Scottis tuke þe iusse of mekilwourte beryis, and mengit it in þair wyne, ayill and brede.' '† micklewort, n.'. OED Online. June 2012. Oxford University Press. 3 August 2012. See also Nicola Royan, 'Bellenden, John (c.1495–1545)', *Oxford Dictionary of National Biography*, Oxford University Press, 2004; online edn, May 2006.

32 Christina Larner, *Enemies of God: The Witch-hunt in Scotland* (Baltimore, MD: Johns Hopkins University Press, 1981), p. 31.

33 Larner, p. 60.

34 Larner, p. 116.

35 Charles Zika, *Exorcising our Demons: Magic, Witchcraft and Visual Culture in Early Modern Europe* (Leiden and Boston: Brill, 2003), p. 271. See Zika's Figure 8.

36 Zika, p. 116.

37 Zika, p. 271.

38 Zika, pp. 271–2.

39 Zika, p. 273. Zika argues that the cauldron served as a complex symbol, identifying 'the witch as female, for it linked witchcraft with the female activities of the hearth and the distribution of food, activities through which relationships could be created and destroyed' (p. 274).

40 William Bradford Smith, 'Food and Deception in the Discourse of Heresy and Witchcraft in Bamberg', in *At the Table: Metaphorical and Material Cultures of Food in Medieval and Early Modern Europe* (Turnhout, Belgium: Brepols, 2007), p. 109.

41 Mary Floyd-Wilson, 'English Epicures and Scottish Witches', *Shakespeare Quarterly* 57.2 (2006), p. 142. For the purposes of my discussion, I am not interested in her argument that Shakespeare, drawing on 'geohumoralism and Neostoicism', interrogates popular notions of Scottish temperance (p. 142). Based in part on a statement in Levinus Lemnius' *The Secret Miracles of Nature* (London, 1658), she argues that evil spirits can mingle with food, humours and air (p. 144). This point seems quite relevant to my argument. Although Lemnius' book was published in 1658, long after *Macbeth*, some of these connections can be traced to an earlier period.

42 Floyd-Wilson, p. 143. I do not, however, find her argument that Shakespeare presents the witches' 'powers as indigenous to Scotland in particular' (p. 143) entirely persuasive; nor do I find a preponderance of evidence to support her conclusion that 'Macbeth recognizes, in other words, that his passions are ecological' (p. 151).

43 See Zika, Fig. 11, p. 217.

44 See Zika, p. 250; see also Fig. 13, p. 249.

45 Peter Stallybrass, '*Macbeth* and Witchcraft', in *Focus on Macbeth*, ed. John Russell Brown (London and Boston:

Routledge & Kegan Paul, 1982), p. 195; and Deborah Willis, *Malevolent Nurture: Witch-Hunting and Maternal Power in Early Modern England* (Ithaca and London: Cornell University Press, 1995), p. 213.

46 Stallybrass, '*Macbeth* and Witchcraft', p. 195.

47 Frederick Kiefer, *Shakespeare's Visual Theatre*, p. 111.

48 Kiefer, p. 112. In *Shakespeare's Speaking Pictures: Studies in Iconic Imagery* (Albuquerque: University of New Mexico Press, 1974), John Doebler argues that the witches serve as 'iconic images uniting the opposites of destiny and freely tempted evil' (p. 120).

49 Frances Dolan, *Dangerous Familiars: Representation of Domestic Crime in England, 1550–1700* (Ithaca and London: Cornell University Press, 1994), p. 225.

50 Dolan, p. 226.

51 Roy Booth, 'Witchcraft, Flight and the Early Modern English Stage', *Early Modern Literary Studies* 13.1 (2007), pp. 1–37.

52 Other methods included 'pricking for the witch's mark, threats of torture, and direct torture', although the rack, regularly used by the Inquisition, was not used in Scotland (Larner, p. 107).

53 Wendy Wall, *Staging Domesticity: Household Work and English Identity in Early Modern Drama* (Cambridge: Cambridge University Press, 2002), p. 199.

54 *A Book of Cookrye*, gathered by A. W. (London, 1591), Fol. 4; 22.

55 *The Good Huswifes Iewell* (London, 1610) Fol. 45.

56 *The Widdowes Treasure, Plentifully furnished with sundry precious and approved secrets in Phisicke and Chirurgery, for the health and pleasure of Mankinde* (London, 1599).

57 STC 10826.

58 James Carmichael, *Newes from Scotland, declaring the damnable life and death of Doctor Fian a notable sorcerer, who was burned at Edenbrough in Ianuary last. 1591* (London, 1592), 10841a, which also appears in STC 10842.3.

59 Gary Taylor and John Lavagnino include the entire text of *Tragedy of Macbeth* in their edition of *Thomas Middleton:*

The Collected Works (Oxford: Oxford University Press, 2007). Gary Taylor edited the text of the play, and he meticulously searched for any trace of Middleton's hand throughout the text. In her introduction, Inga-Stina Ewbank notes that Shakespeare's authorship of most of the text is not in dispute, but, she adds, 'Gary Taylor concluded that Middleton wrote about eleven per cent of the adapted text' (p. 1165). The attributions to Middleton do not affect my argument about the interconnections between cookery and witchcraft in the play. Ewbank admits that 'Shakespeare integrates the cauldron scene with Macbeth's descent into hell of his own making' (p. 1167). For a thoughtful analysis of this matter, see the review, 'The Oxford Middleton', by Kenneth Tucker, *The Shakespeare Newsletter* 61.3 (Winter 2011/12), pp. 93–102, esp. 94.

60 Hieronymus Brunschwig, *Book of Distillation*, trans. Lawrence Andrew (c. 1530), ed. Harold J. Abrahams (New York and London, 1971), p. 9.

61 Sousa, *At Home*, pp. 151–67.

62 Colin Spencer, *British Food: An Extraordinary Thousand Years of History* (New York: Columbia University Press, 2002), p. 116.

63 Daryl W. Palmer, *Hospitable Performances: Dramatic Genre and the Cultural Practices in Early Modern England* (West Lafayette IN: Purdue University Press, 1992), p. 173.

64 Palmer, p. 175.

65 Palmer, p. 175.

66 Palmer, p. 176.

8

The Language of *Macbeth*

Jonathan Hope and Michael Witmore

Macbeth has affected its critics perhaps more intensely than any other Shakespeare play, and its language in particular has been the focus of outrage, puzzled unease, and close examination. Modern responses attest to the play's 'continuous sense of menace' and 'horror', a feeling that the play itself, rather than individuated characters, speaks the lines, and a sense that what is communicated goes beyond the grammar or strict logic of the surface linguistic forms.[1] Perhaps the most resonant account of the play's mysterious effect is Thomas De Quincey's celebrated short note 'On The Knocking At The Gate In *Macbeth*' (1823), which begins with his childhood 'perplexity' at the strength of the feelings produced in him by the knocking at the gate after Duncan's murder:

> [...] it reflected back upon the murder a peculiar awfulness and a depth of solemnity; yet ... I never could see *why* it should produce such an effect.[2]

(p. 389)

De Quincey concludes that the knocking, heard repeatedly both as *actual* knocking and in the echoing vocabulary of the scene ('Here's a knocking indeed... Knock, knock, knock... Knock, knock... Knock, knock, knock... Knock, knock'; 2.3.1–15) serves to mark the point where 'the human', or everyday, starts to reassert itself over 'the fiendish' which has dominated the play hitherto. This manifestation of normality paradoxically makes us more aware of 'the awful parenthesis' that has suspended everyday life. Similarly, it signals the coming focus on Macbeth and his tormented guilt:

> in the murderer ... there must be raging some great storm of passion, – jealousy, ambition, vengeance, hatred, – which will create a hell within him; and *into this hell we are to look*.

(p. 392)

De Quincey's final phrase (emphasis mine) is as threatening as anything in the play itself, but most critics, while agreeing that the play has a particular, uncanny power, locate the source of that power not at the mid-point of the action, nor in stage business, but right at the start, and in the language. For them, the effects of dis-ease produced by what one critic has called the 'infected' language of the play[3] can be traced to vocabulary, metrics, grammar and sound patterning. These features begin with the witches in scene 1 and spread out via 'the mouths of the Macbeths and their porter',[4] so that eventually characters as diverse as the First Murderer, Duncan and Banquo speak 'for the play' rather than themselves.[5]

L. C. Knights fixes the first element of this common language, writing of the 'sickening see-saw rhythm' of the witches, in an early focus on metrical form subsequently extended by David Kranz and Russ McDonald.[6] It is worth unpicking this phrase in precise technical detail, as Knights' insight really does open up the linguistic peculiarity of the play. What Knights means by 'sickening see-saw' is the trochaic tetrameter the witches use:

When shall we three meet again?

When the hurlyburly's done,
When the battle's lost and won.
Fair is foul, and foul is fair

(1.1.1, 3–4, 11)

Trochaic verse uses feet consisting of two syllables arranged in a **strong**-weak pattern ('***hur***-ly***bur***-ly'), which contrasts with Shakespeare's more normal iambic pattern, where syllables are arranged weak-***strong*** ('suc-***cess***', 're-***flect***'). Trochaic verse is more obviously metrical than iambic: we hear the rhythm as insistent because it is less natural in English, and this is what Knights means by the 'sickening' effect:

***When** shall **we** three **meet** a**gain**?*

When** the **hurly***bur***ly's **done**,*
When** the **battle's **lost** and **won**.*

Fair** is **foul**, and **foul** is **fair

(1.1.1, 3–4, 11)

Notice, in contrast, how much more natural, less incantatory, Macbeth's iambic pentameter echo of the witches sounds:

So *foul* and *fair* a *day* I *have* not *seen*.

(1.3.38)

And there is another, perhaps more subtle, metrical disruption in the witches' language. In normal tetrameter, each line has four feet of two syllables each, so in well-behaved trochaic tetrameter, we expect eight syllables per line (4 x 2 = 8). For the weird music of the witches, however, Shakespeare uses what is called a 'catalectic' metre, dropping a syllable: in this case the final syllable of the line. So the witches' lines characteristically have seven rather than eight syllables (see Table 1).

Table 1 *Metrics in* Macbeth *1.1.4*

foot number:		**1**		**2**		**3**		**4**
syllable number:	1	2	3	4	5	6	7	8
stress:	s	w	s	w	s	w	s	w
line:	*Fair* is		*foul* and		*foul* is		*fair* –	

It is tempting to note, as a result of this, that when Macbeth calls the witches 'imperfect speakers' (1.3.70), his words are true metrically, as well as in all their other senses. One consequence of the catalectic nature of the metre is that the witches' lines end on a strong syllable, rather like a 'normal' iambic line. The verse-music of the witches can thus be seen as a partial pre-echo of the dominant metre of the play – an early suggestion that all is not right with the moral world, and that the chaos to come is fated, prefigured in the very metrical forms of the language.

Critics have found this 'see-saw' rhythm in other characters' verse. McDonald (p. 47) detects it in Macbeth's 'This supernatural soliciting / Cannot be ill; cannot be good' (1.3.130–1), and Kranz notes:

> While the witches disappear near the end of 1.3, many of the poetic patterns they engendered do not. The selfsame tune, the aural embodiment of their unholy spirit, makes its way into the mouths of several characters. ('Supernatural Soliciting', p. 357)

It is not only trochaic metre that spreads from the witches' first scene; as Frank Kermode comments:

> Here, perhaps more than in any other of Shakespeare's plays, an idiosyncratic rhythm and a lexical habit establish

themselves with a sort of hypnotic firmness. 'Lost and won', say the Sisters at the beginning of the first scene: 'What he hath lost, noble Macbeth hath won', says Duncan at the end of the second, having just before that rhymed 'Macbeth' with 'death'. (*Shakespeare's Language*, pp. 203–4)

Russ McDonald explores the possible effects on the reader of this dense sonic repetition:

A major result of such extreme verbal compression is to magnify the relations between similar words and sounds, making their identities more audible and more potentially, or at least apparently, significant [...] echoing is aurally satisfying and intellectually tantalising [...] echoing sounds register with unusual force because they reverberate in so short a space. Not only are words repeated ('double, double, toil and trouble') but consonants and vowels are doubled and trebled, rhythmic configurations repeated insistently, and phrases and images reiterated, not just immediately but memorably, across several scenes. (*Late Style*, pp. 45–7)

There is more to this than simple repetition and echo, which are, after all, a normal feature of Renaissance verse. George Walton Williams points out that the echoes of *Macbeth* often have an 'eerie *secondary* force' ('Verbal Echoing', p. 240). When Macbeth apparently repeats the witches' 'fair' and 'foul', for example, he has yet to meet them. For Williams, his use of their words suggests that:

[...] there is a bond between them and him, more significant than mere repetition of diction. He is ready to receive them when they come to him. Macbeth did not hear the Witches, but he knows how they speak and so knows how they think; speaking their words, he speaks their thoughts. (pp. 240–1)

Similar echoes occur elsewhere, perhaps most notably in 1.5 when Lady Macbeth greets her husband with his titles:

> Great Glamis! worthy Cawdor!
> Greater than both, by the all-hail hereafter!
>
> (1.5.53–4)

Here, Lady Macbeth echoes the words of the witches from 1.3: 'All hail, Macbeth! that shalt be King hereafter' (50). She has just read one of those words, 'all-hail', in Macbeth's letter describing his meeting (they *all-hailed me* 1.5.6). But Macbeth does not use 'hereafter' in his letter. Like her husband, Lady Macbeth seems to be able to speak the thoughts of the witches. As Williams notes, the word 'hereafter' echoes repeatedly elsewhere, a sign of the play's concerns with time present and future, and the consequences of actions. Perhaps this 'secondary' repetition is the source of the unsettling power critics have so often detected in the play, but found hard to explain. Normally, as Russ McDonald notes, echo and repetition are aesthetically 'satisfying', but their effect in *Macbeth* seems to be discomforting. This discomfort may come from cognitive dissonance: we recognize the echoes, but are aware that they have no logical explanation in the world of the play.

Stephen Booth offers a further explanation for the unsettling effect of language in the play. For him, it is characterized by indefinition.[7] 'Finality', he argues, is:

> [...] unattainable throughout *Macbeth* [...] the beginnings, sources, causes, of almost everything in the play are at best nebulous [...] it is almost impossible to find the source of any idea in *Macbeth*; every new idea seems already there when it is presented to us. (pp. 93–4)

One of the ways in which this jarring familiarity is achieved is by the dense verbal and metrical pre-echoes we have discussed. Ideas in the play have no single identifiable source because everyone speaks the same language, and seems already to know what others think. This claim is supported by a suggestive performance tradition: *Macbeth* works extremely well when its roles are explicitly doubled.[8]

The presence of this pervasive linguistic style in *Macbeth* marks, for Russ McDonald, a significant shift in Shakespeare's dramatic technique. McDonald believes that in the mid-1590s Shakespeare 'reached professional maturity' by learning:

> [...] to make his speakers sound like themselves [...] one of the triumphs of his craft [...] and by which he is differentiated from lesser dramatists. Prince Hal, Falstaff, King Henry, Hotspur, Owen Glendower – none of these speakers will be confused with the others [...] so confident of their individual voices is their creator that he even allows some speakers to parody others. (*Late Style*, pp. 33–4)

Around 1607, however, McDonald identifies a shift in the focus of Shakespeare's language from character differentiation to plot exploration. Whole plays, rather than individual characters, now have 'styles', and the characters in any one play tend to sound like each other. For McDonald, this constitutes a key feature of Shakespeare's late style.[9]

Literary accounts of the language of *Macbeth* offer, therefore, a clear consensus: the play has a linguistic style that crosses character boundaries, and repetition is a characteristic trope. Can we trace this in more formal linguistic studies? We now propose to investigate the language of *Macbeth* using quantitative techniques as a way of testing literary claims about the play, and to illustrate how linguistic approaches can lead us to surprising findings about literary language.

Given what literary critics have said about the importance of repetition in *Macbeth*, we will begin with word-frequency analysis, as a way of assessing the amount of repetition in the text compared with Shakespeare's other work. Perhaps the simplest measure of vocabulary repetition across texts is the type-token ratio. A text's type-token ratio is calculated by dividing the number of *different words* (types) in that text by the total number of *all words* (tokens). Consider, for example, the text,

Fair is foul and foul is fair

which we analyse in Table 2. The total number of words (tokens) here is seven. But three of those words ('fair', 'is', 'foul') appear twice, so while the number of *tokens* is seven, the number of *types* is four ('fair', 'is', 'foul', 'and'). This gives us a ratio of $4 \div 7 = 0.57$.

Compare this with another text,

So foul and fair a day I have not seen

which we analyse in Table 3. This second text has ten tokens, all of which are distinct types (each word is a different word). So the ratio is $10 \div 10 = 1$.

Any text which has no repetition will have a type-token ratio of 1. However, most texts contain very many repeated words: words like 'a', 'the', 'and' and so on. Any text which repeats words will have a type-token ratio of less than 1, with the figure decreasing as more words are repeated. Lear's

Never, never, never, never, never

(5.3.307)

has five tokens, but only one type, giving a ratio of $1 \div 5 = 0.2$.

Intuitively therefore, type-token ratios ought to be a good measure of the relative vocabulary richness of texts. If we work out the type-token ratio for each of Shakespeare's plays, we should be able to tell which plays have more repetition, since their type-token ratios will be lower. Brian Brainerd calculated these figures in an early study of type token ratios, and gives results for *Macbeth* and the other major tragedies.[10] On Brainerd's figures, *Macbeth* has a

Table 2 *Type-token counting in* **Macbeth** *1.1.4*

Tokens: (cumulative total)	1	2	3	4	5	6	7
	Fair	is	foul	and	foul	is	fair
Types: (cumulative total)	1	2	3	4	4	4	4

Table 3 *Type-token counting in* **Macbeth** *1.3.38*

Tokens: (cumulative total)	1	2	3	4	5	6	7	8	9	10
	So	foul	and	fair	a	day	I	have	not	seen
Types: (cumulative total)	1	2	3	4	5	6	7	8	9	10

type-token ratio of 0.2, which compares with *King Lear*: 0.17; *Hamlet*: 0.16; and *Othello*: 0.15. Given that a higher ratio implies less repetition, these figures suggest that *Macbeth* is *more* diverse in its vocabulary than the other great tragedies!

There are, however, several possible explanations for this surprising finding, one of which is an unfortunate statistical problem with type-token ratios. While the number of tokens in a text increases uniformly (one more token with every word, all the way through a text irrespective of length), the relative number of types tends to decrease steadily. Every word is a new token, but almost all texts consist mainly of repeated types: and the longer a text goes on, the more repetition there is. This means that type-token ratios are highly correlated with the length of the texts being analysed. Longer texts generally have more repetition, relatively fewer types, and therefore lower type-token ratios than short texts. *Macbeth*, as a notably shorter text than the other tragedies, can be expected to have a higher type-token ratio.[11]

If there are statistical problems with type-token ratios as a measure of vocabulary richness, there are also fundamental literary and stylistic questions about the effects of vocabulary richness and repetition. As David Hoover shows, our intuitions about the relative difficulty or quality of an author may not match the facts of their vocabulary use.[12] In a provocative study, Maria Cristina Consiglio compares the type-token ratio of Shakespeare's *King Lear* with that of Nahum Tate's infamous rewriting.[13] Her results confound expectations: Tate's version is more diverse in its vocabulary than Shakespeare's. Similarly, literary critics have frequently assumed that Shakespeare, as an acknowledged genius, must have had a huge vocabulary. Recent linguistic work has shown, however, that Shakespeare's vocabulary was of resolutely average size for his time.[14]

This suggests that we need to move away from crudely mathematical measures of style and effect. As Ward Elliott and Robert Valenza point out:

> Shakespeare learned early how to strike deep, not with an outsize inventory of long, inkhorn words, but with a par-for-the-course inventory, mostly of plain words, surpassingly well chosen and put together. ('Dwarf', p. 47)

Choice and arrangement may be more significant than raw frequency in the production of the kind of stylistic effects critics report for *Macbeth*. It may be that the frequent identification of repetition as crucial in *Macbeth* is because the play repeats certain highly *salient* words, rather than because it has high overall rates of repetition. Frank Kermode's study gives a possible example of this when he states that *Macbeth* 'is greatly

Table 4 *'Time' and 'times' in* Macbeth *and other plays*

Play	Relative frequency	Raw frequency
Macbeth	.267	47
Hamlet	.162	48
King Lear	.107	27
Antony and Cleopatra	.139	33

(Figures quoted from Kermode, *Language*, page 213 – based on Spevack, *Concordance*, vol. 3)

preoccupied with time' (*Shakespeare's Language*, p. 202), citing in support the fact that the words 'time' and 'times' appear 44 times and 3 times respectively. By way of comparison, Kermode offers the much longer *Hamlet*, where the total is 48; *King Lear*: 27; and *Antony and Cleopatra*: 33. He gives Spevack's 'relative frequency' scores, which seek to take play-length into account, and thus allow comparisons between texts of different lengths.[15] These figures are given in Table 4.

We can see, once play-length is taken into account, that 'time' and 'times' appear more frequently in *Macbeth* than elsewhere, though Kermode is reluctant to make much of these figures, relegating them to a footnote, and failing to explain exactly what 'relative frequency' is (the figure is derived by dividing the frequency of the word(s) being studied by the total number of words in a play and multiplying by one hundred to give a percentage).

Kermode's use of word frequencies here is broadly typical of literary critics' use of statistics: the frequency of a highly salient content word is cited as support for an argument that is actually made using traditional 'quote and discuss' methods. And the initial identification of 'time' and 'times' as words to count is made impressionistically, as a result of subjective reading, rather than emerging from a statistical test. Kermode's citation of 'relative frequency' makes his analysis more sophisticated than most, but our understanding of the relationship between the frequency of content words and 'meaning' is poor. Yes, the words 'time' and 'times' are relatively more frequent in *Macbeth* than in *Hamlet*, but someone reading or seeing a performance of the full text of both plays encounters the words almost the same number of times. Does the saliency of the terms increase in *Macbeth* because they are less diluted by other words?

Where Kermode (and literary critics more generally) tend to identify what they see as significant themes first through their own reading, and then use frequency counts to support that claim, there are statistical tests which examine every word in a text, against their observed frequencies in a wider corpus, in order to identify all those words in a text which have unusual frequencies. For example, we can analyse the frequency of every word in *Macbeth* compared to the frequencies of those words in the whole of Shakespeare. The results of such a test (called a log-likelihood test) show us those words that Shakespeare uses more *and less* frequently in *Macbeth* than in his work as a whole.

There are several advantages to such a test over the less systematic method used by Kermode. Perhaps most importantly, log-likelihood identifies words which are unexpectedly reduced in frequency, as well as those which occur more often than normal. Additionally, log-likelihood detects frequency shifts in very common words – notably function words such as pronouns, determiners and prepositions. Again, this is something human readers are relatively poor at doing: we are alert to small increases in rare items such as 'time', but blind even to very large shifts in the frequency of words such as 'and'.

The web-based text analysis tool WordHoard allows anyone to run log-likelihood tests on Shakespeare.[16] For this chapter, we made a log-likelihood comparison between every word in *Macbeth* and the occurrence of each word in all of Shakespeare. The most significant results are shown in Table 5.

The analysis gives a list of 33 words which show a difference between their actual frequency in the play, and their expected frequency given Shakespeare's practice elsewhere. The table may look confusing, so we will use the highest scoring word, 'thane' as an example of what each column means.

The first column, headed 'Lemma' lists the word being analysed.[17] The second column gives its part of speech (in this case 'n' for noun). The third column is crucial, as the '+' or '-' sign indicates whether the frequency of the word is raised or lowered in *Macbeth* compared to Shakespeare's normal use. We can see from the '+' sign that 'thane' occurs more frequently in *Macbeth* than we would expect, given Shakespeare's use of it in his work as a whole. The fourth column gives the log-likelihood score: the higher this is, the greater the shift in frequency over or under expectation. Stars are used to indicate degrees of statistical significance: four indicate a result very unlikely to be due to chance, with the degree of confidence decreasing as the number of stars decreases. 'Thane' has by far the highest log-likelihood score in the play, and is given four stars, indicating that the result is very unlikely to be due to chance (or normal variation).[18]

The next columns are very useful in allowing us to judge the extent of any shift in usage. 'Analysis parts per 10,000' tells us how many times the word occurs every 10,000 words in the analysis text (which in this case is *Macbeth*). So we can see that 'thane' occurs 18 times every 10,000 words in *Macbeth*. We can compare this with the next column, which tells us how many times 'thane' occurs in the 'Reference' sample (which is the whole of Shakespeare's work). Here we see that 'thane' occurs just 0.35 times every 10,000 words in Shakespeare. Another way of assessing this is provided by the next two columns, which give the raw counts for 'thane' in the analysis text (*Macbeth*) and the reference text (the whole of Shakespeare). We can see that 'thane' occurs 30 times in *Macbeth*, and 30 times in the whole of Shakespeare: in other words, every Shakespearean instance of 'thane' comes in *Macbeth*.

Table 5 *Log-likelihood comparisons between* Macbeth *and Shakespeare (top 33 results – generated by WordHoard)*

Lemma	Word class	Relative use	Log likelihood	Analysis parts per 10,000	Reference parts per 10,000	Analysis count	Reference count
thane	n	+	156.1****	18	0.35	30	30
hail	v	+	51****	10	0.82	17	71
knock	v	+	49.8****	11	1.17	19	101
cauldron	n	+	41.6****	4.8	0.09	8	8
our	po	+	41.5****	71	36.76	119	3180
she	pn	-	41.3****	21	53.05	35	4590
the	dt	+	41****	422	327.07	703	28298
tyrant	n	+	40.2****	9	0.89	15	77
sleep	n	+	33.3****	9.6	1.38	16	119
weird	j	+	31.2****	3.6	0.07	6	6
I	pn	-	28.6****	283	359.55	472	31108
trouble	n	+	27.3****	5	0.43	9	37
dagger	n	+	26.3***	6	0.61	10	53
wood	n 1	+	25.9***	6.6	0.8	11	69
fear	n	+	24.5***	13.8	3.88	23	336

nature	n	+	23.1***	15.6	5	26	433
we	pn	+	20.5**	98	67.3	164	5823
double	v	+	20.3**	3.6	0.23	6	20
horror	n	+	20.3**	3.6	0.23	6	20
you	pn	-	19.8**	128	171.26	213	14817
which	crq	+	17.5*	48	28.71	80	2484
upon	acp	+	17.5*	37.8	21.07	63	1823
deed	n	+	17*	10.8	3.32	18	287
new	j	+	16.7*	10	3.05	17	264
castle	n	+	15.5*	4	0.55	7	48
air	n	+	15*	8	2.36	14	204
yet	av	+	14.9*	34	19.41	57	1679
bloody	j	+	14.8	9	2.68	15	232
time	n	+	14.8	28.8	15.50	48	1341
strange	j	+	14.5	10	3.36	17	291
worthy	j	+	14	10.8	3.78	18	327
love	v	-	13.7	4	13.15	7	1138
a	dt	-	13.5	144	181.24	240	15681

Given this, it is hardly surprising that log-likelihood is telling us that the use of 'thane' in *Macbeth* is unusual compared to Shakespeare's normal usage. But it is also fair to say that this result is not very interesting. It is easy to explain why the Scottish word 'thane' appears in Shakespeare's only Scottish play. The presence of the word in this play, and nowhere else, is not an interpretative problem.

There are several other words which have similarly obvious explanations. 'Cauldron' and 'weird' are also found only in *Macbeth*. 'Hail', 'knock', 'tyrant', 'sleep', 'trouble', 'dagger', and 'wood', although used elsewhere, all show a raised frequency over the expected one, and all are clearly linked to particular plot events or themes. *Macbeth* is a play in which daggers feature; characters are murdered in and worry about their sleep; there is an extended passage about knocking at a door; a wood moves. We hardly need computers and advanced statistics to tell us this.

However, log-likelihood comes into its own as a discovery technique if we shift away from obvious content words. There are several function words in the table whose presence is harder to explain. 'Our' is much more frequent than we would expect, occurring almost twice as often (71 times every 10,000 words against Shakespeare's norm of 37 times). 'She' is reduced in frequency, at 21 per 10,000 words versus 53 (which we might find surprising, given the prominence of Lady Macbeth). Perhaps most puzzling, 'the' is raised in frequency to a highly significant degree. It is easy to skip over these words when 'reading' a log-likelihood table, since the content words tend to catch our eye, but it is the function words that often raise the most interesting problems of explanation.

For us, the most intriguing log-likelihood result for *Macbeth* concerns the determiner 'the'. This is exactly the sort of word literary critics tend not to comment on; indeed, it is exactly the sort of word even early quantitative and digital analysts excluded from their work on the assumption that it was too common to be interesting. But experience of log-likelihood tests shows that it is often the most frequent words that prove the most interesting, because they are the most difficult to explain; and they are the words that can only be identified as interesting through the use of digital analysis and complex statistics. Most important of all, the effect of such words can only be explained by returning to the text and looking carefully at their contexts of use. Quantitative and digital analysis does not distance us from the text; it sends us back to it with new questions.

First, let's make the increase in 'the' explicit. WordHoard's figures show that 'the' occurs in *Macbeth* 422 times every 10,000 words. In Shakespeare as a whole, 'the' appears only 327 times every 10,000 words. In terms of actual instances, 'the' appears 703 times in *Macbeth*; but if Shakespeare were behaving 'normally', it would only appear 545 times. So we can say that there are about 150 'extra' 'the' forms in *Macbeth*.

How can we account for this? There are several issues that we should think about here. One possibility is that the play is using the definite article ('the') in situations where Shakespeare would, in other plays, have used the indefinite article ('a'). When we look at the log-likelihood result for 'a' at the bottom of Table 5, we find something very suggestive. A minus sign in the 'Relative use' column tells us that the frequency of 'a' in the play is indeed lower than we would expect given Shakespeare's normal behaviour. However, the log-likelihood score for 'a' is just 13.5 (as opposed to 41 for 'the'), and there are no stars, suggesting that the effect could be due to chance. So we need to be cautious about this result: it is not as strong as that for 'the', but it is interesting. Shakespeare normally uses 'a' about 181 times every 10,000 words. In *Macbeth*, this drops to 144 times every 10,000 words. The observed frequency (240 'a' forms in the play) is about 60 down on the expected (300 forms). So there *is* a shift from 'a' to 'the' in the play, though not enough to explain the whole increase in 'the' forms.

Checking the results for the other determiners produces

some similar results: 'some' and 'this' are also down on expectation, though again, not at the level of significance (these results are not given in Table 5). 'That' and 'those', on the other hand, are raised slightly. So there seems a reasonable statistical case for saying that there is a tendency in *Macbeth*, compared to the canon as a whole, for determiners to be definite ('the', 'that', 'those') rather than indefinite ('a', 'some'). We will return to this.

Another possible explanation is that *Macbeth* has more noun phrases than other plays, and that this allows more opportunities for Shakespeare to use determiners. WordHoard uses a 'deeply tagged' corpus of Shakespeare: that is, all of the words have been tagged for grammatical function. So we can search on 'word class'. This isn't going to answer our question exactly, since WordHoard marks 'nouns' rather than 'noun phrases', but comparisons between the number of nouns in Shakespeare's plays will get us close enough to what we want to know. When we look at the log-likelihood table for word class in *Macbeth*, we find that nouns are raised slightly, though with a very low log-likelihood score of 1.0. There are 2,991 nouns in the play, 90 more than the expected result (2905) given Shakespeare's practice elsewhere. So it is possible that what we are seeing in the very strong result for 'the' is a combination of a shift in determiner choice from 'a' to 'the', and a slight rise in noun frequency, with those 'extra' nouns tending to take definite determiners.[19]

So, this is a finding, but is it an interesting one? Does it tell us anything about the way the play works? Common sense suggests that an increased use of definite articles should make the play more definite than Shakespeare's other work. This is puzzling, though, since the subjective experience of reading the play, as reported by generations of literary scholars, is not one of definiteness, but rather of *indefinition*; looming, overwhelming, but ill-defined, fear and dread. This mismatch between subjective impression and objective finding is interesting, precisely because it is counter-intuitive and difficult to explain. Generally in literary studies, things that are difficult

to explain produce more insightful discussion than things that
are easy to explain.

Is it possible that an increase in the use of 'the' is producing
an effect of indefiniteness? Once we start examining the ways
'the' is used in the play, we notice some fascinating patterns.
Just before the murder, the Macbeths are startled by noises in
the night, which Lady Macbeth explains as follows:

> It was the owl that shriek'd, the fatal bellman,
> Which gives the stern'st good-night.
>
> (2.2.4–5)

A more expected determiner here would have been 'an': 'It
was *an* owl that shriek'd'. This is because Lady Macbeth is
explaining an unexpected event, assigning to it a previously
unknown cause. The expectation in English is that *new*
information, like this, is introduced using indefinite articles,
while *given* information (something we already know about)
is marked with definite articles. So why does Lady Macbeth
use 'the' here? The effect is to present the owl not as an actual,
specific owl, but as a generalized, mythical or proverbial
owl; and this shift is clear in her epithet 'the fatal bellman',
which also, much more expectedly, uses the definite article. So
Lady Macbeth's choice of determiner shifts the owl from the
immediate, specific 'now' of the play, into a less determinate
mythological space and time. The owl becomes an idea, rather
than a thing.

There are further instances elsewhere of 'the' being used
to introduce ideas which, strictly speaking are new to the
discourse of the play:

> To beguile the time,
> Look like the time; bear welcome in your eye,
> Your hand, your tongue: look like th'innocent flower,
> But be the serpent under't.
>
> (1.5.62–5)

Here, 'th'innocent flower' and 'the serpent' are treated as given information: the language acts as though we already know about these things. This assumption of knowledge produces the murky, claustrophobic feeling critics have often detected in *Macbeth*: it gives the feeling that everything has been decided already. Similarly in Macbeth's speech:

> If it were done, when 'tis done, then 'twere well
> It were done quickly: if <u>th'assassination</u>
> Could trammel up <u>the consequence</u>, and catch
> With his surcease success; that but <u>this blow</u>
> Might be <u>the be-all</u> and <u>the end-all</u> – here,
> But here, upon <u>this bank</u> and shoal of time,
> We'd jump <u>the life</u> to come.
>
> (1.7.1–7)

Although these ideas are new (indeed, several of the nouns introduced by 'the' have their first recorded appearance in English in this passage), they are presented as given information. There is thus a tension in the language: unfamiliar, abstract concepts and formal terms are presented as if they were familiar, everyday things. The language behaves as if the things it talks about were certain, but it deals with abstracts, concepts, metaphors.

Elsewhere, we find 'the', and other definite determiners operating to form nouns out of adjectives:

> And you whose places are the nearest
>
> (1.4.36)

to concretize abstract ideas:

> Great Glamis! worthy Cawdor!
> Greater than both, by <u>the all-hail hereafter</u>!
> Thy letters have transported me beyond
> <u>This ignorant present</u>, and I feel now
> <u>The future</u> in <u>the instant</u>.
>
> (1.5.53–7)

and to give definiteness to reference that is general:

> Let not light see my black and deep desires;
> The eye wink at the hand; yet let that be,
> Which the eye fears, when it is done, to see.

(1.4.51–3)

Why does Macbeth not say 'my hand' and 'my eye' here? We would suggest that this is the beginning of the dissociation between desire, act and guilt which wracks him through the play; and which is manifest in his ascribing independent agency to the eye and the hand, achieved linguistically by substituting 'the' for the expected possessive pronoun. We see this process elsewhere in Shakespeare's plays: for example, in Hamlet's descriptions of how the will fails to inspire the body to put its intentions into act. But Hamlet's more intellectual analysis of the distributed nature of human agency is given grammatical form in *Macbeth* as body parts take on an identity of their own; unclaimed, and so perhaps un-owned, by the person to which they belong.

We can link these linguistic observations to Stephen Booth's critical claim about indefinition in *Macbeth*. As we have seen, Booth claims that 'it is almost impossible to find the source of any idea in *Macbeth*; every new idea seems already there when it is presented to us' (*Indefinition*, p. 94). Booth made this claim without knowledge of the statistical rise in 'the' forms in the play, but the mathematics back him up. *Macbeth* is a play which presents the new as old, and the indefinite and uncertain as certain. Paradoxically, the effect of this apparent certainty is uncertainty and dislocation in the reader: the formal structures of the language, the function words, are telling us one thing (things are familiar, things are fixed, things are certain); but the content words are telling us something else ('into this hell we are to look'). A determiner tells us *how* to think about the specifics being mentioned. It doesn't simply specify the number of a noun, but an assumed perspective on the world in which that noun appears: exhaustive, partial, hypothetical, matter-of-fact. That perspective is, in *Macbeth,* a jarring one: the determiner calls attention to the fact that the listener does not know the noun being discussed, and indeed, could not know such a thing. It is as if, in some of these uses, listeners are encountering a certain kind of category mistake, like hearing someone claiming to know just how many hairs are in Macbeth's beard. We reject not the proffered count, but the presumption that such a thing can be counted in the first place.

We can sense this type of ongoing category mistake in the following passage, which alienates the listener by assuming he or she ought to be in the know – or that the characters know something terribly specific that cannot be stated:

> Glamis thou art, and Cawdor; and shalt be
> What thou art promis'd. – Yet do I fear thy nature:
> It is too full o'<u>th' milk of human kindness,</u>
> To catch <u>the nearest way</u>. Thou wouldst be great;
> Art not without ambition, but without
> <u>The illness should attend it</u>: what thou wouldst highly,
> That wouldst thou holily; wouldst not play false,
> And yet wouldst wrongly win; thou'dst have, great Glamis,
> That which cries, 'Thus thou must do,' if thou have it;
> And that which rather thou dost fear to do,
> Than wishest should be undone. Hie thee hither,
> That I may pour my spirits in thine ear,
> And chastise with <u>the valour of my tongue</u>
> All that impedes thee from <u>the golden round,</u>
> Which fate and metaphysical aid doth seem
> To have thee crown'd withal.
>
> $\qquad\qquad\qquad\qquad\qquad$ (1.5.14–29)

'<u>th' milk of human kindness</u>'; '<u>the nearest way</u>'; '<u>The illness should attend it</u>': these all assume, or imply, a knowledge and familiarity that is impossible. The sickening lack of specificity is reinforced by the run of pronouns and pronominal phrases whose referent is assumed, but difficult to identify: 'what thou wouldst'; 'That'; 'That which'; 'it'; 'that which'. And by a set of ellipted verbs and pronouns:

> what thou wouldst *[have]* highly,
> That wouldst thou *[have]* holily; *[thou]* wouldst not play false,
> And yet *[thou]* wouldst wrongly win *[it]*

As much as repetition of content words and sounds, this forms the characteristic, queasy music of *Macbeth*: high density of pronoun replacement and ellipsis – both features that assume shared knowledge on the part of speaker and hearer. When the audience can supply a referent for pronouns, and can fill the ellipsis with a suitable word, the effect is to build a strong bond between speaker and hearer: the hearer guesses the speaker's words without actually hearing them, as the Macbeths do the witches'. But if the referents of pronouns shift without warning, as they do in Macbeth's

> If it were done, when 'tis done, then 'twere well
> It were done quickly

$(1.7.1–2)^{20}$

and if the shared knowledge on which ellipsis depends is absent, then the effect is dislocation, and, ultimately, horror.

Notes

1 For 'menace' and 'horror', see George Walton Williams, '"Time for such a word": verbal echoing in *Macbeth*', in *Shakespeare and Language*, ed. Catherine M. S. Alexander (Cambridge: Cambridge University Press, 2004), pp. 240–50 (originally published in *Shakespeare Survey*, 47 [1994], pp. 153–9), 210 and 211. For the play, rather than characters speaking, see Nicholas Brooke ed., *Macbeth* (Oxford: Oxford University Press, 1990), pp. 12–13. For communication beyond surface

meaning, see Stephen Booth, 'Close reading without reading', in *Shakespeare Reread: The Texts in New Contexts*, ed. Russ McDonald (Ithaca: Cornell, 1984), pp. 42–55; and Russ McDonald, *Shakespeare's Late Style* (Cambridge: Cambridge University Press: 2006), p. 46.

The outrage belongs to Dr Johnson, who objected to what he saw as indecorous vocabulary, though this did not stop him mining the play for examples for his *Dictionary*. Lisa Hopkins, 'Household words: *Macbeth* and the failure of spectacle', *Shakespeare Survey*, 50 (2004), pp. 101–10, gives an account of Johnson's outrage. Arthur Sherbo ('Dr. Johnson on *Macbeth*: 1745 and 1765', *The Review of English Studies*, New Series, 2.5 [1951], pp. 40–7) and Anne McDermott ('The defining language: Johnson's *Dictionary* and *Macbeth*', *The Review of English Studies*, New Series, 44.176 [1993], pp. 521–38) detail the use he made of the play in his *Dictionary*.

Readers wishing to extend work on the play's language beyond this chapter should look to the play's most recent editors for Cambridge and Oxford (A. R. Braunmuller ed., *Macbeth* [Cambridge, 1997] and Brooke – see above); both have extended sections in their introductions on the language of the play. Frank Kermode's chapter in *Shakespeare's Language* (2000) is excellent, but most important, and useful, of all is Russ McDonald's account of the play (*Late Style,* pp. 43–52, 33–4); we would suggest this as the first port of call after this essay.

2   Thomas De Quincey, 'On The Knocking At The Gate In Macbeth', *The Collected Writings of Thomas De Quincey*, ed. David Masson (1896–7), vol. x, pp. 389–94. (I have followed modern editions in correcting 'murderer' to 'murder' in the quotation.)

3   McDonald, *Late Style*, p. 44.

4   David L. Kranz, 'The sounds of supernatural soliciting in *Macbeth*', *Studies in Philology*, 100.3 (2003), p. 367.

5   Brooke ed., *Macbeth*, pp. 12–13.

6   L. C. Knights, *Explorations: Essays in Criticism Mainly on the Literature of the Seventeenth Century* (1946), 20; Kranz 'Supernatural Soliciting', pp. 351–2; McDonald, *Late Style*, pp. 47–8.

7   Stephen Booth, *King Lear, Macbeth, Indefinition and Tragedy*
     (New Haven: Yale University Press, 1983).

8   A recent Japanese production (Tokyo, 2010) had all characters
     except the Macbeths played by the three witches, while the
     2012 National Theatre of Scotland production had Alan
     Cumming's Macbeth locked in a mental hospital, obsessively
     recounting the whole play to himself, taking on the separate
     roles within his own character.

9   *Late Style*, pp. 33–4 and 47. McDonald's claim seems
     impressionistically right to us, but the wide availability of
     digital tools now makes empirical testing possible. It would
     not be hard to make linguistic comparisons between the styles
     of major characters in plays before and after 1607 to establish
     degrees of differentiation. Certainly our own work, based on
     plays rather than characters, tends to suggest that Shakespeare's
     style as a whole becomes more consistent later in his career
     (Michael Witmore and Jonathan Hope, 'Shakespeare's Late
     Plays: Earlier Than You Think' [unpublished paper presented
     at Stratford International Shakespeare Conference, 2012]) –
     though we would push the beginnings of the later style closer to
     1599.

10   Brian Brainerd, 'On the relation between types and tokens
     in literary text', *Journal of Applied Probability*, 9.3 (1982),
     pp. 507–18.

11   A good starting point for exploring measures of vocabulary
     richness is this post on the Corpus Linguistics blog: http://
     corplinguistics.wordpress.com/2011/11/21/vocabulary-richness/
     [accessed 31 October 2013].

12   David L. Hoover, 'Another Perspective on Vocabulary
     Richness', *Computers and the Humanities*, 37 (2003),
     pp. 151–78.

13   Maria Cristina Consiglio, 'e-Lears: a corpus approach to
     Shakespeare and Tate', in *The State of Stylistics: Pala 26*, ed.
     Greg Watson (Amsterdam: Rodopi, 2008), pp. 191–206.

14   See Hugh Craig, 'Shakespeare's vocabulary: myth and reality',
     Shakespeare Quarterly, 62.1 (2011), pp. 53–74; and Ward E.
     Y. Elliott and Robert J. Valenza, 'Shakespeare's vocabulary: did
     it dwarf all others?', in *Stylistics and Shakespeare's Language*:

Transdisciplinary Approaches, Mireille Ravassat and Jonathan Culpeper (eds) (2011), pp. 34–57. Jonathan Hope, 'Shakespeare and the English Language', in *English in the World: History, Diversity, Change*, Philip Seargeant and Joan Swann (eds) (2012), pp. 83–92, gives a summary of this work.

15 Marvin Spevack, *A Complete and Systematic Concordance to the Works of Shakespeare* (Hildesheim: Georg Olms, 1973).

16 WordHoard can be downloaded from: http://wordhoard. northwestern.edu/userman/index.html Log-likelihood is explained in more detail in the excellent user documentation found at the WordHoard site: http://wordhoard.northwestern. edu/userman/analysis-comparewords.html#loglike [accessed 31 October 2013].

17 'Words' are not straightforward entities to define or count. WordHoard distinguishes between 'spelling' and 'lemma'. A 'spelling' count operates strictly on spelling: so 'dagger' and 'daggers' will be treated as two separate words. A 'lemma' count works by dictionary entry: so 'dagger' and 'daggers' would be one word, as would 'am' and 'is'. The choice between using 'spelling' and 'lemma' lies with the researcher. In this study, we have used 'lemma'.

18 We note in passing that Table 5 shows that the lemma 'time' is indeed raised in frequency in *Macbeth*, but not to a level which is accorded statistical significance.

19 While investigating this, we came across a slightly surprising side-result: proper nouns (the names of people and places, not normally able to take any kind of determiner, so not relevant to our central question here) are strongly lowered in frequency in the play. This is surprising, since our subjective impression is that the play is filled with names (Macbeth, Glamis, Cawdor), which contribute to an overpowering, almost claustrophobic sense of location. But the figures do not back this up. Perhaps the subjective effect is produced by the repetition of a few names at highly salient moments. This is another warning of the dangers of assuming too simple a relationship between frequency and literary effect.

20 Jonathan Hope, *Shakespeare's Grammar* (2003), pp. 13–16, discusses this passage in grammatical and stylistic detail.

PART FOUR

Adaptation and Afterlife

9

The Shapes of *Macbeth*: The Staged Text

Sandra Clark

In this chapter I examine evidence from a selection of promptbooks and acting editions and some performance records to explore the changing shape of the *Macbeth* text over the centuries, and the implications of such changes. There is a vast wealth of potential material: Shattuck in his catalogue of Shakespeare promptbooks records around 150 for *Macbeth* up to 1961, a number exceeded only by *Hamlet*.[1] Numerous others for this period alone have been discovered, and for the next fifty years the play has, if anything, become even more popular in the theatre. Almost every leading actor since Betterton has tried his hand at the title role. Consequently, this account will be highly selective. Its focus will be on the staged text rather than on performance as such, and only on the broader effects created by its reshaping. Only productions where the shaping of the text has raised relevant questions will be discussed. By using the expression 'staged text', I mean to consider only performances for live theatre, not versions for other media. I aim to consider the relationship between the staged text and its original in the First Folio, hence I also exclude adaptations. It seems fair to say that all directors make small cuts within speeches, and these are not my subject here, although it is worth bearing in mind that the significance of changes to the text is not necessarily proportionate to the length of the passages that are cut or added. For example, a number of staged texts from Garrick's (1744) onwards include the opening line that Davenant wrote for Macbeth at his first appearance in 1.3: 'Command they make a halt upon the heath', spoken to the military followers with whom he and Banquo have entered. The economically suggestive effects of his first line in F, 'So foul and fair a day I have not seen', commenting at once on the state of the battle and the condition of the weather and linking him implicitly to the paradoxical world of the weird sisters and their characteristic speech styles, are thus blunted. The new line separates Macbeth and Banquo from the rest of the entourage, positing the soldiers as a distant presence, which creates an effect of its own; but it is not the same as in Shakespeare's original.[2]

There are certain key elements in the text and its history that contribute most significantly to the shapes which the play takes in the theatre: the influence of the Davenant version, which persisted in various forms for centuries, and relates particularly to the treatment of the witches; the Porter's scene; the presence or absence of Lady Macbeth in 2.3; the scene of the murders of Lady Macduff and her son; the cutting of 4.3, especially in relation to Malcolm's self-accusations, and the excursus on Edward the Confessor; and the battle scenes that make up the play's ending. Most of these changes take the form of cuts, made for many different sorts of reasons, aesthetic and pragmatic: to shorten the play; to remove verbal difficulties; to trim down the cast; to comply with standards of taste and decorum; to reshape parts to suit the predilections of the main actors; to increase tension, pathos, excitement; and, for a long period, to provide curtain lines. But there are also additions, in particular to the witches' roles, which were for a long time amplified with a new scene after 2.3, as well as extra

songs and dances in 4.1, and also the dying speech which
Garrick wrote for Macbeth, used into the nineteenth century.

Two seventeenth-century promptbooks of the play indicate
something of the shapes that the staged text will assume.
Macbeth is unusual in boasting the existence of a pre-Resto-
ration promptbook, which consists of a text of F1 marked
up with cuts and some stage directions.[3] It is interesting here
for two reasons, the first being that of the c.300 lines cut,
the majority are from scenes which have historically been the
most subject to cuts, up at least to the mid-twentieth century:
2.3, the Porter's scene; 3.1, Macbeth's first interview with
the Murderers; 3.6, the scene of commentary on the state
of Scotland after Banquo's murder; and 4.3, the long scene
centred on Malcolm and Macduff, from which more than
seventy lines are cut. In the absence of any clear evidence
as to the origins of this text, speculation about the rationale
for the cuts has to be limited; but the history of *Macbeth*
onstage demonstrates that they were not simply a matter
of early modern theatrical taste. The second reason for the
significance of this early promptbook is that it is based on
'uncontaminated' F1; it predates Davenant's adaptation of
Macbeth[4] which was to influence the staged text for more than
200 years.

The other early promptbook is that from the Smock Alley
theatre in Dublin, probably to be dated between 1674 and
1682.[5] Unlike the Padua promptbook it has an indisputable
provenance in the professional theatre, and it represents a
transitional stage in the text between basic Shakespeare and
Davenant; the text used is F3, but overlaid with markings by
at least four different hands, some of which show clear, though
limited, borrowings from Davenant. But the actual reshaping
of the text follows Davenant significantly in some key places:
the cutting of the Porter scene, which has continued to
differing extents into the twentieth century, the cutting of
the Apparitions in 4.1 and of Lady Macduff's son in 4.2, and
the management of the ending. Davenant's adaptation was
published (without the playwright's name) as *Macbeth, A*

Tragaedy. With all the Alterations, Amendments, Additions, and New Songs. As it's now Acted at the Duke's Theatre in 1674. It held the stage unchallenged until Garrick in 1744 produced his own version, much closer to, but by no means identical with, Shakespeare's, although it was billed 'as Shakespeare wrote it'.[6] James Quin, who had been playing Macbeth for more than twenty years, was reported as exclaiming: 'What does he mean? Don't I play *Macbeth* as written by Shakespeare?'[7] Much of what Davenant had done in his version was promptly jettisoned, in particular the three extra scenes for Macduff and his wife, the new scene for Macbeth and his Lady in act 4 in which the ghost of Duncan appears, and the encounter between the two wives in 1.5 where Lady Macbeth is prevented from getting at Macbeth's letter by having to console Lady Macduff for her husband's absence at the war. His reformulation of the play as a study of the deluded desire for illicit power, in accord with the politics of the Restoration, was influential in only one respect, its culmination in the line given to the dying Macbeth: 'Farewell vain World, and what's most vain in it, Ambition'.[8] This provided the key for Garrick to compose an eight-line dying speech for Macbeth:

> 'Tis done! The scene of life will quickly close.
> Ambition's vain, delusive dreams are fled,
> And now I wake to darkness, guilt, and horror;
> I cannot bear it! Let me shake it off –
> It will not be; my soul is clogg'd with blood –
> I cannot rise! I dare not ask for mercy –
> It is too late, hell drags me down; I sink,
> I sink – Oh! – my soul is lost for ever!

Despite the disapproval of the poet and critic Francis Gentleman ('we are not fond of characters writhing and flouncing on carpets'),[9] the speech was taken up by several of Garrick's successors including John Philip Kemble, and printed in his version of the text.[10] As Paul Prescott suggests, 'the ostentatious manifestation of remorse' was important for dramatic villains in this period, and this, along with Garrick's cutting of the scene with Lady Macduff's murder, may have helped lessen Macbeth's violence and align his characterization with that of the contemporary ideal of the man of sensibility.[11]

But Davenant's influence was a significant factor in the shaping of the text for some time to come. His reduction of the cast – omitting the bloody Captain, Ross, Angus, Menteith, Caithness, Young Siward, Macduff's Son, the two Doctors, the Third Murderer, and the Old Man – showed what could be done to tidy up the play, although few later stagings have made such radical reductions. But the extra prominence given to Seyton, who acquired many of the lines given to these characters, continued throughout the nineteenth and twentieth centuries. In the Folio text, Seyton is a somewhat mysterious character who appears only in two scenes late in the play. Macbeth summons him by name in 5.3 to help arm him for the coming battle, and in 5.5 he brings news of the death of Lady Macbeth. The play's latest editor suggests that, if his name is pronounced 'Satan' as may have been likely in Shakespeare's time, then he 'represents demonic power'.[12] But such a possibility is diminished if Seyton is present in the play from early on as a household servant or attendant. He figures in such roles, 'a hard-worked functionary',[13] at least from Kemble onwards. In Glen Byam Shaw's 1955 production with Olivier, for example, Seyton first appears in 1.5, in the role of 'the head servant of the Macbeth household', and is distinctively characterized as Macbeth's devoted follower. Trevor Nunn's 1976 production follows suit in combining a number of small messenger/attendant roles into Seyton's, and allocating him, with some significance, the role of Third Murderer.[14]

The play's ending has been the subject of much reshaping, although here the influence of Davenant is less significant. His last act follows the structure of Shakespeare's, alternating scenes featuring the advance of Malcolm's forces with scenes featuring Macbeth. In Shakespeare the two strands of action coalesce in the encounter of Macbeth and Young Siward, while in Davenant Siward is replaced by Lenox and there is no equivalent of Old Siward. In Davenant, after the fight with Macduff, Macbeth, according to the stage direction, 'falls' and Macduff then finishes him off onstage with a series of blows:

This for my Royal Master Duncan,
This for my dearest Friend my Wife,
These for those Pledges of our Loves, my Children.
Hark, I hear a Noise, sure there are more
Reserves to conquer. I'le as a Trophy bear
Away his sword, to witness my Revenge.

                                        (5.9.35–40)[15]

He makes his exit, allowing Macbeth to die alone onstage with the one additional line, 'Farewell vain World, and what's most vain in it, Ambition', thus highlighting the theme which has informed this rewriting of Shakespeare's play throughout. Macbeth's body remains onstage, and it is with his sword (rather than his head) that Macduff makes his triumphal entry, in a final scene that is comparatively close to Shakespeare's. By these means Davenant avoids some of the difficulties of the Folio ending. The original stage direction following Macbeth's last line, 'And damn'd be him that first cries, "Hold, enough!"', reads *'Exeunt fighting. Alarums. Enter fighting, and Macbeth slain. Retreat, and flourish'*. No new scene is indicated. Many editors have found this ambiguous or contradictory.[16] Does Macbeth die on or offstage? One problem is that if he meets his death onstage, somehow or other his head must be available to be brought onstage by Macduff a few lines later. Editors can solve this by inserting a stage direction for the exit of Macduff and removal of Macbeth's body, but in the theatre it is not so simple. Davenant's solution is to leave the body onstage and to have Macduff exit but remove Macbeth's sword, which provides a trophy and dispenses with the less decorous – and for actors and designers more problematic – fake head.[17] The lack of a dying speech for Macbeth is unique for a Shakespearean tragic protagonist, but not apparently regarded as a desideratum for very long.[18]

The offstage death for Macbeth has never been a favoured option, despite its possible textual authenticity. In this respect, the pioneering work of Samuel Phelps should be acknowledged. In his inaugural production of *Macbeth* at the Sadler's Wells Theatre in 1844, Phelps retained the then-traditional onstage death and curtain after 'Hold, enough'. But in 1847 he boldly attempted to present what he saw as a true version of the play as Shakespeare wrote it, and controversially restored both an offstage death and a head on a pole borne in by Macduff. His efforts did not meet with universal acceptance. One critic remarked admiringly on the actor's decision to cut short what might have been his high moment:

> To relinquish the usual close, in which the death of Macbeth in his desperate fight with Macduff concentrates attention on the former, was a piece of self-sacrifice [...] that cannot well be overrated.[19]

Jonas Levy in *Lloyds Weekly London News* also praised the offstage death:

> We have heard many objections to 'bringing on the tyrant's head'; but in our opinion Mr Phelps has done well in adhering strictly to the author. We have no desire for a *regular picturesque* death.[20]

But as Sprague observes, 'the critics disagreed sharply as to the propriety of showing the head – and the business was not retained'.[21] Rosenberg describes some successful stagings which allowed Macbeth to be visible, fighting to the last, but then 'discharge[d] spectacularly into the void' to die, like Olivier in 1955 being driven up a long flight of stairs and then plummeting to his death over the battlements.[22] But a witness to the performance, Kenneth Tynan, was disappointed by the ending after Olivier's brilliance in Macbeth's final scene: '"Exeunt fighting" was a poor end for such a giant warrior. We wanted to see how he would die: and it was not he but Shakespeare who let us down.'[23] He felt, like Bradley, that an onstage death would elicit from the audience 'a rush of passionate admiration, and a glory of the greatness of the soul'.[24] In contrast to this, Godfrey Tearle as Macbeth was forced offstage to die in Anthony Quayle's production of 1949, and his head brought on by Macduff. When Ralph Richardson in 1952 was chased off the stage by Macduff to meet his end, the effect was deemed 'more ludicrous than tragic'.[25]

The handling of the play's conclusion may be related to the often-remarked-upon sense of disappointment experienced in the theatre, and attributed to some lowering of tension in the second part, after the heady excitement of the first part, culminating in the banquet scene.[26] Consequently, not only 4.3 but also the series of scenes after Lady Macbeth's sleepwalking have often been subject to pruning. The acting text prepared for Adelaide Ristori, printed with a parallel translation into Italian in 1866, provides an extreme example of this, no doubt in large part explained by the wish of the actress to retain as much of the audience's attention for Lady Macbeth as possible.[27] In her version, all the scenes featuring Malcolm's army are cut in their entirety; Macbeth's two scenes before the beginning of the battle are run together, Young Siward and all reference to him is cut, and even Macbeth and Macduff's final encounter is shortened. The play ends, uniquely, on Macduff's lines:

> I have no words;
> My voice is in my sword: thou bloodier villain
> Than terms can give thee out!
>
> (5.8.6–8)

After this Macduff is killed onstage, and Malcolm and his followers make a triumphal entrance during which 'Malcolm is raised on a shield' but without any dialogue. It is exceptional that so little stage time as this is allowed to the battle scenes, though Sprague refers to 5.2, where the Scots lords prepare for battle, as 'rarely acted'.[28] Garrick set the trend in this, perhaps, as Rosenberg suggest, to minimize 'implications that Macbeth was anything but an honorable murderer'.[29] The coming of Birnam Wood provided an opportunity for stage spectacle in the nineteenth century, particularly for Macready in 1837 and Phelps in 1860, but 'leafy screens' and all reference to them are cut in some twentieth-century productions such as Komisarjevsky's of 1933 and Trevor Nunn's of 1974.[30] Young Siward's part and his noble death have been regularly cut since Davenant, from Garrick onwards. Rosenberg again descried a wish 'to protect the nobler image of Macbeth', but suggested that Garrick lost more than he gained by doing this.[31] Perhaps nineteenth-century Macbeths, like Phelps, Charles Kean and Macready, who all cut Young Siward, may have shared this wish, but in the twentieth century and also more recently Young Siward's disappearance has served the interests of shortening and sharpening the play's ending rather than of glamorizing its protagonist. Ristori's reasons for abbreviating the battle scenes were personal, but ending the play with no more text after Macbeth's last line and death at the hands of Macduff was common practice in the days when a grand curtain line drew on thunderous applause: Charles Kean (1853), Edwin Booth (1868), Tyrone Power (1907), Frank Benson (1917/8) and many others ended productions in this way. One consequence of such truncation of Shakespeare's text is that the play becomes the personal tragedy of Macbeth; both any sense of restoration and restitution and any political ramifications are diminished.

But it is the case that the play's final moments can appear anticlimactic. The Folio does not assign a separate scene to the concluding forty-two lines, in which various loose ends are tied up: young Siward's death is reported, Macduff enters with Macbeth's head, and Malcolm is hailed king, rewards his followers and prepares for his coronation.[32] The concluding

formal speech in which Malcolm, often regarded as a comparatively secondary and colourless character, curtly dismisses
Macbeth and his lady as 'the dead butcher and his fiendlike
queen' diminishes the play's main characters and appears
reductive. One measure taken to deal with this problem was
reassigning Malcolm's speech to the more dramatically significant Macduff and cutting the line about the Macbeths (the Lee
Salmon acting edition, 1753).[33] Others have included cutting
most of Malcolm's speech (Kemble, Forbes-Robertson, Glen
Byam Shaw and many others) or creating a more dramatic
conclusion than the one provided in F. In earlier times the play
would often end either on Macbeth's last line, 'And damn'd be
he that first cries, "Hold, enough"' (Barry Sullivan, Edmund
Kean, Charles Kean, Macready) or the exclamation, 'Hail,
King of Scotland' (Phelps, Booth, Irving, Tyrone Power, Frank
Benson, and others). Other directors have cut the last scene so
as to include the acknowledgement of Malcolm as King, but
little more. 'All Hail, King of Scotland' provided a curtain line
for Macready (1853), Irving (189?) and Tree (1911). Anthony
Quayle's production for the RSC (1949) allowed Malcolm
just the first and last sentences of his final speech, then notes
in the promptbook: 'Quick curtain down'. Komisarjevsky
reorganized the ending so as to give Malcolm a few lines of
his last speech but to end with Macduff's claim, 'The time is
free', followed by a moment in which 'all salute the dead and
move down on to [the] apron stage'.[34] It is rare that the final
scene is included in its entirety, except in productions which
make a point of working with a very full text; one example is
Garrick, who even gave Macduff some additional lines (from
Davenant) to present Malcolm with Macbeth's sword and to
claim his own status as God's appointed revenger. Another,
three hundred years later, was Peter Hall's National Theatre
production of 1978, done in accordance with his views on
the unacceptability of cutting. But the play's last moments
can be amplified by extra-textual additions; for example, the
English Stage Company's production of 1990 made a political
point by concluding with Malcolm's coronation celebrated

with Scottish piping to the tune of 'O flower of Scotland', which was then drowned out by a band playing 'God save the king'.[35] Such stagings can have the effect of ironizing the ending, as for instance when the witches reappear. In Welles' production of 1936 the all-hailing of Malcolm was followed by a sinister moment when Hecate stepped forward with the line, 'Peace, the charm's wound up', creating what has been termed 'a pessimistic *da capo* ending'.[36] At several recent productions (Dominic Cooke 2004, Liverpool Everyman 2010, Globe 2010) the sisters themselves have reappeared, perhaps implying that, as Terry Eagleton provocatively suggested, they are 'the heroines of the piece'.[37]

The cutting and reshaping of the ending is a major component in the adjustment of the text of F to staging requirements at various periods, but the main area in the reshaping of the stage text over more than two centuries has been the witch scenes. The manner in which this was carried out, from Davenant to the later nineteenth century, affected the shape of the play in a very literal way, by greatly expanding the spectacular elements in the middle of it. While act 3, scene 6 – fifty lines of commentary by Lennox and a Lord – has been almost universally cut from the Smock Alley promptbook until the 1960s, the Hecate scene, 3.5, which has now all but vanished, was always staged. Garrick adopted Davenant's enlargement of it, with lines and music from Middleton's *The Witch,* and in his text it was followed immediately by a version of 4.1 enhanced with much extra witch business, more lines from *The Witch* and many more witches; this accounted for twice as much stage time as Shakespeare's scene. All these changes to the Folio derive from Davenant, whose version was so successfully staged at Dorset Garden in 1672, being, in Downes's description: 'drest in all it's Finery, as new Cloaths, new Scenes, Machines, as flyings for the Witches, with all the Singing and Dancing in it ... being in the nature of an Opera.'[38] In addition to the original three weird sisters, singing witches feature regularly in cast lists from the eighteenth to the later nineteenth centuries. One or more verses of the song indicated

in F only by the cue, 'Black spirits, etc.' in 4.1 are called for
from 'all the singing witches' in the 1753 Lee/Salmon text, in
Kemble, in Oxberry's text (1821), Charles Kean's text, Booth's
text, Irving's text and elsewhere.

Locke's music, specified on the title-page of Charles Kean's
acting edition (1853), for example, which had probably been
composed for the Davenant version,[39] was a regular accompa-
niment. The witches' presence in the play was also sometimes
enlarged by an extra scene including songs and dances, adapted
by Garrick from Davenant and placed at the end of 2.3, the
discovery of Duncan's murder. This was staged at least as late
as Charles Kean (1853). Phelps had attempted to break with
this tradition in his second production of the play at Sadler's
Wells in 1847, announcing that he would offer '*Macbeth* from
the original text, dispensing with the Singing Witches',[40] and
was applauded critically for his boldness. One reviewer who
supported the innovation remarked of the witch element that
'four short scenes, divided between three and sometimes four
individuals, make up the whole of this terrible machinery'.[41]
But the pressure of custom was too great, and in the cast
list for his production of 1858 five singing witches, three of
them men, were credited, and Locke's music reappeared. The
discerning Henry Morley, a professor at University College,
London, who attended a Phelps production of *Macbeth* in
1864, wished it could be acted 'for a few nights at least,
without Locke's music, and the corps of witches jigging to
Davenant's misfitting rhymes', but this was not to be for some
years.[42] Irving in 1888 regarded himself as an innovator by
having female witches, and aiming 'to divest [them] of that
semi-comic element which at one time threatened to obscure,
if not altogether to efface, their supernatural significance'.[43]
Since Davenant's time the witches had been played by male
actors as a comic turn.[44] Macklin in 1773 attempted to break
with this tradition and treat the witches seriously, as did
Kemble in 1794 in his staging of their scenes:

The scenes were all new, and the witches no longer wore

mittens, plaited caps, laced aprons, red stomachers, ruff, etc. (which was the dress of those weird sisters, when Mess. Beard, Champness, etc. represented them with Garrick's Macbeth) or any human garb, but appeared as preternatural beings, distinguishable only by the fellness of their purposes, and the fatality of their delusions.[45]

But neither Macklin, Kemble nor Irving attempted to pare down their parts, as Phelps had done, and Irving's production, like other landmark productions of the period, such as Kemble's of 1794 and Charles Kean's of 1853, made the spectacular effects of the combined scenes 3.5 and 4.1 central to its attractions. Kemble not only had a chorus of fifty or sixty singing witches, but also a group of children to represent the 'black spirits and white, / Red spirits and grey'.[46] Irving's Hecate was attended by sixty spirits, 'clad mystically in greenish white gauze' who performed to an 'exquisite choral setting of "Black spirits"'.[47] Such spectacle lengthened the playing time; despite heavy cutting of the text itself, productions would run to three hours or more. Probably the last major *Macbeth* to take this shape was that of Herbert Beerbohm Tree in 1911. He cut 4.2 and most of 4.3, also nearly fifty lines from 4.1; but he staged the Hecate material (including 3.5) elaborately, with extra witches, songs and dances and the appearance of a 'wraith-like horde' behind the Apparitions.[48] His staging was much admired, but not simply as spectacle; the witches were said to represent 'the psychic realities usually glimpsed only in dream and nightmare', and in the words of the reviewer for the *Daily Express*, contributed to the transformation of Macbeth into 'a dream play, as essentially unrealistic as Maeterlinck's Pelléas and Melisande'.[49]

The effect of the enlargement of this part of the play was more pronounced when, as regularly happened over a period of at least 100 years, the scene of the murder of Lady Macduff and her young son (4.2) was totally omitted, and the next scene heavily cut. The fourth act thus came to consist largely of 4.1, after which the narrative proceeded rapidly to the next theatrical highpoint: Lady Macbeth's sleepwalking.[50] We cannot know to what extent the Folio text represents what was actually staged when the play was first written, but there is no doubt that, with brief exceptions like the 1847 Phelps production, the distance between F and the staged text for much of the eighteenth and all of the nineteenth century was very considerable. In the late nineteenth century William Poel attempted to lessen it, and in 1927 claimed (not entirely accurately) that in his radical production of 1909 for the Elizabethan Stage Society, done 'in the Elizabethan manner', 'Lady Macduff made her appearance on the stage after more than two hundred years' absence'.[51] (He did however also include Hecate and three extra witches as her attendants, all dressed in masque costumes, the attendants representing the three Fates.)[52] Poel's desire to restore the text of F[53] was part of a wholesale wish to revolutionize the staging of Shakespeare, to rid the theatre of spectacular Shakespeare as represented by the productions of Irving and Tree, and to restore Elizabethan theatrical techniques. It became part of a larger movement in which the rise of so-called directors' theatre resulted in productions driven conceptually rather than by the need to showcase the skills of leading actors or the creation of spectacle for its own sake.

The fortunes of the witches in the twentieth and twenty-first centuries have been various. In the early part of the twentieth century there were attempts to diminish their roles. Komisarjevsky's radically expressionist production in 1933 cut their lines considerably in his attempt to demystify their roles; they were no longer supernatural beings but, in the opening scene, they are old women 'picking up souvenirs as the curtain rises' and later, fortune-tellers.[54] Tyrone Guthrie in 1934 cut the opening scene completely, aiming to refocus the play by getting rid of 'the implication that they are a governing influence of the tragedy'.[55] Stagings of 3.5 have been rare and exceptional in this period. Orson Welles in his so-called 'Voodoo *Macbeth*' of 1936, in which the Folio text is radically rearranged, reacted against current tendencies by expanding the role of Hecate, who, played by a male actor, appeared in six of the production's eight scenes and is a pervasive presence.[56] Mark Rylance, in a maverick production of 1995, included Hecate as, in the words of one reviewer, a 'drag lollipop lady', apparently in the belief that restoring the witch scenes regularly cut would lift the curse that has long hung over the play.[57] A better-justified restoration of Hecate was made by Peter Hall in his production of 1978. Hall in the mid-twentieth century typified a current view, following Poel, in his feeling that 'any cutting which alters or affects the theme of the play must be immoral' and that cutting should only be 'within speeches'.[58] His first *Macbeth* at Stratford in 1967/8 had minimal cutting of Hecate's part in 4.1. He had initially intended to include 3.5, but was obliged to cut it on account of staging difficulties. (Unusually, his promptbook marks no cuts at all for 4.3.) In his production for the National Theatre in 1978, Hall, to some extent guided by John Russell Brown, whom he acknowledged as a co-director, included all the Hecate material in 3.5 and 4.1. He did this because of a belief in the authenticity of 3.5 as Shakespearean, but also because he had a clear notion of what Hecate might represent:

> She gives metaphorical presence to God or, rather, anti-God. This is essential to the dramatic action, like the later Shakespearean masque world, the arrival of Jupiter or Diana [...] I think of Hecate and the cauldron scene as I think of the most potent manifestations of the masque in Inigo Jones and Ben Jonson, and that is no small thing.[59]

He believed that 4.1 should be staged as a masque or a 'show', comparing Shakespeare's stagecraft here with that in later plays such as *Cymbeline* and *The Tempest*, and hoped for it to show 'different levels of reality' in the play.[60] He chose a young and beautiful actress to play Hecate in his wish 'to make evil look as wholesome and innocent and good as possible'.[61] Hall's production was not well received. His intentions for the Hecate scenes were not generally understood, and they were thought intrusive by critics convinced that they were not Shakespeare's work. But D. J. Palmer, reviewing the production, albeit from an assuredly Middletonian standpoint, praised Hall's achievement. He admired the presentation of Hecate as 'a figure of radiant fair-haired beauty in a splendid blue-black gown [...] in contrast to the grotesquely bearded and ragged witches', and saw in 4.1 the staging of Hecate 'aloft' as a visual counterpart to the enthronement of Lady Macbeth at the top table in the banquet scene.[62]

Hall's production was played on the large stage of the Olivier Theatre without an interval. He managed to get it down to just over two-and-a-half hours, even with an almost complete text, but this was thought too long by disgruntled reviewers. In the nineteenth century productions regularly ran over three hours. Tree's (with a severely cut text) extended to four, but with fifteen scene changes and nearly an hour taken up in intervals, no one seems to have complained. Hall's production, however, had the misfortune to follow closely on the heels of Trevor Nunn's of 1976, also staged without an interval but on a small scale and in a small theatre, which seems to have created a model for the ideal *Macbeth*. Currently small-scale Macbeths tend to be preferred. Greg Doran's 1999 production at the Swan Theatre, Stratford-upon-Avon was so regarded; it ran without interval for less than two-and-a-quarter hours. Dominic Cooke's of 2004 was similar. But heavy cutting is often required to achieve such compression, as in Out of Joint's production (Max Stafford-Clark, 2004/5) and Cheek by Jowl (Declan Donnellan, 2009/10).

In his handling of Hecate, Hall had hoped to redefine the significance of the supernatural, but from the general critical response he seems to have been unsuccessful. However, the witches themselves are returning to productions of the later twentieth and early twenty-first centuries in new forms. Sometimes male actors again play the roles;[63] not uncommonly they are present in various scenes and guises throughout the play;[64] and they also reappear at the end, suggesting that the evil they represent has not been eradicated. In the most recent RSC production of 2011[65] they were played by children and their lines radically cut down (and adjusted where necessary, to identify them as 'the weird children'); they did not open the play, and they did not conjure. But they were present on many occasions, running screaming over the stage while the killing of Duncan is taking place, representing the murdered children of Lady Macduff, and bringing in the boughs of Birnam Wood. Reviewers commented on the sinister qualities they helped to create. As with Hall's beauteous Hecate, they seemed, in their embodiment of both innocence and duplicity, to stand for those opposites that are so disturbingly combined from the start in the play in the witches' formulation: 'Fair is foul and foul is fair'.

The staged text of *Macbeth*, then, continues to take new forms. This is not a process of evolution, but one which will never, in the nature of live theatre, end. While it may be possible to deduce from the long history of the staged text that some parts of the play have regularly been found problematic onstage, the reasons for this will vary according to all sorts of factors, including not just contemporary standards of taste and morality but also theatrical conditions and cultural norms prevalent at different times. The significance of the gap between stage and page can be variously evaluated; what is 'privileged by performance'[66] may, as it has been argued, conceal or misrepresent what can be discovered by reading the text, but not necessarily. This account of the staged text also raises the important question of whether there is such a thing as an 'essential *Macbeth*', and if so, how much deviation from F can be tolerated before its identity is lost. While William Winter's assertion in 1911 that 'not one of Shakespeare's plays has been subject to so much misdirected experiment [as *Macbeth*]'[67] implies the existence of a distinct standard, it is doubtful if anyone nowadays would attempt to define it.

Notes

1   Charles H. Shattuck, *The Shakespeare Promptbooks: A Descriptive Catalogue* (Urbana and London: University of Illinois Press, 1965).

2   The line was recognized as spurious by some playgoers at least as early as 1773, but it had a lasting appeal. See the discussion of the line by Arthur Colby Sprague, *Shakespeare and the Actors: The Stage Business in His Plays (1660–1905)*, (Cambridge, MA, 1945), pp. 228–9.

3   See G. Blakemore Evans ed., *Shakespearean Promptbooks of the Seventeenth Century*, 7 vols. (1960–89), vol. 5, and 'New Evidence on the Provenance of the Padua Promptbooks of Shakespeare's *Macbeth, Measure for Measure* and *The Winter's Tale*', *SB* 20 (1967), pp. 239–42. Evans had originally dated the promptbooks in the 1620s, but subsequent evidence suggested that a date in the 1640s was more likely.

4   Composed probably in the early 1660s though not published until 1674.

5   Blakemore Evans favours the latter end of this period.

6   Nonetheless, Garrick cut the Porter, the murders of Lady Macduff and her son, and much of Malcolm's self-accusation in 4.3. See Kalman Burnin, *David Garrick, Director* (1961), p. 103ff. On Garrick's cuts, see also Vanessa Cunningham, *Shakespeare and Garrick* (2008), p. 50ff.

7   *The Plays of David Garrick*, Harry William Pedicord and Frederick Louis Bergmann (eds), 3 vols. (1981), vol. 3, p. 398.

8   The Yale MS version of the play, which was not printed, also includes a six-line speech from Lennox to Malcolm in 5.2 on the evils of ambition. See Christopher Spencer ed., *Five Restoration Adaptations of Shakespeare* (Urbana: University of Illinois Press, 1965), p. 16.

9   Gentleman's comments on Garrick's *Macbeth* appear in his annotations to the text in Bell's acting edition of 1773. See *The Plays of David Garrick*, Harry W. Pedicord and Frederick L. Bergmann (eds) (1981), vol. 3, pp. 72–3. In this period a green baize carpet (the 'tragic carpet') was put out for death

scenes so that actors would not dirty their costumes on the bare boards.

10 Kemble published his text of *Macbeth* several times: 1794 (twice), 1803, 1814, 1818.

11 Paul Prescott, 'Doing all that becomes a man: The Reception and Afterlife of the Macbeth Actor, 1744–1889', *Shakespeare Survey* 57 (2004), p. 85. Prescott examines how ideals of masculinity influenced the portrayal of Macbeth by other actors such as Kemble, Kean, Macready and Irving.

12 A. R. Braunmuller ed., *Macbeth* (Cambridge, 1997), note on 5.3.19, and also supplementary note, p. 244.

13 Sprague, p. 237.

14 This was also the case in Dominic Cooke's production for the RSC in 2004. In Macready's production of 1846, Seyton also served as the Porter.

15 Quotation from Spencer, *Five Restoration Adaptations*.

16 Many editors from Pope onwards insert one. See the comments of Braunmuller, pp. 236, 249–50, and Nicholas Brooke ed., *Macbeth* (Oxford, 1990), p. 209.

17 See discussions of staging problems to do with the head in Sprague, pp. 279–80, and Marvin Rosenberg, *The Masks of Macbeth* (1978), pp. 651–2.

18 Sprague, 279, cites *The Theatrical Inquisitor*, November 1814, as objecting to the retention of the dying speech by Edmund Kean. I have found no references to its use onstage later than this. Macready, who first played Macbeth in 1820, did not use it (Dennis Bartholomeusz, *Macbeth and the Players* [1969], p. 169).

19 John Westlake Marston, *Our Recent Actors* (1888), quoted in Rosenberg, p. 647.

20 Quoted in W. May Phelps and John Forbes-Robertson, *The Life and Life-Work of Samuel Phelps* (1886), p. 100.

21 Sprague, p. 279.

22 Rosenberg, pp. 647–8. Other Macbeths who have died offstage include Maurice Evans (1941), Michael Redgrave (1947), Nicol Williamson (1974) and Ian McKellen (1976). McKellen,

discussing his performance, remarks: 'The death takes place offstage, which is presumably because Shakespeare wants the head brought back on.' See his account in *Shakespeare on Stage*, ed. Julian Curry (2010), pp. 147–69.

23 Kenneth Tynan, from *Curtains* (1961), quoted in William Shakespeare's *'Macbeth': A Sourcebook*, ed. Alexander Leggatt (2006), p. 109.

24 A. C. Bradley, *Oxford Lectures on Poetry* (1909), p. 77, quoted in Prescott, 'Doing all that becomes a man', p. 85.

25 John Wilders ed., *Shakespeare in Production: Macbeth* (2004), p. 214, quoting from a review in the *New Statesman*, 21 June 1952.

26 See Wilders, pp. 61–2. Ian McKellen, one of the most successful Macbeths of the twentieth century, praises his director, Trevor Nunn, for cuts made to the battle scenes so as to focus on Macbeth's dilemma, saying bluntly of the last act: 'It isn't very good' (*Shakespeare on Stage*, p. 147).

27 *Shakespeare's Tragedy of Macbeth Adapted Expressly for Madame Ristori and her Italian Dramatic Company*, trans. Giulio Carcano (1866). A contemporary playgoer, Henry Morley, observed that in Ristori's version, Macbeth was rendered very much subsidiary to his wife (Henry Morley, *Journal of a London Playgoer. From 1851–1866*) [1866], p. 186).

28 Sprague, p. 272.

29 Rosenberg, p. 592.

30 This is also the case in recent productions such as those by Cheek by Jowl (2009/10), the Globe (2010), and the Liverpool Playhouse (2011).

31 Rosenberg, p. 613.

32 Many editors, following Pope, create a separate scene at this point. See Braunmuller's comment, pp. 236, 249–50.

33 *The Historical Tragedy of Macbeth (Written originally by Shakespeare). Newly adapted to the Stage, with Alterations, as performed in the Theatre at Edinburgh* (Edinburgh: W. Cheyne, 1753).

34 SD from Komisarjevsky's promptbook (Shakespeare Centre, Stratford-upon-Avon).

35 Keith Parsons and Pamela Mason (eds), *Shakespeare in Performance* (London: Salamander, 1995), p. 129.

36 Dennis Kennedy, *Looking at Shakespeare: A Visual History of Twentieth Century Performance* (Cambridge: Cambridge University Press, 1993, 1996), p. 147.

37 Terry Eagleton, *William Shakespeare* (Oxford: Blackwell, 1986), 2. Rosenberg (pp. 654–5) gives several examples of foreign productions which have ended in this way.

38 John Downes, *Roscius Anglicanus* (1708), p. 33.

39 Though Robert E. Moore, 'The Music to Macbeth', *The Musical Quarterly* 47 (1961), p. 28, has some doubts about this.

40 W. May Phelps and John Forbes-Robertson, *The Life and Life-Work of Samuel Phelps* (London: Sampson Low, 1886), p. 96.

41 Ibid., p. 97.

42 Morley, *Journal of a London Playgoer*, 349.

43 From the Preface to the printed text as performed at the Lyceum in 1880, in *Sir Henry Irving. Theatre, Culture and Society. Essays, Addresses and Lectures*, ed. Jeffrey Richards (Keele: Ryburn Publishing, 1994), p. 255.

44 Sandra Clark. '*Macbeth* and the Weird Sisters', *Shakespeare Studies. The Shakespeare Society of Japan*, 46 (2008), pp. 62–76, 62ff.

45 W. C. Oulton, *The History of the Theatres*, 2 vols. (1796), vol. 2, p. 139, quoted in A. M. Nagler, *A Source Book in Theatrical History* (New York: Dover Publications, 1952), p. 413.

46 Joseph W. Donohue, 'Kemble's Production of *Macbeth* (1794)', *Theatre Notebook* 21 (1966/7), pp. 163–74, 69.

47 Rosenberg, p. 508. The largest number recorded was in Phelps' production of 1864, which boasted a chorus of 100 singing witches (*Daily News*, 4 November 1864).

48 Michael Mullin, 'Strange Images of Death: Sir Herbert Beerbohm Tree's *Macbeth*, 1911', *Theatre Survey* 17.2 (1976), pp. 125–42, 134.

49 Mullin, p. 135.

50 The only exception to this was the eccentric text produced for
    Adelaide Ristori, which cut all of 4.1 and 4.2 as well as much
    of 4.3.

51 Bartholmeusz, pp. 220–1. Phelps had in fact restored part
    of 4.2, including Lady Macduff, though not her son, in
    productions of 1847 and 1850 (Robert Speaight, *William
    Poel and the Elizabethan Revival* [London: Heinemann, 1954],
    p. 187).

52 Edward M. Moore, 'William Poel', *SQ* 23.1 (1972), pp. 21–36,
    32.

53 At least in the case of *Macbeth*. He was not always consistent
    here. See Moore, pp. 32–4.

54 Komisarjevsky's promptbook. For an account of his production,
    see Michael Mullin, 'Augures and Understood Relations:
    Theodore Komisarjevsky's *Macbeth*', *Educational Theatre
    Journal* 26.1 (1974), pp. 20–30.

55 Guthrie's programme note for the production, quoted in
    Bartholomeusz, p. 238. Bartholomeusz notes that Guthrie
    was influenced by the views of Harley Granville-Barker, who
    believed that the opening scene was not by Shakespeare.

56 The text is reproduced with discussion in Richard France ed.,
    *Orson Welles on Shakespeare. The W.P.A. and Mercury Theater
    Playscripts* (New York: Cambridge University Press, 1990).

57 Paul Taylor, *Independent*, 27 September 1995.

58 Claris Glick, 'William Poel: His Theories and Influence', *SQ*
    15.1 (1964), pp. 15–25, 23.

59 Peter Hall, 'Directing *Macbeth*', in *Focus on 'Macbeth'*, ed.
    John Russell Brown (London: Routledge & Kegan Paul, 1982),
    pp. 231–48, 242, 244. Hall gives his reasons for believing 3.5 to
    be Shakespearean on p. 243. Russell Brown, in correspondence
    with Hall about the production, compares the Hecate speech
    in 3.5 with that of the Duke in *Measure for Measure* at the
    end of 3.1: 'The speech itself is undeniably powerful (like the
    sudden clarity of the Duke in *Measure for Measure* [...] or the
    unexpected advent of Hymen in *As You Like It*.' (From a memo
    in the National Theatre Archives.)

60 Hall, 'Directing *Macbeth*', p. 245.

61 Hall's note to the designer John Bury (National Theatre Archives).

62 D. J. Palmer, '*Macbeth* at the National Theatre, 1978', *Critical Quarterly* 20.3 (1978 v), pp. 71–5.

63 As at a production in 2001 staged at Ludlow Castle, directed by James Roose-Evans, with three tall black shaven-headed actors in the roles, and at the Liverpool Everyman in 2011, directed by Gemma Bodinetz, where one of the witches was a boy in drag, who also doubled as Fleance.

64 As at the Almeida production directed by John Caird in 2005, at Rupert Goold's production in 2007/8, at Conall Morrison's RSC production in 2007 and at the Globe, directed by Lucy Bailey in 2011.

65 Directed by Michael Boyd as the inaugural production of the reopened Royal Shakespeare Theatre at Stratford-upon-Avon.

66 Harry Berger Jr., 'Text against Performance in Shakespeare: The Example of *Macbeth*', in *The Power of Forms in the English Renaissance*, ed. Stephen Greenblatt (Norman, OK: Pilgrim Books, 1982), pp. 49–80, 73.

67 William Winter, *Shakespeare on the Stage*. First Series (New York: Moffat, Yard and Co., 1911), p. 473.

10

Raising the Violence while Lowering the Stakes: Geoffrey Wright's Screen Adaptation of *Macbeth*

Philippa Sheppard

Australian filmmaker Geoffrey Wright, who in 1992 directed the notoriously graphic *Romper Stomper*, in 2006 adapted Shakespeare's tragedy *Macbeth* for the screen. In an interview on the DVD, he claims that his film is no more violent than Shakespeare's play, but this is disingenuous. By shifting the setting to present-day Melbourne, and transforming the cast from kings and thanes to drug-smuggling gang-members, he has invited the inclusion of more violence than in the original, while simultaneously excluding meditation on the state and on the soul. Wright does this in three ways: he strips his protagonists of any redeeming characteristics; he shows us violent scenes that in Shakespeare's play occur offstage, *and* adds new ones; and he cuts almost all the speeches in which Macbeth reflects on his leadership, his gradual loss of humanity, and his eternal damnation. In sum, Wright's approach is reductive, narrowing the rich Jacobean variety of theme and ambiguity of character so that it fits the conventions of a streamlined gangster film. The point of this essay is not to fault Wright for lack of fidelity to Shakespeare's text. Obviously, if all an adaptation entailed was a slavish illustration of an existing text, few directors would embrace the task. Rather, this essay seeks to evaluate whether or not Wright's *Macbeth* is *in itself* a successful piece of work, as cultural history has deemed Shakespeare's to be.

In adapting a Shakespeare play for the screen, a director will naturally make much of scenes that are inherently visual and downplay those that are wordy or static. Almost invariably, in Wright's estimation, the film-worthy scenes in Shakespeare's *Macbeth* (admittedly one of his bloodiest plays) are the violent ones, whereas scenes boasting humour (the Porter scene), shared love, religious or political debate, rarely make the cut. It is inevitable, perhaps, that in the transition from a stage play to the more visual medium of film, a medium that has an almost magnetic pull towards realistic effects, the violence in the play should loom even larger. What is significant, however, is that in Wright's version, violence itself becomes the story, replacing Shakespeare's more psychologically and intellectually profound, and therefore satisfying, narrative. This was an accusation made against Roman Polanski's 1971 film; Pauline Kael commented that 'slaughter is the star'.[1] Wright's film, however, makes Polanski's look like a Sunday school picnic. Viewing Wright's *Macbeth* highlights the brilliant qualities of Shakespeare's play by their complete absence in the film. Shakespeare's *Macbeth* traces the moral deterioration and self-damnation of two people with potential, and charts the fate of a nation from rightful rule to usurpation to rightful rule restored. It is Macbeth's nuanced and imaginative reflections on his own decline that elevate the plot to tragedy in the grand style. Of course, the chronological and cultural primacy of Shakespeare's work unavoidably colours the spectator's judgement. If the viewer has any prior knowledge of the source material, it becomes virtually impossible to assess an adaptation entirely on its own merits. Graham Holderness sternly declared that evaluating 'a film version against a conception of its "original" is, since Shakespeare did not make films, a meaningless procedure'.[2] With this warning in mind, I will be assessing Wright's film with reference to several other screen adaptations.

Given that Wright reduces Shakespeare's dialogue to its barest bones, and is clearly more interested in the violent actions than in the characterization or philosophy of the play, one cannot help wondering why he chose to base his film on Shakespeare's tragedy rather than writing his own film about Melbourne gangsters. From the interviews cited here, it does not seem as if Wright had any intention of satirizing or degrading the play; rather, he speaks as if he were responding to what he thinks is essential to the play itself: an exploration of violence. Is it possible, however, to explore anything with any profundity while using so few words? Wright cuts Macbeth's musings on the effects his violent actions have had on him. Is showing images of violence again and again an 'exploration'? After watching Wright's film, the spectator could come away with little more than the obvious conclusion, likely held before watching the movie, that 'violence is reprehensible' – or, more disturbingly, seduced by the notion that 'violence is power'. What, then, does such a film add to our society's discourse on the subject? If the response is 'nothing', then is such a revelling in violent images a kind of pornography?

Wright may have chosen to call his gangster film *Macbeth*, and to maintain the original language, to exploit the cultural capital of Shakespeare. He has selected the one play that most people have studied at school – it is arguably even more familiar territory than *Hamlet* or *Romeo and Juliet*. However, his attempt to capitalize on the fame of the play obviously backfired, as the film grossed only $9,613 in the United States[3] and received very poor reviews. The box office failure may be partially attributed to its 'Restricted' rating, and the fact that it opened in the US on only *one* screen, so there was little chance of the film gaining attention through word-of-mouth, despite the film's sensationalism, on which Wright was banking.

When one examines both the history of Wright as a director and his own words about his *Macbeth*, it becomes clear that he has a fetishistic fascination with guns, daggers, blood and guts. His previous films, *Romper Stomper, Metal Skin*[4] and *Cherry Falls*,[5] are blood-saturated, and by his own admission, Wright is drawn to characters 'who approach life like a head-on collision'.[6] His leading actor, Sam Worthington, revealed in the DVD interview: 'Geoff pitched it [*Macbeth*] to me as the most violent Australian film ever made and he wanted it to get banned.' Wright, then, may have seized on Shakespeare's play because of the opportunities to film violent scenes while still maintaining a veneer of artistry.[7]

The effects of Wright's criminalization of the leads

By casting Duncan as a gang chieftain, responsible for violent crimes, Wright has changed the nature of Macbeth's own transgression. He is, of course, by no means the first director to have made this transformation – although in an interview, speaking of the various routes to update Shakespeare, he appears unaware of this: 'You can take the corporate model or the gangster model and I haven't seen the latter.'[8] Ken Hughes in his 1955 *Joe Macbeth*, William Reilly in his 1990 *Men of Respect* and Vishal Bhardwaj in his 2003 *Maqbool* all adopted a gangster setting, with similar effects. In Shakespeare's play, Macbeth violates all kinds of taboos in murdering Duncan: Duncan is Macbeth's king, and benevolent and wise in his office; he is Macbeth's houseguest whom he should protect; and Duncan is a venerable kinsman who has recently showered Macbeth with blessings. Macbeth in Shakespeare's play acts out of unadulterated ambition; Duncan in no way deserves his fate. Shakespeare rendered the contrast between Duncan and Macbeth even starker than he found it in Holinshed,[9] by adding to Duncan's virtues and neglecting to mention Macbeth's historical claim to the throne. In Wright's film, and in the other gangster adaptations listed, Duncan is one criminal lowlife and Macbeth another. How, then, can the audience feel truly aggrieved at Duncan's annihilation and Macbeth's descent into evil? Wright's *Macbeth* is thus a gangster film, not a tragedy. Gone is the catharsis of tragedy because there is almost no sense of lost potential. It is clear that Shakespeare was aware of this Aristotelian criterion for tragedy, as his contemporary, Sir Philip Sidney, writes of it in his *Defence of Poetry* (1595).[10] In fact, Sidney refers to Aristotle nine times. About tragedy, Aristotle wrote:

> Nor, again, should the fall of a very bad man from prosperous to adverse fortune be represented: because, though such a subject may be pleasing from its moral tendency, it will produce neither pity nor terror. For our pity is excited by misfortunes undeservedly suffered, and our terror by some resemblance between the sufferer and ourselves.[11]

While Shakespeare's Macbeth by the conclusion deserves his suffering, certainly in the first half of the play we pity him, because he has so recently been like ourselves, and because initially he merited some admiration. Furthermore, we are aware that as a king of his time, and even of Shakespeare's, he is not unusually evil in offing his political opponents. In championing the tragic genre, Sidney writes that 'with stirring the affects of admiration and commiseration, [tragedy] teacheth the uncertainty of this world, and upon how weak foundations gilden roofs are builded'.[12] Of course, a contemporary film director is unlikely to have an agenda to teach wisdom and humility, as Sidney is claiming (perhaps largely to win his case) that Elizabethan poets had. Obviously, no playwright or director is bound to observe Aristotle's rules for tragedy, but these rules remain compelling observations on the ways in which representing certain patterns of human action affect those who watch them. 'The affects of admiration and commiseration' Sidney describes are not merely pedagogical tools, but also an effective means of achieving audience satisfaction, and that, presumably, is something which interests contemporary directors also.

In Shakespeare's drama, Macbeth is introduced to us as a valiant and loyal soldier, defending his homeland against a Norwegian lord supported by rebel thanes (1.2.31). Granted, in the original, Macbeth is portrayed as a ferocious killer – we are given the nasty detail of his unseaming Macdonwald 'from the nave to th' chops' (1.2.22), and as Michael L. Hays points out, Macbeth forgoes chivalric niceties before he fights.[13] However, we do not *see* any of this onstage, and that is a critical difference. In Wright's film, we are shown Macbeth's grisly handiwork. Shakespeare's Macbeth may be a formidable soldier, suggesting his ease with shedding blood, but there was and is a distinction between killing in defence of your country (a culturally sanctioned act) and murdering for money (a criminal act).

After the credits, Wright's Macbeth is first properly introduced escorting a suitcase of cocaine to an Asian gang, and then mowing this rival gang down when they seize both drugs and money. There is nothing remotely heroic about his acts of violence except that he shows little fear. As *Variety* reviewer Richard Kuipers points out, 'the initial heroism' is 'critical to making grand tragedy of his road to ruin'.[14] However, a sense of tragedy is possible without a specific military sort of heroism; two other recent adaptations of *Macbeth* open with Macbeth as a cook. Admittedly, the fate of a nation does not rest on these cooks' actions, but in each case, the Macbeth character is singled out as special in his particular context, which grants the audience a sense of his potential. A restaurant is a particularly resonant place to set an adaptation of *Macbeth*, not only because of the dominance of food imagery (as discussed by Katherine Knowles in her fascinating article 'Appetite and Ambition: The Influence of Hunger in *Macbeth*'[15]), but also because a professional kitchen is an obvious place to find strange ingredients, cauldrons, sharp knives and pools of blood. Long before these restaurant adaptations, Ionesco highlighted the connection between appetite and ambition in his 1972 play *Macbett*.[16]

Billy Morrissette's 2001 dark comedy *Scotland, PA*[17] shifts the setting to a burger joint in the imaginary small town of Scotland, Pennsylvania in the 1970s. The leading couple are underachievers. Thirty-somethings Patricia (Maura Tierney) and Joe Mcbeth (James Le Gros) flip burgers at Duncan's fast-food restaurant. (Fast food and a certain hamburger chain also loom large in Rick Miller's *MacHomer*.) Yet Joe Mcbeth is distinguished from the other small-town denizens, initially by his ability to rid the restaurant of unruly food-slinging customers in a mock-battle scene, and later with his ideas, deemed brilliant by his wife and fellow burger-flipper, Banko (Kevin Corrigan). Mcbeth thinks the restaurant should offer small, fried, breaded pieces of chicken with dipping sauce and have a travelling van which serves fries. Morrissette here, with the benefit of hindsight, suggests his Mcbeth is prescient by predicting trends which characterize the current fast-food industry. Pat Mcbeth also has something resembling high status in Scotland, PA, as she is considered the town beauty. Mcbeth is regarded as fortunate, not only for being married to the local belle, but also because she is shown to be loyal to him when propositioned by other men; the couple are clearly passionately in love. Pat and Joe Mcbeth are thus admired and reasonably happy at the beginning of the film, fulfilling at least some of the Aristotelian and Shakespearean criteria for tragic heroes. They begin the film with something of value to lose.

The Macbeth couple in the brilliant 2003 BBC *Shakespeare Retold* adaptation, written by Peter Moffat, have even more to lose. Joe Macbeth, wonderfully played by James MacAvoy, is the head chef in one of the top Glasgow restaurants; his wife,

Ella (Keeley Hawes) is the *maître d'*. Duncan (Vincent Regan) owns the restaurant, and hosts a popular cooking show in which he prepares recipes sometimes stolen from Joe. Joe's wife resents the fame and attention Duncan receives as she believes her husband is the real culinary genius, and she goads him into killing Duncan when he stays the night after his boozy celebration of the restaurant gaining three Michelin stars. At the beginning of the film, it is clear that the Macbeths have a degree of happiness: they are passionate about their work and each other. After the murder of Duncan, Macbeth suffers an identity crisis, much as in Shakespeare's play. His wife Ella observes that she doesn't know what he is thinking any more, and asks him where the old Joe is. He answers: 'Who is that?... The guy who puts everything he has into cooking the best food he can, or the man who stabs people in their sleep?' Both directors in these adaptations have managed to keep the stakes high enough that the audience is moved by the characters' reversal of fortune.

As highlighted in these two adaptations, often in production the other point in the tragic trajectory is the sense of great potential in the couple's marriage. Shakespeare's couple begin the play eager to share their thoughts with one another. They constantly use endearments, and they comfort each other when the strain of their increasingly violent lifestyle becomes too much. They have been cited as one of Shakespeare's most affectionate married couples.[18] Certainly their marriage is portrayed as passionate in Roman Polanski's 1971 film. Not so in Wright's film. In their second scene together, Worthington's Macbeth strokes and kisses his wife, and she is utterly unresponsive. Victoria Hill, who plays Lady Macbeth and co-wrote the screenplay, reveals the film's interpretation in the DVD interview: 'The marriage that she's in is falling apart and there's a lot of resentment towards her husband.' In other words, they are the dysfunctional couple so typical of contemporary film. Worthington's Macbeth is suffering from unrequited love, the one small grain of potential Wright allows him. But even this leads to violence, as Worthington reveals in the same interview: 'Our spin on it is that all he wants is love from his wife [...] if you're going to stand in his way from getting that loving, you're dead. It's as simple as that.' Wright also discusses the influence Lady Macbeth wields over her husband. He credits her with giving Macbeth the notion that he is an Alpha Male: 'Then he realizes he's quite good at it [power-broking] when she begins to fade.'[19] Amanda Kane Rooks chooses to focus on this 'alleged dangerous sexual power of women' in the film.[20]

Wright's Macbeths are damaged people from the outset. They are not only drug and alcohol addicts, locked in a miserable marriage, but they have recently lost their only child as a consequence of some negligence on Lady Macbeth's part, as Hill mentions in the DVD interview. (The Macbeths' childless state has long been an issue for investigation, from Knights onwards.[21] Several recent productions on stage and screen have used the dead child as a source for creating an eerie atmosphere.[22]) Their mental health is fragile: Macbeth hallucinates about witches, while Lady Macbeth is depressive. Macbeth assumes she has killed herself when, in their second scene, he finds her asleep in her bath. Perhaps she has made previous attempts. In contrast, Shakespeare's Lady Macbeth in the first two acts seems vibrant and strong. Shakespeare's Macbeths have much to lose: a loving marriage (in many productions), esteem in their community, and their immortal souls. Wright's Macbeths have lost everything before the movie even starts – they are hollow people. This gives the film no emotional trajectory. Wright's efforts to make the tragedy more realistic and timely thus backfire. In Shakespeare's play, it is because they were formerly unsullied people that the murders of Duncan, Banquo and Macduff's family unhinge the Macbeths. For Wright's couple, murder is just business as usual. Their moral descent is shallow: they betray fellow gang-members. Is guilt from this betrayal enough to destroy two hardened criminals? This same problem besets the other gangster adaptations of *Macbeth* listed above. In each case, the Macbeth character rises in status as a result of coolly murdering members of a rival gang. The ethical slide is just a matter of turning on members of your own gang – a question of disloyalty. Is it enough for an audience to care? Certainly *Joe Macbeth*[23] and *Men of Respect*[24] were critical and box-office failures, and *Maqbool*[25] did poorly in the box office also, which seems to imply it was not enough. The *Time Out Film Guide* acknowledges *Joe Macbeth*'s reputation as 'a total disaster' and *Men of Respect* grossed only $139,155 in the USA.[26] Interestingly, as if in recognition of the difficulty of producing a successful adaptation of *Macbeth*[27] with lowered, gangster stakes, two new adaptations of *Macbeth* (both released in 2012), the Caribbean film *Macbett* directed by Aleta Chappelle and the English-German-Austrian co-production video of *Macbeth* directed by Daniel Coll, return to a royal setting, the stakes restored to the fate of a nation.

Wright has also changed Macbeth's motivation. Shakespeare's Macbeth is driven to murder Duncan by his own and his wife's ambition for the throne. Wright's Macbeth kills Duncan to save his wife from suicidal despair. In the film, Lady Macbeth seems numb, almost catatonic, only coming alive when plotting to replace Duncan with Macbeth.

The effects of Wright's additional violence

Shakespeare opens the tragedy with the weird sisters' short dialogue in which they prepare to meet with Macbeth. Wright's interpretation of this scene is quite successful, but, typically, more violent. Shakespeare's witches just talk; Wright's witches, nubile uniformed schoolgirls, desecrate gravestones. They gleefully poke out the eyes of stone angels and spray them with red paint so they appear, Gloucester-like, to be bleeding from their eye sockets. Hill reveals in the DVD interview that in this interpretation, the witches are

entirely figments of Macbeth's imagination. This again has
the effect of making Macbeth seem lost from the beginning.
In Shakespeare's play, the witches are real. Banquo sees them
too. The evil starts off being outside Macbeth – he must invite
it in, an act of free will. In the contemporary film, the evil is
inside Macbeth from the outset. Also, Macbeth's fantasies
about these sexy weird sisters, including a nude *ménage à
quatre* later in the film, seem to render his primary motivation
as articulated by the actors – to regain his wife's love – more
uncertain.

In Shakespeare's second scene, a battlefield report is
delivered to the King. The blood on the injured messenger
and his description are the audience's only access to the
offstage violence. In Wright's version, the gang battle is fully
realized, and filmed in a way that glorifies violence. Duncan's
band walk towards the rendezvous in a line, clad in trendy
jackets, with an upbeat instrumental rock soundtrack playing,
reminiscent of Quentin Tarantino's *Reservoir Dogs*.[28] When
a hidden sniper is suddenly heard emerging from an elevator,
everyone starts shooting, and a high-pitched, synthesized
screaming sound is added to the soundtrack. The scene is
gory and fast-paced, and Macbeth seems tough, powerful
and cool as he wields his gun. When the battle ends, only
a couple of men are left standing, the hand-held camera
panning over the others, now corpses, crumpled in pools of
blood.

The next scene, only reported in Shakespeare, which
Wright chooses to film, is the execution of Cawdor – an
easy scene to excise. The audience only needs to know that
Duncan has been too trusting, and that with Cawdor's death,
Macbeth inherits his estate, fulfilling the witches' prophecy.
Wright shows us Cawdor, miserably tied up and then shot,
his blood splattering his executioner. Cawdor is such a minor
character that his death elicits no emotion, so why show it
unless the intention is to squeeze the play for every last drop
of violence?

Despite his up-to-the-minute setting, Wright chooses to

have Macbeth murder Duncan with the guards' daggers, not with their guns and silencers. His camera fetishistically zooms in on each gleaming dagger as Macbeth's hand extracts it from the guards' pockets. In Shakespeare, the murder of Duncan takes place offstage. In the film, Duncan wakes up and stares at Macbeth before he murders him. Duncan then takes an inordinately long time to die, so that Macbeth needs to plunge his knife in repeatedly, leaving the bed a mass of blood. Wright chooses a canted frame and low-angle camera which looks up to Macbeth, so that the audience shares Duncan's ghastly, dying point of view.

Macbeth's murder of the guards, which again is only reported in the play, is shown in the film, even though the guards are cameo roles in whom the audience takes minimal interest. The murder of Banquo, shown in the play, is also enacted in the film, and again, Wright chooses to forgo the convenience of gun and silencer for the sanguinary dagger. Moreover, Banquo's ghost tries to garrotte Macbeth at the banquet.

In Shakespeare's play, only Macduff's son's murder is shown onstage, but Wright chooses to display Lady Macduff garrotted at length against her fridge, which bears the typical suburban decoration of magnets and a family photo. Geoffrey Wright commented on this choice in a web interview:

> The murder of Macduff's family looks a lot more brutal in contemporary terms than if it had been shot in a period way. It's a good way to remind the audience that the violence in the film isn't ceremonial or symbolic, it's a representation of 'real' brutality. The period costumes can 'protect' or insulate an audience from the horror of the story, but the contemporary look makes it appear to be something more immediate, much closer to 'home' and happening to people who look like 'us'.[29]

Again, in this interview, Wright avoids any revelation of his aim, confessed to his leading actor, to titillate his audience with violence. Certainly, he permitted his marketing team to sell the film using the typical attractions of 'babes' and guns. In the trailer, Lady Macduff appears with a frequency out of proportion to her small role in the film, because she is played by a pretty blonde. For the same reason, the trailer also features Malcolm's girlfriend, who has a tiny role in the film. The violent and sexy images are interspersed with the words POWER, MURDER and REVENGE in bold lettering. Trailers are characteristically and necessarily blunter than the films they promote, but this trailer was a fairly accurate representation of the film's substance.

In Shakespeare's play, Lady Macbeth's suicide is represented by the offstage screams of her ladies-in-waiting and the report of a messenger. In Wright's film, Macbeth finds his wife lying dead in her bloody bath after she has slit her wrists. Again, Wright peddles a disturbing blend of sex and violence. Her white, naked body is beautiful floating in the red water, and it is not the first time the audience has seen it.

The film does boast occasional flashes of wit. Sam Worthington's Macbeth wryly acknowledges the original play shortly before he meets his end by donning a black leather kilt and performing an impromptu jig for his baffled bodyguard. Earlier, Birnam Wood came to Dunsinane in the clever modern parallel form of a truck bearing lumber. Perhaps Wright was influenced here by Tom Stoppard's play *Cahoot's Macbeth*[30] (London, 1979) in which the Czech main characters are former professional actors who are forbidden to perform publicly, and have had to take on menial jobs. They are mounting a private performance of *Macbeth* as part of the Living Room Theatre form of protest. Their Shakespearean performance is interrupted by the entrance of a police inspector, who interrogates the performers on their act of subversion against a repressive state. The actors protest by making a stage out of lumber that has arrived in a truck – Birnam wood. The inspector retaliates by building a wall across the proscenium opening.

The prophecy of Birnam Wood coming to Dunsinane seems to have been a source of creativity to many of the adapters of *Macbeth*, perhaps because it is seen as a difficult reality to swallow for a modern audience. Barbara Garson's play *Macbird* (1966),[31] satirizing Lyndon Johnson's rise to the US Presidency using Shakespeare's tragedy as a vehicle, has the riots of 1966 as a march of 'burning wood' on Washington. In *Scotland, PA,* Birnam Wood comes to Dunsinane when Pat Mcbeth dons a new outfit adorned with a pattern of bare black branches. The Canadian one-man show, *MacHomer,* by Rick Miller (Montreal, 2005), is upfront about the way in which hewing down a forest stretches a contemporary audience's credulity:

Ross: Why ruin a perfectly good forest? What kind of environmental message would we be sending our children?
Willie: It's in the script, man.
Ross: Script, schmipt. We've mangled it this far, let's go all the way! You're a stereotypical Scotsman, do you have your golf clubs on you?

Ross then throws a golf club through the castle window where, offstage, it strikes Lady MacHomer on the head, killing her. When MacHomer demands his wife's cause of death, he is told: 'A Burn'Em Wood.'[32]

Instead of Shakespeare's final sword duel between Macduff and Macbeth, Wright has them slash at each other with broken bottles and engage in a brutal fist fight, throughout which Macduff's face is a mask of blood. Wright then adds a scene in which Fleance follows the injured Macbeth up to his bedroom to finish him off, but ends up killing the luckless maid who surprises him instead. The witches are truly prescient – Fleance is heading for gang lord status. This scene ends the film in as dark a way as possible, suggesting that the next generation will continue the meaningless slaughter perpetuated by their fathers. Malcolm, who is often performed as representing the restitution of order, both political and spiritual, in Shakespeare's tragedy, here grins wickedly at the corpses of Macbeth and his wife. This dark interpretation of Fleance and Malcolm was also a feature of *Men of Respect*, and obviously fits with the gangster aesthetic. It makes for a certain monotony of tone, however.

It is clear from the loving shots of weapons, the blending of 'babes' and blood, and the interpretation of Macbeth as a kind of 'rock star' revealed in the DVD, that the message underpinning the film is that violence is power, and power is 'cool'. Wright in two different interviews articulates this:

> [*Macbeth* is] about power: we're all interested in the Alpha chimp, aren't we? We might be the Beta chimp or the Gamma chimp, working for the Alpha chimp, but human strategy is hard wired to the use and abuse of power. Most people can handle a lack of power, but very, very few of us can handle a lot of power. We're not very good at it. And a lot of Alpha males fail; they can get there, but they can't keep it. And Macbeth is the classic flawed Alpha male.[33]

Alpha chimps achieve their supremacy over other chimps through displays of aggression and violence. While not necessarily the largest physical specimen, the Alpha chimp is usually best at creating a threatening impression, posturing. In a separate interview, Wright expresses his sense that being a skilful killer is what transforms a man into the Alpha Male: 'Macbeth is a difficult character because he has to change from a hen-pecked husband to a tyrant. He has to develop a sense of confidence that enables him to go so far with the killing.'[34] In Shakespeare's play too, Macbeth gains power and status through killing, but once the killing becomes criminal rather than sanctioned, his position is precarious. All the killing in Wright's film is criminal.

Shakespeare had valid reasons to report most of the carnage. Staging murder is challenging. If realistic effects are desired, fake blood has to be provided, possibly staining costumes. Then there is the awkwardness of the actor's breathing when he is supposed to be dead, and the necessity of moving his body offstage. Furthermore, Shakespeare's awareness of the Classical prohibition against showing violence onstage may have restrained him. In contrast, Wright, working in a visual medium with a different set of conventions, cannot rely on reports all the time – his audience would feel cheated and his film might well be dull. At the same time, he consistently opts to show violence even when the victim is a minor character, uninteresting to the audience. We need not have seen the deaths of Cawdor, the guards, or the murderers. These are not characters in whom we have much emotional investment. Why choose to show these deaths instead of allowing Macbeth some of his speeches? Wright cut the dialogue radically, thus losing what many have found compelling about the play: the downward psychological spiral of the lead characters, and the disquisitions about effective rule and eternal judgement. Naturally, the latter two may inspire less interest in a contemporary audience than a Jacobean one, but the former would only contribute to the 'character arc' much promoted by screenwriting gurus.

The effect of Wright's dialogue cuts

Successful film adaptations generally allow images to do more of the work than dialogue, but Wright's cuts strip the play of what makes it emotionally and intellectually satisfying. Shakespeare's Macbeth has eleven speeches in which he reflects on his actions. These speeches are characterized by a genuine anxiety about his identity and eternal destination. As G. K. Hunter observed:

> As a crime-does-not-pay story [the play] is less concerned with the uncovering of the crime to others than with the uncovering of the criminal *to himself*. The play spreads out from our interest in the hero [...] a man obsessed by his

relation to those criminal tendencies that are so universal that we best describe them by speaking of 'evil'.[35]

Macbeth uncovers the truth about himself to himself through his speeches, which Wright slashes or cuts altogether. Macbeth is worried from the start about the way the killing will affect him: 'I dare do all that may become a man; / Who dares do more is none' (1.7.46–7). Directly after murdering Duncan, he says: 'To know my deed 'twere best not know myself' (2.2.71). In the opening acts of the play, he is alert to the implications of his actions, and those of others. We watch as the number of murders slowly undoes him. He is unable to sleep; he stops communicating with his wife; and finally, he is so benumbed that his only reaction to her death is: 'She should have died hereafter. / There would have been a time for such a word' (5.5.17–18). Shakespeare thus builds into his play Macbeth's gradual moral destruction. He ends the play having lost his honour, his love, his friends, his peace of mind, and his immortal soul.

These eleven speeches give us the sense of Macbeth's tragic 'what might have been'. When he speaks, we are conscious of his febrile imagination and intelligence. He first reacts to the witches by debating the moral implications of internalizing their prophecies: 'This supernatural soliciting / Cannot be ill, cannot be good' (1.3.129f.). Wright cuts this speech. Macbeth in his next soliloquy weighs the pros and cons of killing Duncan: 'If it were done when 'tis done, then 'twere well / It were done quickly …' (1.7.1–26). He here discovers that the only motivation he has for killing Duncan is ambition, the satisfaction of which is not worth the loss of his soul. Wright maintains only a few lines.

Of the famous dagger speech, Wright keeps only six of the thirty lines, thus reducing the vividness of Macbeth's gothic imagination. When he returns to his wife after dispatching Duncan, Shakespeare's Macbeth frets over his inability to say 'Amen' and anticipates his future insomnia. Wright maintains only two of these twenty lines (2.2). As Robert Miola convincingly argues, Macbeth's 'desire to say "Amen" testifies to his goodness, to his deep and deeply denied need for grace and blessings'.[36] This reminder of his goodness, at the moment when he has thrown it away, is an essential ingredient for tragedy. Furthermore, Wright excises completely Macbeth's two musings on his own sense of insecurity and impermanence: 'To be thus is nothing / But to be safely thus' (3.1.49f.), and 'We have scorched the snake, not killed it' (3.2.15f.). He cuts most of Macbeth's expressions of anguish over Fleance's escape (3.4.20f.) and all of his description of being trapped in a murderous way of life: 'I am in blood / Stepped in so far ...' (3.4.121–43). Wright edits out entirely Macbeth's 'I am sick at heart ...' speech (5.3.20), which recognizes the bleak future awaiting him, since he has lost honour and friendship through his bloody course. He also cuts 'I have almost forgot the taste of fears', in which Macbeth reflects on his complete desensitization.

Macbeth's 'Tomorrow' soliloquy, Wright neuters: Worthington delivers it posthumously in voice-over, and leaves off the final sentence. When the protagonist is reduced to a taciturn man of action, like any other Hollywood thug, the story is no longer a tragedy of a brave and imaginative leader, destroyed and damned by his ambition; it becomes merely the account of a gang's dissolution as a consequence of – as Worthington puts it in the DVD interview – 'your mate [Macbeth] going a bit loopy'.

Wright doesn't *sell* his film that way, of course. In interviews, he speaks about purposeful characterization in the film:

> On a personal emotional level, I have this fascination with characters that persist with their struggle after it is obvious that they are doomed [...] There's something totally absorbing about the poetry of the gesture, about a person who's being driven on only by the sheer force of their personality.[37]

This comment bears some analysis. The film actually reveals little of Macbeth's personality because it gives him no time to share his reflections with the audience. The internal struggle between ambition and integrity that Shakespeare dramatizes is necessarily eradicated in a hero who has long made murder a way of life. Consequently, Worthington's Macbeth is a cipher. Worthington's often impassive face further contributes to the audience's alienation from Macbeth. Why did Wright cast him?

> We had to justify the idea that Macbeth was a gangster. Does he look edgy and unpredictable? I think yes. Sam's the kind of guy who's dangled people over the railing of balconies when in an altercation; I respect that and I'm impressed and I take notice of these things.[38]

In both these comments, Wright reveals himself as nostalgically seduced by a retrograde image of manliness. Macbeth's futile persistence in fighting at the end despite his recognition that he is doomed achieves nothing but an increased death count. Wright seems to admire the violent gesture because it suggests a kind of bestial (Alpha male) power to him. In the original setting of Shakespeare's play, however, Macbeth's persistence when doomed suggests that Macbeth is quixotically adhering to an ideal of dying with honour. His verbal efforts to spare Macduff seem to support this. Shakespeare thus maintains a complex ambiguity in his nature right until the end; some vestige of Macbeth's original goodness and honour clearly remain.

Wright's setting and treatment of Malcolm

For a story to be successful or satisfying, there has to be something or someone for the audience to care about. This is a cliché of script-writing workshops and books. Shakespeare makes us care about many of his characters: Duncan,

Macbeth, Lady Macbeth, Macduff and his family, and, in some interpretations, Malcolm. He also makes us care about the fate of Scotland. One of the ways he achieves this is by revealing the virtues and strengths of the characters, and the manifold benefits of living under a sacred king, like Duncan or England's Edward the Confessor (McCoy 30).[39] Wright immediately lowers the stakes by having Duncan preside over a small, illegal drug-smuggling business instead of a nation, and by presenting him as little better than Macbeth. As Michael L. Hays has persuasively argued, Shakespeare's play is as much about the restoration of right rule as it is about the destruction of the central couple. Garson's play *Macbird* (1966) demonstrates the way in which it is possible to set *Macbeth* in contemporary times while emphasizing rather than eradicating the political interpretation. In fact, *Macbeth* has a venerable history in adapted form of being used as a vehicle for political comment and change. In addition to the political contribution made by *Macbird*, and *Cahoot's Macbeth*, Welcome Msomi's *Umabatha*,[40] the Zulu Macbeth (1970), became an important 'part of an intercultural movement towards liberation and literary self-apprehension of the black South African population'.[41] This is not to dictate a political agenda to every adapter, just to acknowledge that this dimension of Shakespeare's play adds to its richness, and its loss is felt in Wright's curiously hollow interpretation. In Shakespeare's tragedy, Malcolm is a key figure in the play, a counterweight of kingly virtue to Macbeth's evil, and the scene in which he interviews Macduff (4.3.) a key scene. While it would be natural for a filmmaker to radically edit this scene, as it is largely a theoretical debate, and Malcolm's methods of ascertaining Macduff's loyalty are ambiguous and even confusing, Wright cuts the dialogue altogether. One criminal can hardly test another for virtue and fidelity. As mentioned earlier, Malcolm's last look at the Macbeths in the film suggests that, despite his cooperation with the police, he is far from providing a real, salutary alternative to Macbeth.

The Christian framework of Shakespeare's play also enlarges its scope. As Robert Miola contends, *Macbeth* is 'a drama of damnation that purposefully evokes and engages contemporary theology'.[42] Wright's brief, nostalgic homage to this aspect of the play is not in Shakespeare's words, and is granted to a character who does not even appear in the original; he has his Cawdor deliver the Our Father before his execution. In Shakespeare's play, Duncan and Malcolm (and English Edward) are not merely good kings, but divinely appointed rulers, whereas Macbeth is a usurper. Under his rule, Scotland is blighted by horrific prodigies, barrenness and disease (2.3.55–63; 2.4.1–19; 3.6.32–7; 4.3.4–8; 4.3.164–73), a witness to God's disapprobation. Malcolm restores Scotland to harmony by assuming the throne. As Hays observes: 'None of the other major tragedies is so clearly romantic and so frankly idealistic in showing the ultimate triumph of good over evil.'[43] Wright's setting in contemporary Melbourne's gangland thus narrows the frame once again; his characters' actions have little effect outside their underworld of crime. While Malcolm appears to have cooperated with the law to bring Macbeth down, he is motivated solely by revenge in Wright's film, while in Shakespeare's play, he fights 'a just and holy war to restore [Scotland's] well-being'.[44] Fleance seems to presage a continuation of the gang-violence in the future. This cynical conclusion, which departs from Shakespeare, is typical of twentieth- and twenty-first-century adaptations, both of *Macbeth* and other tragedies, and may demonstrate the enduring influence of Jan Kott's *Shakespeare Our Contemporary*, with its insistence on the parallels between absolute kingship in Shakespeare and totalitarian regimes in recent history. For instance, Polanski's *Macbeth*[45] concludes with Malcolm about to enter the witches' lair with the suggestion that the cycle of self-fulfilling destructive prophecies is about to recur. The malign implications of Fleance's corruption in *Men of Respect* have already been mentioned. *MacHomer* ends with a ghostly King Duncan, played by the ruthless capitalist boss from the Simpsons, Mr Burns, wresting the crown from Malcolm. At the conclusions of both Branagh and Almereyda's films of *Hamlet*, a sinister Fortinbras assumes control.

Conclusion

Wright sounds a conciliatory note for the real gangsters on whom his *Macbeth* is based: 'It's about what happens when you take on too much death, what happens to your soul. The Melbourne gangsters were caught up in a machinery that they couldn't stop, that was clearly out of control. The result was thirty-four unsolved murders.' Wright expresses himself in a way that casts the criminals as victims, powerless to end the violence, and not to be held accountable for it. Also, the idea of Macbeth's soul having taken on '*too much* death' seems indicative of Wright's unconscious acceptance of violence; isn't even *one* death too much?

Shakespeare's play explores the Macbeths' self-discovery – they find out how far they are willing to go for power and how much this journey transforms them. Lady Macbeth discovers she is not nearly as ruthless as she thought she was, while Macbeth finds he is much more so, and consequently, much less human. At the end of the play, he expresses his bitter understanding of all that he has lost: 'honour, love, obedience, troops of friends' (5.5.27). His selfish quest for power has left him isolated. His articulation of this reveals to the audience that Macbeth has learned (too late) from his experiences over the course of the play to value the benefits of a virtuous life which he abandoned when he set out on his course of inexorable self-promotion. This *anagnorisis* is integral to the tragic genre. Wright affords us no such hook.

Peter Keough, in his edited volume, *Flesh and Blood: Film Critics on Sex, Violence and Censorship*, asks: 'Is excess in the defence of artistic integrity a virtue or a vice? When does the artistic exploration of extreme violence become exploitation?'[46] Wright with his 2006 *Macbeth* has crossed the line into exploitation. One of many elements that distinguishes Shakespeare's *Macbeth* from a mere 'portrait of a psychopath', which shows us evil but teaches us nothing about it (the character Nahum describes it thus in the Canadian television series *Slings and Arrows*[47]), is the protagonist's eloquent meditation on his actions. Wright has stripped this dimension away and, in its place, offers nothing but empty violence. This makes the film unfulfilling, and not just for an audience of Shakespeare-lovers. As the *Variety* reviewer expressed it, the film 'is oversupplied with particularly nasty bloodletting and underdone as an involving portrait of one of the Bard's mightiest and most psychologically intriguing tragic figures'.[48] Wright himself almost admits his reductive strategy: '[Sex and death] are the big issues and they like the camera very much.'[49] One can perceive the same intellectual passivity in this statement as in some of Wright's earlier ones. Socrates said that the unexamined life is not worth living; Wright has inadvertently shown us that unexamined filmed violence is not worth watching.

Notes

1 Pauline Kael, 'The Current Cinema', *The New Yorker*, 5 February 1972, p. 76.

2 Graham Holderness, *Taming of the Shrew: Shakespeare in Performance* (Manchester: Manchester University Press, 1989), p. 67.

3 International Movie Database, Box Office Mojo.

4 *Metal Skin*, Dir. Geoffrey White. Perf. Tara Morice, Aden Young. Daniel Scharf Productions, 1994.

5 *Cherry Falls*, Dir. Geoffrey White. Perf. Brittany Murphy, Jay Mohr. Fresh Produce Company, 2000.

6 'An Interview with Geoffrey Wright'. www.screenwize.com/archives/55 [accessed 22 May 2008].

7 *Macbeth*, Dir. Geoffrey White. Perf. Sam Worthington, Victoria Hill (Arclight, 2007).

8   Andrew L. Urban, 'Simple as Alphabeth: Interview with Geoffrey
     Wright', *Urbancinefile: the World of Film in Australia* (22 May
     2008), Edition no. 585. http://www.urbancinephile.com.au/
     home/view.asp?Article_ID=12251&p=y [accessed 22 May 2008].

9   Raphael Holinshed, *Chronicles: England, Scotland, and Ireland*
     (London, 1965) facsimile.

10   Sidney, Sir Philip, *A Defence of Poetry*, ed. J. A. Van Dorsten
     (Oxford: Oxford University Press, 1989).

11   Aristotle, *Poetics and Demetrius's On Style* (London, 1941), XI
     25.

12   Ibid, p. 45.

13   Michael H. Hays, *Shakespearean Tragedy as Chivalric
     Romance: Rethinking Macbeth, Hamlet, Othello and King
     Lear* (Cambridge: D. S. Brewer, 2003), p. 108. Shakespeare
     references and quotations are to Nicholas Brooke ed., *Macbeth*
     (Oxford: Oxford University Press, 1990).

14   Richard Kuipers, 'Macbeth', *Variety*, 10 September 2006. http://
     www.variety.com/story.asp?1=story&r=VE1117931531&c=31
     [accessed 22 May 2008].

15   Katherine Knowles, 'Appetite and Ambition: The Influence of
     Hunger in *Macbeth*', *Early English Studies* (Vol. 2, 2009). See
     also Ramona Wray's essay in this volume.

16   Ionesco, Eugene, *Macbett*, trans. Charles Marowitz (New York,
     1973).

17   *Scotland, PA*, Dir. Billy Morrissette. Perf. Maura Tierney, James
     Le Gros. Abandon Pictures, 2001.

18   See A. C. Bradley, *Shakespearean Tragedy* (New York: St
     Martin's Press, 1967), p. 290; Harold Bloom, *Shakespeare: The
     Invention of the Human* (New York: Penguin-Putnam, 1998),
     p. 518; G. K. Hunter ed., *Macbeth* (Harmondsworth: Penguin,
     1982), p. 15.

19   Andrew L. Urban, 'Simple as Alphabeth: Interview with
     Geoffrey Wright'. http://www.urbancinephile.com.au/home/
     view.asp?Article_ID=12251&p=y [accessed 22 May 2008].

20   Amanda Kane Rooks, 'Macbeth's Wicked Women: Sexualized
     Evil in Geoffrey Wright's *Macbeth*', 'Macbeth' Dir. Mark
     Brozel. Perf. James McAvoy, Keeley Hawes, BBC, 2005.

21 Knights, L. C., 'How Many Children Had Lady Macbeth', *Explorations* (Harmondsworth, 1964).

22 In the *BBC Shakespeare Retold*, Ella breaks down in the restaurant, in front of customers, babbling about her premature baby's last hours. Michael Caven's production with Second Age Theatre Company, Dublin, 2003, had an empty crib in an attic room.

23 *Joe Macbeth*, Dir. Ken Hughes. Perf. Paul Douglas, Ruth Roman. Columbia Pictures, 1955.

24 *Men of Respect*, Dir. William Reilly. Perf. John Turturro, Katherine Borowitz. Arthur Goldblatt Productions, 1990.

25 *Maqbool*, Dir. Vishal Bhardwaj. Perf. Irrfan Khan, Tabu. Kaleidoscope Entertainment, 2003.

26 International Movie Database, Box Office Mojo.

27 *Macbett*, Dir Aleta Chappelle. Perf. Terence Howard, Sanaa Lathan. Moonshadow, 2012.

28 *Reservoir Dogs*, Dir. Quentin Tarantino. Perf. Harvey Keitel, Tim Roth. Live Entertainment, 1992.

29 Nicanor Loreti, 'Interview: Director Geoffrey Wright'. www.fearzone.com/blog

30 Tom Stoppard, *Dogg's Hamlet, Cahoot's Macbeth* (London, 1980).

31 Barbara Garson, *Macbird* (New York, 1966).

32 Rick Miller, *MacHomer* (Montreal, 2011), Scenes 7–8.

33 Andrew L. Urban, 'Simple as Alphabeth: Interview with Geoffrey Wright'. http://www.urbancinephile.com.au/home/view.asp?Article_ID=12251&p=y [accessed 22 May 2008].

34 'An Interview with Geoffrey Wright'. www.screenwize.com/archives/55 [accessed 22 May 2008].

35 G. K. Hunter ed., *Macbeth* (Harmondsworth: Penguin, 1982), p. 7.

36 Robert Miola, 'I could not say "Amen": Prayer and Providence in *Macbeth*', *Shakespeare's Christianity: The Protestant and Catholic Poetics of 'Julius Caesar', 'Macbeth' and 'Hamlet'*, ed. Beatrice Batson (Waco, TX: Baylor University Press, 2006), pp. 57–71, 61.

37 'An Interview with Geoffrey Wright'. www.screenwize.com/
    archives/55 [accessed 22 May 2008].

38 Andrew L. Urban, 'Simple as Alphabeth: Interview with
    Geoffrey Wright'. http://www.urbancinephile.com.au/home/
    view.asp?Article_ID=12251&p=y [accessed 22 May 2008].

39 Richard C. McCoy, '"The Grace of Grace" and Double-Talk in
    Macbeth', *Shakespeare Survey 57* (2004), pp. 27–37.

40 Msomi, Welcome, *Umabatha* (Johannesburg, 1996).

41 Sven Rank, *Twentieth-Century Interpretations of Macbeth*
    (Frankfurt am Main: Peter Lang, 2010), p. 298.

42 Robert Miola, 'I could not say "Amen": Prayer and Providence
    in *Macbeth*', p. 67.

43 Michael Hays, *Shakespearean Tragedy as Chivalric Romance*,
    p. 100.

44 Ibid., p. 122.

45 *Macbeth*, Dir. Roman Polanski. Perf. Jon Finch, Francesca
    Annis. Playboy Pictures, 1971.

46 Peter Keough, 'Introduction to Poets of Blood', *Flesh and
    Blood: The National Society of Film Critics on Sex, Violence
    and Censorship* (San Francisco: Mercury House, 1995), p. 177.

47 *Slings and Arrows*, Dir. Peter Wellington. Perf. Paul Gross,
    Martha Burns. Episode 1 'Season's End', Season 2. Acorn
    Media, 2003–6.

48 Richard Kuipers, 'Macbeth', *Variety*, 10 September 2006. http://
    www.variety.com/story.asp?1=story&r=VE1117931531&c=31,
    1 [accessed 22 May 2008].

49 'An Interview with Geoffrey Wright'. www.screenwize.com/
    archives/55 [accessed 22 May 2008].

11

The Butcher and the Text: Adaptation, Theatricality and the 'Shakespea(Re)-Told' *Macbeth*

Ramona Wray

In the British educational system, schoolchildren taking an examination on Shakespeare's *Macbeth* are regularly invited to reflect on act 5's infamous assessment of the protagonist and his partner: 'this dead butcher, and his fiend-like Queen' (5.9.35).[1] Pupils must struggle to encapsulate the trajectory and significations of Macbeth within the 'butcher' designation: how far is 'butcher' an adequate summation for all that our hero represents?

A 2005 film, *Macbeth*, made for television as part of the BBC's 'Shakespea(Re)-Told' season, removes any need for such reflection by making literal the Macbeth/butcher equation.[2] Joe Macbeth (James McAvoy) is Head Chef at

the fiercely hierarchical London restaurant which stands
in for Shakespeare's Scottish court. His wife, Ella/Lady
Macbeth (Keeley Hawes), is the restaurant's *maître d'*, the
role operating as a neat translation of the play's concern
with hosting and hospitality. 'Nose to Tail' is a high-class,
gastronomique establishment; it is at the opposite end of
the culinary spectrum to the fast-food outlet, 'McBeth's', in
the US cinematic satire, *Scotland, PA* (dir. Billy Morrissette,
2001), discussed elsewhere in this book. At 'Nose to Tail', the
menu is almost entirely meat-based (Macbeth's signature dish
is rabbit stuffed with black pudding wrapped in parma ham).
Explicitly conjuring what Ayanna Thompson has described as
'the play's very rhetoric of blood and staining', the kitchen's
work-surfaces (and occasionally floors) swim in blood, and
the red-stained Chef's whites reimagine the 'bloody man'
(1.2.1) of the 'original' drama's inauguration.[3] A visceral feel
is achieved throughout via a *mise-en-scène* which prioritizes
hanging carcasses and slaughtered animals, while processes
of food creation are rendered in graphically visual terms.[4]
Evisceration and execution are Macbeth's *forte*. We witness
him disembowelling a pigeon and killing live lobsters ('the
meat tastes better if the death is less stressful', he instructs
in his natural Scottish burr). Pivotal is the early sequence
introducing the protagonist which reveals him deftly skinning
and dissecting a pig's head. The severed head prefigures the
display of the 'usurper's … head' (5.9.21) in the final stages
of Shakespeare's play (a parallel reinforced when Macbeth
later unveils a tattoo of the animal on his upper arm). More
immediately, Macbeth's maestro manipulation of knife and
cleaver are ciphers for his professional pre-eminence. In
extreme close-up – and in a neat recasting of act one's 'Bloody
instructions' (1.7.9) – the pig's head is expertly cleaved in two,
dissected and arranged as part of a kitchen tutorial. Macbeth
cuts quickly and without hesitation, a series of reaction shots
revealing who has – and has not – a stomach for this kind of
knife-work (sous-chef Billy Banquo [Joseph Millson] looks
on admiringly, but commis-chef Malcolm [Toby Kebbell]

visibly blanches at the display). The episode is an innovative reworking of the Captain's description of Macbeth's single combat with Macdonald ('with his brandish'd steel ... he unseam'd him from the nave to th' chops' [1.2.17, 22]). As the battlefield morphs into the professional kitchen, the Chef is seen as purveying to his *protégés* what he labels the 'poetry' of cookery; iambic pentameter is translated into the sights and sounds of television and encapsulated in Macbeth's consummate demonstrations of butchery as an art-form.

Presiding over 'Shakespea(Re)-Told' (one of the BBC's rare forays into adaptation, the series is unique in replacing Shakespeare's language with modern equivalencies), director Peter Moffat was accused at the time of a different kind of butchery. In this instance, the charge was of amputating Shakespeare's text, of carving up the verse. As Margaret Jane Kidnie notes, several commentators 'spoke out against the decision to rescript the plays, insisting that fidelity to language is the touchstone of the work'.[5] According to this logic, to be exposed to the language is to be made cognizant of core Shakespearean values and realities. Occupying a contrary camp of opinion is Jonathan Bate, who observes that this 'superlative' *Macbeth* showcases 'some glorious allusions to the original language'.[6] In this chapter, I build on Bate's brief assessment and, through close analytical engagement, make a case for the film as one of the most ambitious and significant *Macbeth* adaptations to date. In particular, I argue that the corporal forms so central to this production represent a vital means of conveying the play's metaphysical concerns. What is corporal applies not only to the carcasses of animals but also to the bodies of the chefs; this *Macbeth* is notable for its sexualization and fraught homoeroticism, both of which are integral to the film's figuration of the competitive animus of the kitchen world. Part of the production's impact, I suggest, can be traced to its self-conscious intertextuality and, in particular, to its commerce with cultures of the celebrity chef. In this sense, the 'Shakespea(Re)-Told' *Macbeth* demonstrates how new meanings may be produced out of old and how dynamism and creativity lie at the heart of the adaptation process. The loss of Shakespeare's language, and the butchery visited upon the 'original', are paradoxically generative. Fresh modalities of accessing Shakespeare are inscribed in the televisual medium, even as that medium, as I will show, simultaneously summons and plays upon the drama's theatrical antecedents.

I

In the production, our first glimpse of Macbeth is via a shamelessly voyeuristic shot. Dressed only in leather trousers, and with sexily dishevelled hair and a gym-honed chest, he is represented opening a huge fridge freezer and reaching behind the multiple bottles of beer for a pint of milk. In a typically playful transposition, the chef is associated with the 'milk of human kindness' (1.5.16), a move that, at an immediate level, approximates the character description of Lady Macbeth's letter. Yet, as we watch Macbeth drinking greedily, the camera's close-up on his throat and mouth suggests more forcefully the association between consumption and masculinity, or sexuality and food, characteristic of the production as a whole. Functioning in such a manner, the protagonist brings to mind the recent stress on 'testosterone in the kitchen' and the emergence of 'chefs who smouldered rather than simmered'; the 'Shakespea(Re)-Told' *Macbeth*, to adopt a formulation of food critic Elspeth Probyn, occupies a prominent place in the 'sexy food mecca stakes'.[7] Certainly, the portrayal of Macbeth takes energy from the early images that launched Marco Pierre White's career, his being famously photographed '*torse nu* ... with a shark in his crotch'.[8] Viewers are encouraged to spectate on Macbeth in precisely this eroticized capacity.

As he drinks, Macbeth watches his boss on television; this is the celebrity chef, Duncan Docherty (Vincent Regan), performing on the restaurant's spin-off show, 'Dining with Docherty'. The doubled method of spectatorship (there is watching within watching) encourages an audience to compare the two personalities; hence Duncan, with his mature good looks and phoney 'Irishness', is set against Macbeth, typified by youth and boyish charm. The age difference between the two simultaneously evokes ideas about Duncan as father and patriarch (he is affectionately referred to in the kitchen as 'the old man').[9] Hierarchies are economically established not only through previous roles (Regan's parts in the television mini-series, *Empire* [2005], and the film, *Troy* [dir. Wolfgang Petersen, 2004], lend him a classical gravitas) but also through properties and appearances. Particularly communicative are Duncan's suit, Mercedes and media empire, which mark him out as 'King'; by contrast, Macbeth lacks these trappings of power, being firmly identified as the underling who runs his proprietor's kitchen behind the scenes. The imbalance in authority is suggested in a glance at the screen that confirms Macbeth's feelings of resentment and disentitlement. Later, in a voice charged with emotion, Duncan informs Ella that, thanks to her husband's labour, the restaurant has been awarded 'three big beautiful Michelin stars'. These markers of achievement (Michelin stars are awarded for the quality and consistency of the food and the technical versatility and mastery of the chef) work in this version of *Macbeth* both to reference the highest accolade of the restaurant world and to recall the play's construction of the kudos attached to the transfer of the Thane of Cawdor title. 'Have the guest room made up for me', Duncan orders, planning a party for the following evening, but it is clear that, in this celebration of 'success' (1.3.90), he will claim the star status. Later, Ella is quick to harp on the injustice as she reminds her husband that he is the one who has 'done all the work'.[10] The adaptation takes its cue from the pecking-order realities of high-end restaurant regimes in which an under-appreciated kitchen aspirant bides his time before stepping out of the shadows to claim overdue glory.

This manifestation of a backstory, as well as insets like the fictional 'Dining with Docherty' show, lend *Macbeth* a heightened intertextuality. The production makes a virtue of appealing outside of itself to programmes that are premised on kitchen hierarchies and attendant personnel conflicts. Educated in the premises of culinary broadcasting, we are invited to recognize in the work of adaptation the aesthetic markers of a professional kitchen environment. Hence, the cold, stainless steel backdrop, the gleaming floors and surfaces, and the stark blue of the kitchen lights assist Shakespearean exposition in the same moment as they establish parameters of interpretation. Characteristically, Macbeth is conceived of as energetic, inspired and capable of cooking with brio. His strict command in the kitchen is matched only by his passion as a chef working at the highest of levels. Mistakes in the kitchen cause him 'actual physical pain', Macbeth patiently explains to Malcolm, his dedication to his craft establishing him as a culinary perfectionist along the lines of any famous kitchen name. Like celebrity kitchen scenes, these fictional kitchen episodes are full of aggressive acts of phallocentric camaraderie. Male bonding seals the relation between Macbeth and Banquo, as testified to by the prevalence of hugs, massages and even a full-frontal kiss. Moreover, the language of these scenes – including the frequent recourse to 'dick' and 'arse' – is modelled on an equivalent kitchen programming demotic, emphasizing a homoerotic dynamic as central to the thrust of Shakespearean reinvention. By incorporating into itself echoes of, for example, *Kitchen Confidential* and *Ramsay's Kitchen Nightmares*, *Macbeth* reveals the extent to which its dominant conceits rely upon consanguinity with particular television genres.

Perhaps the most felicitous transposition of the *Macbeth* production inheres in the mapping of the hierarchies of Shakespeare's England onto the cultures of discipline inherent in a contemporary kitchen. This is an environment in which, as the narrative establishes, everyone, from the executive-chef to the cleaner, knows his place. Such modes of internal organization are deployed to analogize the social order of Renaissance England which survives in attenuated guise in the kitchen setting, as conveyed in the syncopated 'Yes chef, no chef' refrain. Here, it is implied, the lower culinary orders enjoy little freedom or independence. Or, as director Peter Moffat puts it, 'The eleventh-century warrior castle and the boiling hot kitchen on a Saturday night in London's Soho have everything in common'.[11] In a teasing out of the parallel, the kitchen in *Macbeth* is portrayed as a pressurized milieu, defined by stress and heat, a metaphor for the exercise of power and the pursuit of ambition. More subliminally, the hellish interstices of Shakespeare's Scottish play are registered in the modern construction of the competitive kitchen as an inferno, as the title of the television show, *Hell's Kitchen*, or as Marco Pierre White's autobiography, *The Devil in the Kitchen*, suggest.[12] Most obviously, it is the potential for movement up the kitchen hierarchy that provokes the aspirational bent. As Macbeth states, 'Anyone can make it in a kitchen if they've got the guts and the passion, doesn't matter what their background is or their history'. The 'poor boy made good' is a staple of the celebrity chef phenomenon, with types such as Marco Pierre White recording a bleak upbringing ('Dad was a gambler ... I was a bit of a loner [and] ... suffered from dyslexia ... There was little affection', he narrates) as a concomitant and shaping component of an impassioned drive to overcome adversity through creativity.[13] The energies of upward social mobility are held in play in the production in the representation of Duncan (the 'peasant Irish boy' who becomes 'the toast of the culinary world') and Macbeth himself. In this connection, McAvoy's working-class roots, and association with gritty council estate dramas such as *Shameless*, are constitutive elements in the adaptation's fantasy of an escape from inhibiting origins. Notions of lineage are subsumed here to a reification of work and commitment, making the kitchen the natural arena for the Shakespearean over-reacher.

Intertextuality and theatricality inform each other when the production comically references the superstitions surrounding the play's staging history. Hence, Banquo warns Malcolm: 'Don't say "Gordon Ramsay": it's bad luck to say it out loud. Call him "The Scottish Chef".' With this instance, the celebrity chef takes on the cursed mantle of the 'Scottish play', his name surrogating for the superstitions circulating around the Shakespearean work's performance. Lending substance to this notion of the restaurant as a theatrical space are the arresting red curtains shrouding the walls. More importantly, a significant montage sees as integrally co-dependent the preparations for a performance and the countdown to the restaurant's opening for its nightly trade. As the montage cross-cuts between Macbeth dressing in his ubiquitous whites, Ella perfecting her make-up and correcting the position of the cutlery, and Duncan returning to play his (fictional) role as chef, the suggestion is that a successful restaurant business, like the theatre, depends on collaborative modes of production. Throughout this early montage, a distinctive tune is heard, the first of only two thematic leitmotifs in Kevin Sargent's original soundtrack. Because it accompanies the preparations for the restaurant's opening, this first musical theme communicates the notion of high-end dining as a performance or theatrical undertaking. This sequence, in particular, establishes the theme – reminiscent, in its use of jaunty and ambient keyboards, xylophone and drums, of the instrumentals accompanying 1970s' cookery programmes – as indivisible from the smooth performance of the restaurant. In contradistinction, the kitchen scenes are notable for the absence of non-diegetic sound. By implication, the work of the kitchen is to be taken as an informing 'reality', while the actions of the restaurant are akin to theatre – they belong to a semi-fictional mode.

Notably, with the exception of the occasion of their first appearance, the same musical leitmotif – the leitmotif which signals performance – sounds whenever the witches are glimpsed. The witches and the restaurant, then, are allied through highly characteristic mood music and placed in league with each other as complementary performance expressions. In the adaptation, Shakespeare's 'Weird Sisters' (1.5.7–8) are envisaged as bin-men or rubbish collectors, a reading that carries with it some metaphorical freight. The dustbin suggests itself as a kind of cauldron, or even a repository of secrets, in the same moment as it figures as the ultimate resting-place for what can be discarded, for things that have served their use (prophesies that, as in the play, turn out to possess limited utility). The production's bin-men are also connected with the theatrical in that they are discovered as acting as a chorus line. For example, their prophetic promise to Banquo – 'You get nothing but your son does ... and his son, and his son, and his son' – is sung as a musical refrain in a vernacular parody of Shakespeare's 'line of kings' (3.1.59). Because the refrain is chanted to the tune of the football hymn, 'Here we go', the idea is that the witches are to be understood as articulations of a popular feeling or *mentalité* – the responses of the demotic crowd. And later, when Duncan dies to the diegesis of football hooligans on the street shouting 'England' in unison, a connection to the bin-men is skilfully maintained.

The witches are important not simply as a parody chorus line but also as frames for the narrative. In keeping with the play, the action begins with the witches and a slow pan across the landfill which substitutes for the 'blasted heath' (1.3.77), camerawork establishing the thematic of detritus and consumption that undergirds the production overall. Storm clouds gather and gulls screech overhead as incongruous music ('Night Fever' by the Bee Gees) sounds on the radio; imagery of scavenging and natural upset consorts with suggestions of the nocturnal and a witch-like pop trio. As the camera zooms in on the red refuse lorry, the landscape shot is replaced by a tight close-up on the rubbish collectors discussing their sandwich fillings amid snippets of Shakespearean dialogue. The effect of the references to 'corned beef', 'anchovy' and 'tongue' is to make contemporary the contents of the witches' brew ('Scale of dragon, tooth of wolf' [4.1.22]) and to point up a quotidian conception of restaurant conversations. And, in their incantatory rhythms and stylized pronouncements, the bin-men's exchanges ring the superstitious, prophetic notes central to any *Macbeth* adaptation. That the bin-men are linked to 'Nose to Tail' is clarified at the point where their remarks identify their shift as the so-called 'restaurant slop slot': 'when the hurlyburly's done, when the last mouthful hits the belly of the last diner ... in we go ... to meet the kitchen warrior, the cooking braveheart', they exclaim together. The doubled descriptors are resonant, encapsulating, as they do, archetypal qualities of Scottish heroism and feminine skills that are kitchen-specific. Indeed, the expressions bespeak a conjunction of apparent opposites that are almost Shakespearean in their paradoxical force. After the witches have delivered these pronouncements, the camera moves outward, cutting to Macbeth himself. The transition registers in filmic terms the 'There to meet with Macbeth' (1.1.7) statement while, at the same time, suggesting that the protagonist is the witches' quarry, the intended victim of their projected machinations.

And, in its early stages, the adaptation constructs Macbeth as infernal prey. For instance, the kitchen knives, adorning the white-tiled walls on magnetic boards, are shot in a circular arrangement around Macbeth's head, the idea being that he is a natural target. A more complicated suggestion is that Macbeth is the witches' co-conspirator, for the production repeatedly draws attention to discourses and locales that bring them into close proximity. Hence, the pig's head at the start not only refracts Macbeth's prowess as butcher, it also echoes the second witch's line in the play: 'Killing swine' (1.3.2). Because Macbeth's most nefarious transactions (such as hiring the murderers) are conducted in the bin-lined and dimly lit alley outside the restaurant, he is further allied with the witches and their dark practices. Most damningly, the witches ventriloquize the Shakespearean Macbeth's words, assuming responsibility for most of his soliloquies, as their use of formulations such as 'all our yesterdays' (5.5.22) and 'sound and fury' (5.5.27) indicates. Not so much a manifestation of the control the witches exercise over Macbeth, these appropriations of an anterior language point to the subconscious desires and instincts the protagonist attempts to ignore. The witches, in many respects, stand in for Macbeth and his aspirations and self-delusions. For instance, Macbeth's opening mantra, 'First rule of the kitchen, no waste', is repeatedly unhinged by the realities of his kitchen world ('waste' that is banished to the bins of the alley environment) and his later despotism when he becomes restaurant owner (the 'wasteland' that his rise to power produces). The bin-men, and their actions, stand as forceful reminders of the fact that Macbeth is unable either to escape 'waste' or the guilt and repression attendant on its attempted exclusion.

II

One of the imperatives animating the 'Shakespea(Re)-Told' series is the maximization of the power of female roles – a conscious broadcasting strategy whereby a predominantly female audience for television drama is targeted in a direct appeal.[14] Because the witches are male (a casting move that immediately reduces the symbolic potential attached to female parts), Ella becomes the only significant woman in the production as a whole. Accordingly, and in a compensatory gesture, Ella, from the outset, is figured in an amplified fashion: that is, she is discovered as dominant and in charge, both at work (her control of the restaurant is second to none) and at home (where she has the upper hand in a romantic and highly sexualized relationship). Casting is instrumental in the quick establishment of Ella's exercise of influence. Keeley Hawes, who plays Ella, has accrued an aura of authority through having successfully executed a number of key classical and literary parts (including Dickensian and Shakespearean adaptations). Her history stamps her as a performer who has experience of, and who is at ease with,

Shakespeare. In a comparable way, but discharging authority in a more populist vein, Hawes is the voice of Lara Croft in the *Tomb Raider* series, with the result that her silky tones are subliminally evocative of expressions of female force and will. This is communicated at a physical level; as is obvious from a longshot of the 'butcher, and his fiend-like Queen' pacing the restaurant, Ella is older and taller than her baby-faced husband. Her cut-glass pronunciation contrasts markedly with Macbeth's regional accent and, again, identifies her as more elevated in manner and style. In a typical verbal flirtation with the 'original', Duncan describes Ella as a 'bewitching lady' with 'massive bollocks'; the formula-tions emerge from the Shakespearean construction of Lady Macbeth as a female warrior who has embraced masculinity, and abandoned 'compunctious visitings of Nature' (1.5.44), so as the better to achieve her desires. In this adaptation of *Macbeth*, then, Ella is at centre stage precisely because she brings sexual extremes, and stereotypical markers of gender, into captivating co-existence.

These are among the contexts that mean that Ella is elaborated as achieving through manipulation. Particularly revealing is the initial conversation about the murder of Duncan; taking place on the restaurant roof, it is clear from the exchange of words that Macbeth buckles easily under the pressure of his wife's inducements. With Ella attired in black, and Macbeth in white, the episode suggests a primal temptation, with the widescreen shot of London standing in for the possibility of owning the world. Sexual temptations are on offer, too, as intimated in the champagne-laced scenes that take place in the bedroom, where dark reds and browns, and the flicker of half-light, underscore the entanglements of erotic *frisson* and the lure of dominion. Camerawork is vital to the sequence's effects: although a lengthy close-up shows Macbeth in a narrow plane of focus, the suggestion of his commanding the frame is upset by the appearance of Ella, who rises up from the shadows behind him and begins a coaxing persuasion next to his right ear. The shot replicates a key cinematic and theatrical image of Iago whispering in Othello's ear, conjuring the notion of Ella as a type of aide or lieutenant who will bring about her husband-general's ruin. In addition, the backlit image of Ella hovering above Macbeth's shoulder, and the match-cuts that show her as imposing herself, make visible the power imbalance. Throughout, indeed, character blocking indicts Ella's use of space for personal advantage. Sound is a contributory factor here. It is during these bedroom scenes that we hear, for the first time, the slow and heavy piano notes (the second of the two thematic leitmotifs) which come to be associated with Duncan's demise. In the same way that shady visuals incriminate Ella, so does the score hint at the extent of her guilty involvement.

Crucially, it is Ella who is the presiding inspiration behind putting in place details of Duncan's murder. Organizing some 'washer-uppers ... from the eleventh century' (or illegal immigrants in this production), she masterminds her deadly plan with a suitably arcane air of medievalism. Given the fact that she is envisioned as arranging the murderers' flight, and working to dispose of the duplicate knives in the alley's bins, she both comes to inhabit the same marginal territory as the witches and exceeds the narrative parameters of her Shakespearean counterpart – this Lady Macbeth is distinguished by her proactive role in pursuing and concealing criminality. Immediately after Duncan's murder, the camera pauses on Ella's face in close-up. The suggestion is that she is the one who has assumed responsibility, not least because hers is the first countenance an audience sees now that the fatal deed has been executed. Similarly, when Macbeth returns, the focus falls upon the knife and Ella in the background, the composition displacing the protagonist as the centre of attention and distancing him from individual culpability.

Beside the articulate and polished Ella, Joe is realized as fearful, ashamed, inadequate and, above all, silent. The production robs him of the majority of his soliloquies, leaving him just one sustained reflection. In an adaptation that otherwise dispenses with the rhetorical forms of Macbeth's introspection, this single surviving speech functions, by definition, as a set-piece. Delivered in the locker-room adjoining the kitchen, the speech takes on some of the colouring of its masculine setting even as it also sounds a variation on the production's themes of performance and performativity. In the play, Shakespeare's Macbeth is represented as impersonating grief to absolve himself from public suspicion, as his lines indicate:

Had I but died an hour before this chance,
I had liv'd a blessed time; for, from this instant,
There's nothing serious in mortality;
All is but toys; renown, and grace, is dead;
The wine of life is drawn, and the mere lees
Is left this vault to brag of.

(2.3.89–94)

The adaptation's vernacular gloss on the speech – 'If I'd have died an hour before Duncan Docherty, I'd have died a happy man, but now, it's as if everything that was important in life has gone: nothing can ever be serious again' – captures the emotional beats of the 'original', but modulates them, turning the whole into a soliloquy reflective of some integrity. Here, the sentiments are registered as utterly genuine, a transformation that is assisted by the shift from a public declaration (as in the play) to a moment of private rumination. The idea that the lines are central is foregrounded via their repeated emphasis. Macbeth's solitary pronouncement is reiterated at the press conference following Duncan's murder where Ella echoes her husband's words, appropriating them to serve the needs of the occasion. When the first musical leitmotif sounds during the sequence, the idea that Ella is engaged in a performance is suggested (and then clarified in the camera's pan over Banquo's suspicious expressions). Finally, the adapted lines are heard in the scene in which Macbeth and Ella watch the press conference on a television screen; at this point, the speech, mediated and traversed, is emptied out of 'authentic' emotion.

Television figures again when Macbeth takes on the cookery slot previously occupied by his boss. Macbeth assumes the crown of chef on the 'Dining with Docherty' programme and publishes his own cookery book, an index of his influence and prestige. Yet, as the significance of the thrice-repeated reflection on 'everything that was important' indicates, all is not as it seems. The point is nicely made via a return to the earlier montage countdown to the restaurant opening; the same sequence of shots is replayed and in same order but, on this occasion, glamour and excitement are notably absent. The revised montage reinforces the ways in which actions recur but without the core values of passion and exuberance. Enthusiastic greetings have disappeared, to be replaced by cold nods and an avoidance of touch. Particularly arresting is the colour change in the milk that Macbeth drinks – from naturally white to blood red. Finally, augmenting the sense of a hollowed-out rehearsal of earlier experiences, the soundtrack's jaunty performance leitmotif has been abandoned in favour of that associated with Duncan's murder. This notion of difference within sameness is theatrically meaningful, recalling, as it does, the play's nihilistic cogitation: 'Life's but a walking shadow, a poor player, / That struts and frets his hour upon the stage, / And then is heard no more: it is a tale / Told by an idiot' (5.5.24–7). In a comparable vein, the *Macbeth* adaptation foregrounds in its concluding stages empty gestures and vacant repetition. Macbeth's rules of the kitchen – 'respect' and 'no waste' – are gone, and in their place is a pronounced sense of Shakespearean nothingness.

The scenes that unfold after the murder refract the play's preoccupation with forms of insomnia. Neither Macbeth nor Ella is able to sleep once Duncan has been removed. We are treated to a glut of images of the couple in bed together, but the protagonist and his wife (with eyes staring fixedly awake) do not make physical contact. Blocking foregrounds a growing divide, showing bodies in disharmonious relation, while any sense of intimacy is positioned historically; as Ella states, 'we were together once'. The representation of Ella enters traditional interpretative territory at the point where the audience becomes privy to her awareness of responsibility, a crux in the journey of the character that is announced via scenes of continual hand-washing. But her confrontation with guilt takes second place to the development of Macbeth and his conscience-stricken decline. 'I imagine things, terrible things', he informs Ella, again to the musical leitmotif connected with Duncan, sound and speech pointing to the fatal event that has determined Macbeth's psychic condition. The visions to which viewers are granted access, interestingly, belong not to Ella but to Macbeth – he is revealed as focalizing the production's horrors. Accordingly, in the kitchen, we see from his point of view; the meat that he is frying discharges blood in the pan, as if the steak bears in its material manifestation the wounds and injuries of the protagonist's victims. On another occasion, Macbeth spectates upon his wife taking a shower, only to see the water in which she immerses herself turn to blood. There is no ablution or cleansing here, simply a deeper engulfment by the forms of a murderous regime. For Macbeth at this point, Ella appears 'in blood / Stepp'd in so far, that ... Returning were as tedious as go o'er' (3.4.135–7). The scene lends graphic illustration to the stimulus of guilty fantasy.

The death of Duncan is also the prompt for a series of increasingly tyrannical kitchen acts. In contrast with before, the kitchen is marked by the disappearance of chat, song and tactility – indexes of men operating productively via teamwork. It is in this environment that the authoritarian tendencies of Macbeth are granted their most succinct and recognizable statement – his declaring, uncompromisingly: 'I run this kitchen – mine is the only voice.' Exemplifying the collapse of camaraderie, Macbeth orders his staff to 'lick up' spilt sauce and attempts to burn Malcolm with the *crème brûlée* blow-torch; the episodes draw imaginative power both from the popular construction of the medieval torture-chamber and from the parodic gloss placed on the protagonist's supposed professionalism. Finally, Macbeth is represented as launching himself, enraged, into the restaurant and attacking a diner who has dared to complain; as the customers leave, it is clear that a delicate balance between locales has been upset, that boundaries have been transgressed, and that a carefully gradated system of working relations is in disrepair. Exceeding the limit of his authority, Macbeth becomes here a trope for a mode of political injustice, his brand of excess pointing up a grotesque absolutism.

At this stage in the narrative, Macbeth is imagined as having moved away from the enabling possibilities of a dynamic partnership; thus, he arranges for the murder of Banquo on his own, significantly without Ella's assistance. Revealingly, the idea for dispatching Banquo is precipitated by the latter's confidence: 'we're having another baby', he informs Macbeth. Earlier, Macbeth's sensitivity around issues relating to Banquo's sons was given an obvious emphasis, the suggestion being that the witches' prophecy ignites ambition in part because it caters to the protagonist's vexed attitude towards his own childlessness. A significant dimension of Macbeth's pain – and male envy – is his and Ella's inability to reproduce. In this, a registration of responsiveness to a late twentieth- and early twenty-first-century preoccupation with infertility, the adaptation reorients Lady Macbeth's fraught admission: 'I have given suck, and know / How tender 'tis to love the babe that milks me' (1.7.54–5). The equivalent moment in the production – 'I know how it feels to have a baby feed at my breast: do you remember?' – contains the additional suggestion of a child who lived only briefly and works to establish Ella as shaped by a species of maternal grief. In subsequent scenes, possessed by madness, Ella harangues the restaurant's diners, recalling her child who died at three days old. A more stridently accented maternity is attached to Ella here, a symptom or mediation of contemporary discourses around stillbirth and postnatal depression. Carol Chillington Rutter, reflecting upon Shakespeare's *Macbeth*'s reproductive connotations, notes that:

[...] the image of the child draws together the play's stake in history, its yearning aspirations for 'tomorrow and tomorrow and tomorrow', its frustrated desires for 'blessed' yesterday, a time of grace before 'memory' came to figure as a wasteland rooted only with sorrow.[15]

Her assessment chimes with the *Macbeth* production, particularly in the stress placed on lack as motive, on forms of hierarchy mediated through children or a child-like status and dependency, and on the ways in which competitiveness between men is conducted through constructions of familial 'success'.

The failure of Macbeth's familial 'succession' within the restaurant hierarchy is highlighted in the deaths with which the production culminates. Margaret Jane Kidnie comments that the scene of Ella's death is 'heavily augmented for television with the dramatization of what is transparently a suicide'.[16] Where in Shakespeare's play the death of Lady Macbeth is left unresolved in terms of reason and cause, the 'Shakespea(Re)-Told' film specifies that Ella takes her own life, jumping from the roof of the restaurant as she vainly calls out for Macbeth to come to her aid. A backstage event is thus lent a front-end kind of representational interpretation and prominence. Intercut with Ella's fatal leap is the piercing sound of Macduff's scream, his response to the news that his family has been slaughtered. The editorial juxtaposition is illuminating, for Macduff's fall to the ground mimics the mortal arc traced by Ella, suggesting that both are to be understood as ranking high among Macbeth's casualties. More importantly, the bringing together of a pair of victims has the effect of telescoping the action. Typically, the method of the adaptation is to deal deftly and economically with the play's second half. As a result, the final stages proceed at a more exaggerated and frenetic pace, suiting an escalation of tension, suspense and excitement, tried-and-trusted features of this genre of television programming. Macbeth's reaction to Ella's death – 'Am I sorry? Do I still have that in me? What do I feel about the death of my wife? Nothing' – is treated less as a nihilistic climax and more as a continuation of the 'everything that was important in life has gone' address. With nothing left to say – or do – Macbeth is in prime position for his final confrontation. The underpinning conceit of the adaptation comes into its own in the duel in the kitchen in which Macbeth, having donned his chain-mail apron (or 'armour'), takes on Macduff in a knife fight. In an eerie revisiting, Ella's madness – or a type of it – comes to inhabit Macbeth, his crying out 'I'm immortal!' as he engages in combat. And the particular complexion of the protagonist's insane hubris is reinforced not only in the exclamatory dialogue but also in the blue emergency lights that bathe the culinary adversaries in a hallucinogenic and other-worldly glow.

Only the police helicopter landing on the roof of the restaurant – a response to Ella's suicide – forces Macbeth to recognize the disintegration of the witches' promises. 'Pigs will drop on your head before you're harmed', the leading bin-man had stated reassuringly, only for Macbeth to realize, as he strikes his head in frustration, the slang equivalents through which the witches commune; 'Pigs will fly', he agonizingly acknowledges. Dropping his knife and opening his shirt for Macduff's blade, Macbeth is discovered as creating the opportunity for his own self-destruction. With a grim appositeness, the protagonist is turned into a piece of meat – Macduff hoists his nemesis onto the work-surface and executes his own brand of butchery. As in act 1, scene 7 of the play, 'Bloody instructions' (Macbeth's butchery tutorial), being 'taught, return / To plague th'inventor' (1.7.9–10). Bleeding to death, Macbeth is imaged as – and becomes synonymous with – the pig's head of the opening.

At the very close, Malcolm, whom we know has no passion for cookery or food, takes over the restaurant and assumes the coveted television slot, complete with stolen recipes and faux Irish blarney. Unlike Shakespeare's text, however, the 'Shakespea(Re)-Told' *Macbeth* does not end here; rather, a distinctive coda returns us, in typically daring form, to the witches. As Malcolm takes a break in the alleyway, he contemplates the departing bin-lorry and finds himself stunned, as the vehicle turns, by the appearance of Fleance, who, balanced on his bicycle, looks on accusingly. The boy – his presence prioritizes and prolongs the place of the child in the production – is accompanied by a flashing blue light, suggestive of warning or imminent calamity. In addition, the ghostly nature of his re-entry into the narrative hints at vengeful memories and stories inadequately concluded. It is, of course, a highly theatrical moment, one in keeping with the adaptation's emphases and its innovative reworking of textual implication, absences and possibilities. And Malcolm is represented as visibly disconcerted. As the musical leitmotif associated with performance sounds once more, it is clear the show will go on. The story of *Macbeth*, and its endless potential for adaptation, continues.

Notes

1   Quotations are taken from the Arden Complete Works. This chapter originated in a very stimulating seminar on *Macbeth* at the SAA meeting in Seattle, 2011. I am grateful to the participants and, in particular, to Ann Thompson, the seminar leader, for sharpening my thinking on this play.

2   The 'Shakespea(Re)-Told' season prioritized television adaptations, 'spin offs' that translated into a modern vernacular the Shakespearean parlance while simultaneously retaining the drama's structural schemes. Four 're-tellings' were commissioned (in order of transmission, *Much Ado About Nothing*, *Macbeth*, *The Taming of the Shrew* and *A Midsummer Night's Dream*).

3   Ayanna Thompson, 'What Is a "Weyward" *Macbeth*?' in *Weyward 'Macbeth': Intersections of Race and Performance*, Scott L. Newstok and Ayanna Thompson (eds) (New York: Palgrave Macmillan, 2010), p. 4.

4   The emphasis on food products, and their corporal places of origin, is of a piece with a sombre atmosphere in which a fashionably offal-laced *cuisine* and dark moods easily consort with each other.

5 Margaret Jane Kidnie, *Shakespeare and the Problem of Adaptation* (London and New York: Routledge, 2009), p. 114.

6 Jonathan Bate, 'Skilful remixes off a bard for all seasons', *THE*, 9 December (2005), http://www.timeshighereducation.co.uk [accessed 30 August 2012].

7 John Newton, 'Flesh Pots', *The Age*, 5 October (1999), p. 5; Elspeth Probyn, *Carnal Appetites: Food/Sex/Identities* (London and New York: Routledge, 2000), p. 66.

8 Probyn, *Carnal*, 66. The decision to place the photograph on permanent display in the National Portrait Gallery, London, is an index of its cultural significance.

9 The Shakespearean reference here is to Duncan as 'the old man' (5.1.40).

10 While the kitchen is a set, the restaurant scenes were filmed at Prism Restaurant, Leadenhall Street, London (Chris Barber, 'Banquet's Ghost', *Olive*, December [2005], pp. 26–7).

11 'Editorial', *Daily Mail Weekend: TV Magazine*, 29 October (2007), p. 8.

12 Marco Pierre White, *The Devil in the Kitchen: The Autobiography* (London: Orion Books, 2007).

13 White, *Devil*, pp. 8, 13, 15.

14 The *Much Ado About Nothing* and *The Taming of the Shrew* adaptations, for example, demonstrate an assured sense of modern equivalents for Shakespeare and a considered awareness of the ways in which post-feminist understandings of gender and genre push into productive proximity early modern constructions of 'woman' and twenty-first-century reflections on love, marriage and heterosexual relations. See Ramona Wray, 'Shakespeare and the Singletons, or, Beatrice Meets Bridget Jones: Post-Feminism, Popular Culture and "Shakespea(Re)-Told"', in *Screening Shakespeare in the Twenty-First Century*, Mark Thornton Burnett and Ramona Wray (eds) (Edinburgh: Edinburgh University Press, 2006), p. 186.

15 Carol Chillington Rutter, 'Remind Me: How Many Children Had Lady Macbeth?', *Shakespeare Survey 57* (2004), p. 39.

16 Kidnie, *Shakespeare*, p. 115.

INDEX